PRAISE FOR

How to Make a French Family

"Like its author, Samantha Vérant's new book is sweet and sassy, told from the heart. Her story of creating a new family and becoming a different kind of mom is brave and vulnerable. A tale of what happens when we go looking for our best lives and best selves."

—Elizabeth Bard, *New York Times* bestselling author of *Lunch in Paris* and *Picnic in Provence*

"An honest, heartwarming—and at times—heartbreaking account of the struggles that occur when you dare to make your dreams come true."

—Janice MacLeod, author of *New York Times* bestseller *Paris Letters*

"A charming and insightful memoir about what follows happily ever after. The fact that Samantha's quest to create a new family is set in France (and filled with recipes) makes it all the more delicious!"

—Jennifer Coburn, author of *We'll Always Have Paris*

"Love has no boundaries in Samantha Vérant's honest and courageous memoir about leaving it all behind to marry her French husband. *How to Make a French Family* is a testament to her perseverance to adapt to a new life in southwestern France. In the tradition of *Seven Letters from Paris*, readers will laugh, cry, and cheer for Vérant until the final page."

—Susan Blumberg-Kason, author of *Good Chinese Wife*

"*How to Make a French Family* shares the ups and downs, good, bad, and funny moments of building a new life and family in France, never letting us forget that, in the end, love saves the day."

—Kristen Beddard, author of *Bonjour Kale*

"Samantha Vérant dishes up a funny and tender memoir in *How to Make a French Family*. The setup is pure fairy tale, but the tale's power is in the ever after. Vérant's story is genuine, romantic, sometimes heartbreaking, and, in the end, as wonderfully satisfying and rich as the French cuisine detailed on its pages."

—Michelle Gable, *New York Times* bestselling author of *A Paris Apartment* and *I'll See You in Paris*

How to Make a
FRENCH
FAMILY

How to Make a

FRENCH

FAMILY

A MEMOIR *of* LOVE, FOOD, *and* FAUX PAS

SAMANTHA VÉRANT

 sourcebooks

Published by Sourcebooks, Inc.
P.O. Box 4410, Naperville, Illinois 60567-4410
(630) 961-3900
Fax: (630) 961-2168
www.sourcebooks.com

Library of Congress Cataloging-in-Publication data is on file with the publisher.

Printed and bound in the United States of America.
VP 10 9 8 7 6 5 4 3 2 1

To Max and Elvire.
Thank you for opening up your hearts to me.

Je vous aime.
Beaucoup! Beaucoup! Beaucoup!

xox

TABLE OF CONTENTS

AUTHOR'S NOTE

THIS MEMOIR CHRONICLES WHAT HAPPENS to a fairy-tale romance when an American woman, me, marries a Frenchman by the name of Jean-Luc and jumps into a new life in southwestern France. This is a true story. There are no composite characters; however, I did change the names of select individuals to protect their identities. There are some composite scenes; if I didn't do this, the book would be more repetitive than *Groundhog Day*. Some sequences of events have been compressed, moved around, or omitted completely in order to ensure a well-paced story. And, rather than writing two more years of life (again, *Groundhog Day*), I did include our problems with the "renter" in this story. Conversations are not verbatim, but reconstructed from my elephant-like memory. Unless they are with Jean-Luc or my family and expat friends, most of the conversations I have are in conversational French. Well, broken French and a mix of Franglais. To simplify things, I've written the majority of the conversations in English or we'd get lost in translations.

As for the recipes included in this book, season them to your taste, especially when it comes to salt and pepper; take shortcuts, like using a food processor to finely mince, when needed; and get creative! Also, if you have a convection oven, a general rule of thumb is to lower the temperature or diminish the cooking time by 20 percent.

With all that said, I invite you, dear reader, to join me on a— sometimes bumpy—family adventure filled with love, food, and *faux pas*.

HOW TO MAKE
A FRENCH FAMILY

S IMPLY PUT, LOVE IS THE main ingredient needed to make a French family, the same as for any other family in the world, whether blended or traditional. But if you need an actual recipe for inspiration, I'm at your disposal, and here it is:

FAMILLE À LA FRANÇAISE

Prep time: Every day, 24/7

Cook time: Simmer until your heart bubbles over with laughter.

Great for: A lifetime of happiness

Wine suggestion: Forget about wine—celebrate your wonderful life with champagne!

INGREDIENTS:

- Communication
- Friendship
- Adventure
- Passion
- Love
- Marry a sexy Frenchman, win over his two kids, and move to southwestern France*

Blend all ingredients together. Open up your heart to everything and everybody. Don't let fear, insecurities, or regret hold you back. Take a leap. Shake up your life; don't stir it. When we dare to follow our hearts, the risk is worth it. Focus on the little things that make you happy, even when times are tough and messy. It will all work out in the end. Dreams change. And people can, too. Love bigger, live stronger, and don't let anybody tell you that something isn't possible. Dare to follow your heart. And, most importantly, believe in yourself. A happy family is made when all the members in it are happy. Season with an extra dash of love. Serve to everybody in your world.

*   *Optional, but not necessary.*

HOW TO MARRY A FRENCHMAN YOU'VE IGNORED FOR TWENTY YEARS

IT WAS THE ADVENTURE OF a lifetime.

In 1989, my parents moved from a suburb of Boston to London, England, and I was to spend the summer with them, taking a break from advertising design studies at Syracuse University. The moment Tracey found out, she called my dorm room.

"I'm visiting you," she said.

"Of course you are," I replied. We'd often joked that we'd been able to see the world because of my parents' moves—from Chicago, where I grew up, to Boston, Boston to London, London to California, California to Virginia to Tucson, then back to Virginia and back to California again. My home may have changed over the years, but one thing has remained constant: my friendship with Tracey. She's been by my side for every major life change.

"But I have a better idea," I said. "Rather than staying in London, let's travel Europe while we have the chance. First London. Then Paris."

"And then the south of France. And Italy…"

"Don't forget Greece," I said. "Can you take off three weeks of work?"

Tracey worked at the Chicago Board of Trade, clerking for a few traders.

"Are you kidding? I don't care if they fire me. Shots of ouzo? Plates broken on our heads? I'm so in."

The planning began.

Over the summer, I worked three jobs—two waitressing gigs and an internship at an art studio—to save up money for the trip. By the time July rolled around, I'd saved over one thousand dollars, and it was a done deal. Tracey flew to London, and after touring the city, clubbing at the Hippodrome, and dressing my little sister Jessica up like Madonna, it was on to our first stop: Paris.

There was something about the French way of *joie de vivre* that reeled us in like little fishes—from enjoying the sites—the chocolate and perfume shops—to getting lost on the cobbled streets. Paris, the City of Lights, the city of our girlhood dreams, the city of passion, seduced our souls. Of course, we hadn't planned to meet two sexy Frenchmen at a café. But we did.

Tracey had a much better view of their table. She didn't even try to hide her ogling. I had to crane my neck and peer over my right shoulder, trying not to be too obvious. But I was, and he caught me in his gaze for a brief moment. A dark emerald-green button-down shirt complemented his hazel eyes. His hair was thick, dark. He had a cute cleft in his chin. It was love at first sight, or as the French would say, *un coup de foudre*—a bolt of lightning, a shock to the system. The attraction I felt toward this handsome stranger, simply put, was magnetic. Soon, the electricity (or Tracey's blatant staring) pulled the guys over, and they positioned themselves in front of our table. Then, they insulted us.

"No self-respecting Frenchwoman would ever order a bottle of wine sans *bouchon*," said the object of my affection, referring to the screw cap on the only offering we could afford. I was about to speak when he said, "We'd like to propose you a good bottle. But on one condition: if you would allow us the honor, we would like to join you at your table."

Introductions were made. Jean-Luc, the guy in the emerald button-down shirt, and Patrick, his friend, had obviously mastered the "neg" long before the term was coined, but we took no offense. Not with those spine-tingling, sexy French accents. Pleased with our fate, I smiled at Tracey, and she shot me a wicked grin.

Like Jean-Luc, Patrick was a perfect specimen of a man with movie-star good looks. His hair was dark brown, almost black, and he had beautiful crystalline blue eyes. Yet something about him was too perfect—for my taste, at least. But that didn't matter. Tracey was drooling over Patrick, and, after some minor flirting confusion, the coupling was set.

Jean-Luc was unlike any guy I'd ever met. In addition to being ridiculously handsome, at the age of twenty-six, he had just finished up his required military-service officer training in Salon de Provence— and now worked at the French equivalent of NASA while finishing up his PhD. He spoke four or five languages, including Russian. His charm, his intelligence, and his sexy French accent had me hooked. Tracey and Patrick also got along famously, and our night didn't end after dinner. The boys took us for drinks on the Champs-Élysées, where we sat under the stars, the Arc de Triomphe glowing in the distance, and where I tried Porto for the very first time. From there, it was off to a private discothèque, where we danced until the sun came up and exchanged a few stolen kisses. After dropping us off at our youth hostel, they soon returned so that they could show us a bit more of Paris. But Tracey and I only had nine hours left in the City of Lights, and the clock was ticking down quickly. Soon, it was time to go. The guys tried to convince us to stay, but it wasn't an option, seeing that Tracey and I had booked one-way train tickets that we couldn't change. With our hearts racing, we made it to the platform at Gare de Lyon with sixty seconds to spare. Jean-Luc and I shared one final kiss. The train whistle blew. I stepped into the passenger car. "This isn't a good-bye," I said.

The train lurched forward. Jean-Luc and Patrick became tiny specks in the distance. As the train rolled along, my good-bye had already turned into the more permanent *adieu*.

Jean-Luc was too perfect, too smart. He was seven years older than I was, ready for a relationship. The timing wasn't right. As an insecure nineteen-year-old, I figured there must have been something wrong with him if he liked me.

That fall, I returned to my studies at Syracuse University to find six of Jean-Luc's letters waiting. I tried writing him back, but my words came out wrong, sounded stupid, could never match the passion in his. Incoherent scribbles filled the garbage bin in my dorm room. By the time his seventh letter arrived in November, guilt had rendered me numb. I tucked his letters into a blue plastic folder and got back to college living.

Fast forward to May of 2009, twenty years later.

My life hadn't turned out at all like I planned; it was one hot mess. My career and my marriage had fallen apart. I was in debt. And I was miserable. At Tracey's suggestion, I pulled out the seven old love letters that Jean-Luc had written to me two decades prior. Instead of the inspiration I was looking for, I found regret. Because I had never written him back. I had just left Jean-Luc standing on the train platform of the Gare de Lyon, blowing kisses.

Something in my gut told me that in order to change the state of my world, I needed to face past mistakes. I certainly didn't have anything to lose. After a twenty-year delay, I decided to apologize to Jean-Luc. But I couldn't just send him an arbitrary email. What if he'd forgotten about me? To jog his memory, on May 7, 2009, I wrote the first post of a seven-post blog, recounting the twenty-four hours Jean-Luc and I spent together. Then, on May 10, 2009, I sent Jean-Luc the link to the blog, along with my very delayed letter. A few days later, he responded. "I'd experienced train station syndrome," he'd said. For three months, we exchanged over two hundred emails. The emails soon turned into phone calls.

I didn't realize one heartfelt "I'm sorry" would change my life…for the better. On August 2, 2009, I dared to follow my heart, and I flew to France to meet him. The connection between us was instantaneous, just as it had been in 1989.

After circumnavigating the blue, white, and red tape that came with an American woman getting hitched to a Frenchman, we were married in a five-minute ceremony performed at our local *mairie* in France on

May 7, 2010. We were finally able to celebrate our union with our family and friends at my parents' home in California on July 24.

Life and love were, indeed, an adventure.

So let the adventure begin.

Ingredient One

COMMUNICATION

A BEAUTIFUL MESS

ROSE PETALS. THEY WERE EVERYWHERE. Scattered up the stairs leading to the bedroom. Shaped into a heart on the carpet. Blanketing the bed in an explosion of hot pink and orange insanity.

Jean-Luc shook the duvet, launching a hurricane of silver-dollar-size puffs into the air. A breeze blew in from the open window, which turned the petals into a colorful troupe of whirling dervishes spinning around on the floor.

"There must be hundreds of them. Maybe thousands," said Jean-Luc. "It's madness."

In my post-wedding haze, I'd forgotten about the botanical war zone that had had us giggling in delight the evening before. Jean-Luc and I had fallen into bed, exhausted, happy, and filled with relief. This was our second chance at love and—after a twenty-year hiatus—we'd finally tied the knot.

The evening had gone off without a hitch—the weather perfect, the food delicious, and the music outstanding. Buzzed on love and a few glasses of champagne, Jean-Luc and I danced under a full moon, a blanket of stars sparkling over our heads, the perfume of Californian jasmine and roses enveloping us. The morning after, however, it took us a few moments to come to terms with the amorous aftermath of our wedding night.

Jean-Luc nudged my shoulder. He eyed the roses. "Sam, seriously, who did this?"

"I thought you did," I said. "I mean, it's romantic, but, wow. I mean…wow."

"I didn't do this," said Jean-Luc, eyeing me with suspicion.

Whereas I was more of an occasionally neurotic, bottle-blond Lucille Ball, Jean-Luc was a smart and savvy French Desi Arnaz. An artist, I liked to dream big or go home. He was pragmatic, a scientist who investigated facts. He grounded me when my head floated into the clouds. I opened his mathematical mind to creative (and sometimes odd) possibilities. And, sure, I might do nutty things like fly five thousand miles to meet up with a man I'd only known for twenty-four hours and over email, but I wasn't responsible for the rose petals.

"I swear it wasn't me."

"Your mom?"

"She wouldn't dare. You know what a neat freak she is," I said. My thoughts went to my mother, who was hosting my now-stepdaughter, Elvire, at her house. "The state of Elvire's room must be giving her hives. There are clothes all over the floor, wet bikinis and towels on the chair, and she leaves the drawers open. I mean, why? Why does she leave drawers open?"

"I'll tell her to clean it up."

"Good luck with that," I said.

"*Deux secondes*," we said in unison. "Two seconds"—the universal response for any teenaged girl on the planet.

For a moment, Jean-Luc and I sat motionless, watching the rose petals dancing across the floor, our mouths agape. Who was responsible for this botanical bomb? By process of elimination, two lovable but devious delinquents came to mind: my sister, Jessica, and my best friend of more than twenty-five years, Tracey. Frankly, it wouldn't have surprised me if the two of them had plotted and planned together for weeks. But people were always innocent until proven guilty. And I didn't have proof.

Cleaning up what appeared to be thousands of rose petals wasn't exactly what I'd envisioned doing the morning after our wedding, but because of Jean-Luc, my views had shifted; he'd opened up my heart to love and I didn't sweat the small stuff anymore. We'd survived the perils of a long-distance relationship through unbridled communication, consisting of two-hour long telephone calls and emails. Whatever problems we faced, we overcame them together, and not one single argument threatening to shake our system along the way. Rose petals? Hardly a crisis.

Jean-Luc jumped out of bed. "I'll sweep. You gather."

"What a mess," I said, holding back a laugh.

"A beautiful mess." Jean-Luc gingerly removed a rose petal tangled in my hair. "Like you."

"Ha-ha," I said, scrambling out of bed to throw on a pair of shorts and a T-shirt.

"Where are you going?"

"To get a trash bag and a broom."

"*Mais*, Madame Vérant, you haven't given me my morning kiss."

We finished sweeping and gathering, Jean-Luc jumped in the shower, and I headed downstairs to the kitchen. My mom and dad were drinking coffee. A new French habit: I kissed my parents on both cheeks. "Morning, sweetie," said my dad.

"Oh good, you're up," said my mom. She closed her iPad and clapped her hands together with excitement. "That was the best wedding ever. And I didn't even have to leave my own house. Let's keep the party going."

I held up a finger. "Party Anne-imal," I said, referring to the nickname I'd given my mom, Anne. "I haven't had my coffee yet."

"But there are a couple of bottles of champagne left. Mimosa?"

My sister bounced into the kitchen and headed straight to the fridge. "Did somebody say mimosas?" asked Jessica. She placed a bottle of champagne and a jug of orange juice on the kitchen table, and then raced to the dining room, returning with five crystal glasses. "Where's Jean-Luc?"

"He's cleaning up the rest of the rose petals. Somebody, probably Tracey, dumped around a thousand of them in our room last night." I raised an eyebrow.

"Oh no." Jessica's smile faded. "I thought it was beautiful."

"A-ha!" I said. "It *was* you."

Jessica set the champagne glasses down and headed for the door. "I'll help him clean up."

I could have played with her mind for a little bit, but I really appreciated her grandiose—although slightly diabolical—gesture. "Don't worry about it. They're already swept up and bagged," I said.

"Are you sure?" Jess asked.

"Seriously, he's in the shower. He'll be down in a minute." I paused, noting the disappointed expression on Jessica's face. "The heart on the carpet was a nice touch," I said. "And where in the world did you get all those petals?"

"The flower shop down the hill sells them by the bucket."

"How many buckets did you buy?"

"Four."

"Because one wasn't enough?"

She grinned wickedly. "Nope."

My father looked up from his paper. "Sam, your baby sister loves you."

"I do, Eeyah," said Jessica, referring to the way she said my name when she was two and couldn't pronounce my name. Where Eeyah had come from nobody knew. When I was a "cool" teenager, she used to follow me around, clinging to my side like a baby octopus; sometimes it was hard shaking her off. We may have been ten and a half years apart in age, but now that Jessica was twenty-nine, we were close as peas in a pod, and she could almost read my mind. Jessica popped open the bottle and poured, the champagne fizzing to the top of the glasses. She was light on the orange juice. Very light. She handed me a glass, and we sat at the table with my parents.

"Mom, Dad," I said, "Thank you so, so much for everything. Really, I don't know where to begin. It was a perfect night."

"Well, everything was perfect," said my dad, "until the cops arrived."

"What?" questioned Jess.

"What?" I repeated, louder.

He explained how the Malibu Police department had received a complaint at around 11:30, and how the cops didn't show up until two hours later, after all the guests had left. Apparently, the officers felt terrible about coming to the house to deliver a noise violation at a wedding, especially one that had already ended. They apologized profusely and left as peacefully as they'd come.

Jessica held up her glass for a toast. "We rocked the canyon. And escaped the po-po."

Clink.

"Speaking of last night, did you see the moon? It was so full, and so close we could practically touch it," said my mom. Instead of howling like one of the mangy coyotes in the canyon that had kept me awake many a night, as I thought she'd do, my mother broke out into tears. "This past year with you has been incredible, Sam. And now it's over. You're moving to France, and you'll be so far away. What am I going to do without you?"

"Mom, I'll only be a plane ride away. And I can always come back home to visit—at least once or twice a year. And just think! You get to travel to France, to Toulouse and to Provence, and see things you've never seen. Plus, we can Skype."

"I know, Sam. But it's not the same."

I gulped. Mom was right. This was different. I'd been so busy planning the wedding I hadn't taken much time to think about this life-changing move. Until now.

After a twenty-plus-hour travel day, I was going to be far from my family and friends, starting a new life with a new man in a new country, speaking a language in which I only had limited conversational skills, and taking on a somewhat intimidating role: an instant American stepmother to two French kids who had lost their own mother to cancer. It was hard to assuage my mother's sadness while swallowing back my fears.

Dad piped in. "I'm really looking forward to seeing more of France."

"Me too," said Jess.

Mom shook her head and sniffled.

My now-stepchildren, Maxence and Elvire, saved the morning when they sauntered into the kitchen in their pajamas. Mom pretended to wipe something out of her eyes to hide her tears as the kids did the rounds, kissing everybody on each cheek. I sighed. These two beautiful children were now a big part of my life.

Elvire was pale, like a porcelain doll. Her thick, long, auburn hair brought out the blue in her eyes. At thirteen, she was now going through that awkward stage of the occasional pimple and the insecurities puberty brings on. She didn't know how beautiful she was yet, and her shoulders always slumped over, making her tiny frame appear even thinner.

Max's complexion was Mediterranean, his skin tanned darker by the summer sun. Soon turning eleven, he was a little man with a big personality. He was also super cute with his coiffed sun-kissed hair, which brought out the green in his eyes. Both of the kids had Jean-Luc's perfect lips.

"Juice?" I asked the kids as they sat down.

"Who wants pancakes with whipped cream and strawberries?" asked my mom, pulling herself together. When my mother followed that with the promise of American bacon, however, Max and Elvire's eyes lit up. Even Bodhi, my parents' golden retriever, stopped barking and raced into the house, his eyes glowing with bacon lust.

After downing my mimosa, I excused myself and went upstairs. Jean-Luc was still in the bathroom, shaving. I sat down on the bed, willing my nerves to calm down. I'd dreamed of changing everything in my world and, through more than a few adjustments and heart palpitations, it had happened…maybe too quickly. Was I ready for all of this? In ten short days, I was leaving my old life behind me for a new one in France. My mom's unexpected outburst had me on edge.

In her twenties, my mom had carried a paper bag around to stop herself from hyperventilating. My biggest problem was internalizing everything, keeping all those pesky emotions inside, and, sometimes, I held my breath. Before I turned blue in the face or passed out, I focused on the bedroom window and watched the mist creeping up the canyon, hoping it would disintegrate into thin air just like the worries clouding my brain.

Let it out. Don't keep it in. Breathe. Breathe. Breathe.

A quick flash of iridescent green reflected in the window. I bolted to the French doors, threw them open, and walked onto the deck, letting out the breath I'd been holding in one quick whoosh, my heart no longer feeling like it was going to catapult out of my rib cage. My hummingbird had returned.

Many times, right when I needed a reminder to focus on the tiny, beautiful things in life—especially when things appeared to be overly complicated or messy—this hummingbird had appeared. He'd even showed up at our wedding the night before, settling on a branch and chirping loudly, as if to say *"Félicitations,"* before flying away.

Perhaps it wasn't the same bird, but I'd like to think it was.

I pinched my lips together into a kiss, sucked my bottom lip in so it pressed against my teeth, and did my best hummingbird call—a squeaky chirp. The bird landed on the branch of the eucalyptus tree, whose pink and green leaves reminded me of heart-shaped rose petals, and tilted his head, answering my call. His low trill escalated in volume and excitement. Of course, I trilled back.

A pair of strong hands slid down my sides, gripping my waist. "I heard voices. Who were you talking to?" asked Jean-Luc.

I pointed to the tree. "My hummingbird."

Jean-Luc raised an inquisitive eyebrow. "You're talking to birds?"

"If I said yes, what would you say?"

Jean-Luc laughed. "My crazy American girl."

"That's why you love me."

The hummingbird flew off his perch and zipped toward the clouds like a crazed kamikaze pilot, then he plunged down into the canyon haze, came back up in a swirl of white, chased another bird while twittering madly, and finally settled himself back on his perch. I raised a brow, thinking, *See! See! I'm not a weirdo. It's not my imagination!* Instead I said, "I haven't seen one hummingbird in France."

"There aren't any," said Jean-Luc, gripping my waist tighter before pointing to the pool. "But I have seen quite a few of those. *Les libellules.*"

Surely, he wasn't indicating the swimming pool or he would have said *la piscine.* I repeated the word, "*libellules,*" as best I could. It came out more like *le-blah-blah-bi-da-blah-lue*—not my best attempt. With a hearty laugh, Jean-Luc corrected my pronunciation, and the word twisted uncomfortably on my tongue until I managed to get it somewhat right—not perfect, but not too bad.

"*Les libellules?*" I questioned, focusing on each syllable. At least I was fluent in hummingbird, if not French.

"Dragonflies."

"Right," I said.

Between the hummingbirds, the mist creeping up the canyon, and the dragonflies, nature was truly putting on a show. I wouldn't have been surprised if the local deer had hopped over the fence and joined in on the action. It was truly a fairy-tale moment, and I found myself wondering how long this kind of perfection could last.

That summer, the June gloom typical of California—overcast skies, thick fogs, and nippy drizzles—had extended far into July. Thankfully, we'd lucked out with good weather for our big weekend. The clouds had parted for Friday's family barbecue and held off for Saturday's wedding celebration. But now the chill was back. I shuddered. Just as the weather had changed in the blink of an eye, my life was about to change swiftly too.

LEAPING INTO *L'AMOUR*

H ow did one pack for a new life? What did I absolutely need? What couldn't I live without?

My pile of clothes to give away—mostly items given to me by a former dog-walking client (oddly, a nudist) and shoes I'd held onto for years but never worn—was growing into an island of what-was-I-thinking mistakes. I glanced at a wool sweater I hadn't worn in half a decade. Did it give me joy? Would I ever wear it again? Probably not. *Adieu*, sweater.

Some decisions were easy to make if I deliberated long enough; others were just plain tough. I was holding a set of green Emile Henry mixing bowls—one large, one medium, and one small—when Jean-Luc walked into the bedroom.

"Where do you think I can put these?" I asked. "I'm bringing breakables, like the silver-rimmed glass plates my grandmother gave me, in my carry-on."

Jean-Luc shook his head in disbelief. He took the bowls from my hands and set them down on the bed. "These are too heavy. You can buy new ones."

"But why buy something when I already have them? Plus, they're French."

"Give them to your mom, Sam."

Jean-Luc rifled through an open suitcase, pulling out a handheld lemon press, an OXO can opener, and an OXO vegetable peeler—three of my "I-can't-live-without-them" kitchen tools, packed inside a green Emile Henry ceramic pie plate. He smirked and raised his eyebrows.

"Fine. I'll give the bowls to Mom. But all that"—I jutted out my chin and rotated my index finger in a "don't mess with me" motion—"is coming to France."

After a week of packing and unpacking and then packing again, weighing each suitcase to make sure it was under the fifty-pound limit, I was almost ready for the big move. Six pieces of art—two French lithograph posters I'd bought in the Marais district of Paris, two Italian oil paintings, and two framed Chinese textiles from some ancient dynasty—were snuggled into Jean-Luc's hard-sided bag for safety, wrapped carefully in his clothes. Along with the OXO vegetable peeler and its friends, my life had been reduced to three suitcases containing my clothes, shoes, picture frames, photos, my art direction portfolio, and items like candlesticks, salt and pepper shakers, serving bowls and platters, a gravy boat, serving spoons, two small boxes of Christmas decorations, and a few of my favorite cookbooks, such as *The Joy of Cooking* and Jean-Georges Vongerichten's *Simple to Spectacular*.

"You're not moving to a third-world country," said Jean-Luc as we shuffled goods from one case to another, trying to make weight. He held up a melon baller. "Are you serious?"

I was.

"With the right tools, you can do anything," I said, parroting Jean-Luc's answer when I'd questioned him why he owned every hardware tool ever known to man. "And, just so you know, I gave the mixing bowls to my mom."

"We'll get new ones," he said with a sigh.

I grinned. He blew out the air between his lips—the French way. *Pffffftp*.

Forget about clothes and shoes—put me in a store with kitchen goods and I was in heaven. Although she didn't slave over the stove as much anymore as she had in the past, my mother was a force of nature when it came to serving up delicious meals, often preparing recipes handed down from my grandmother, Nanny, and Nanny's sister, my great aunt Bobbi, like rack of lamb with a mint chutney, beef stroganoff, crab cakes, roast beef with Yorkshire pudding, or—one of my personal favorites—a chunky gazpacho. Passed down from one generation to the next, the love for cooking was in my blood.

At the age of nine, I first experimented with simple dishes—meatloaf and salads being my specialty. By twelve, I was thumbing through *Bon Appétit* and *Gourmet* magazine looking for inspiration, and my first grand attempt came in the form of sundae pie decorated with chocolate leaves—molded from actual leaves I'd picked from the garden. From there, I moved on to more inspired experiments, either trying recipes on my own or helping my mom out in the kitchen.

The first time I visited Jean-Luc's home after we reconnected, I was promised a glimpse of daily life with him and the children. And daily life was exactly what I got. In the evenings, Jean-Luc taught me how to cook basic French cuisine, a skill he was more than familiar with, having been a single dad for such a long time. I'd open up a bottle of wine and we'd have a glass while he instructed me on the finer points of quiche making—the secrets being premade crusts, little cubes of salted pork called *lardons*, *crème fraîche*, *herbes de Provence*, and, of course, adding a tablespoon of Dijon mustard to the egg mixture if making a vegetable quiche. I'd cook up the *lardons* while Jean-Luc whipped the eggs with a whisk, a *fouet*. I learned to remove the green germ from garlic cloves to avoid bitterness. I loved the fact that he enjoyed cooking as much as I did, and I was looking forward to incorporating more French meals into my repertoire. Thanks to Jean-Luc and a few of his family's Provençal recipes, I was already off to a great start.

Jean-Luc picked up my OXO garlic press. "Do you really need this?"

I took it from his hand and hugged it to my chest. "I do. I really do."

What I couldn't fit into my suitcases was stored in the guest room closet—two plastic containers filled with more cookbooks, old drawings from my days at Syracuse University, and childhood keepsakes like my first nubby, brown teddy bear that now had one eye (he'd been well loved), which I'd saved just in case I had a child of my own—which was still a possibility.

I'd always thought I would be a young, cool mom, like my mother. When I was a kid, she took me everywhere with her. When I was an adult, we were closer than close. But with my ex's constant excuses, a baby hadn't been in the cards for me in the past. The world was in shambles. Kids were expensive; we couldn't afford them. We needed to spend more time together. We wouldn't have a life anymore, wouldn't be able to travel, go out. What if the child had birth defects? Things weren't stable enough. Then, according to him, we were too old. But the fact of the matter was that if I had really wanted to have children with Chris, we would have had them.

I held the teddy bear and couldn't help but remember the words Jean-Luc had said when were on our "rekindle the romance" tour in August of 2009. We were standing outside Château d'Ussé—reputed to be both the inspiration behind Charles Perrault's *Sleeping Beauty—La Belle au Bois Dormant*—and Walt Disney's iconic castle. A true fairy-tale setting, it was located on the edge of the Chinon Forest, on the banks of the Indre River, overlooking terraced gardens. Another couple walked by, holding the hands of their daughter, who must have been about three years old. They swung her up into the air and her toes pointed toward the blue sky. Jean-Luc's eyes had locked onto mine and he'd said, "Samantha, I want to give you everything. Everything I have. I don't have much, but what I have is yours. I want you to know joy. You're so special and so unique. I want to give you something you've never had. I want to give you the gift of a child."

Never before had I heard such words come out of an actual human mouth. That was the exact moment I knew our lives would be intertwined. That was the exact moment I knew I was in love with him—and not a giddy schoolgirl love that would fade over time. Real love. In my heart, I'd always wanted a child. And now I was with a man I wanted to have a baby with.

. . . .

On August 6, it was time to head to France. My mother choked back her tears as we loaded up the rental car. "Maybe, one day, you guys can move to California," she said, her face hopeful. "Maybe Jean-Luc could work for JPL." Managed for NASA by the California Institute of Technology, Jet Propulsion Laboratory was located in Pasadena.

Jean-Luc was a seasoned scientist and the head of his department, in charge of a team of twenty-four engineers and technicians. At the age of sixty-five, his French retirement plan would come into play, and he would receive around 65 percent of his salary for the rest of his life. Plus, the cost of living in southern California, especially the housing market, was much higher than it was in southwestern France. I knew a move to the States would never happen, but I didn't want to set my mother off into a thunderstorm of tears and sobs.

"Maybe," I said. "You never know."

"Are you sure you don't want your china?" asked my mom.

"What would I say if I was hosting a dinner party and people asked me where I got it? Oh, this set was a wedding gift from my first marriage? Plus, you use them every day."

"They're just plates. And they're pretty. If you decide you want them, I'll send them to you."

"Thanks," I said. "But they have plates in France."

Jean-Luc nudged me in ribs. "They also have garlic presses."

Max and Elvire hugged my parents and kissed them on both cheeks, said their thank-yous, and jumped into the back seat of the rental car. I bit down on my bottom lip, glancing at my parents' house. This was it. No looking back.

"I'm going to cry," said my mom.

If she started up, I'd be in tears, too.

Uncertainty tugged on one arm, hopefulness on the other. This was my second chance at life and at love, and I didn't want to screw it up, but the fear of failure hadn't truly left my system. I needed to be deprogrammed and quick, knowing, deep down, that there was only one person who could reset my outlook: me. I let out the breath that, once again, I'd been holding in.

"Please don't cry, Mom," I said, my chin quivering. "Dad, for Mom's sake, you have to plan a visit to France…soon."

"Sweetie," said my dad, rubbing my shoulders. "You can count on that."

Jean-Luc slammed the trunk closed, and my dad said, "Take care of my girl."

"I will, Tony. She used to be a boomerang, bouncing back and forth from France to California. This time I've caught her."

"I'm holding you to that," said my dad, and he and Jean-Luc laughed.

My mom grabbed my hands, gripping them tightly as if she were holding on to them for dear life. "Call me when you land," she said.

"I will," I said.

Seconds later, Jean-Luc careened down the canyon road to the Pacific Coast Highway. I sat in the passenger seat, looking out the window as we passed the beaches and the Santa Monica pier, my heart racing with excitement and fear.

My nerves kicked into overdrive at the airport as a hiccup immediately arose in our plans. Jean-Luc had booked my ticket with his frequent flyer miles, and Air France upgraded my seat to economy plus. They'd overbooked the flight and were not able to seat me with Jean-Luc and the kids. On the plane, when I turned to see my family sitting together, the flight attendant closed the curtains. I sat alone, feeling disconnected and like an outsider.

After two extended trips to France while building my relationship with Jean-Luc, one lasting a month over Christmas and the other two months in the spring, I'd had a tiny glimpse of what my life would be like with Jean-Luc and the kids, and I shouldn't have been so nervous about relocating to France. But I was. I considered myself a city girl, but I wasn't moving to Paris. Jean-Luc and the kids lived in Cugnaux, a small town of thirteen thousand people thirteen kilometers south of Toulouse in the Midi-Pyrénées region of southwestern France. Acting as the constant cheerleader in my life, Jean-Luc had assured me that everything would be fine; we had each other and the kids. Yet I wondered: would that be enough? Although I'd spent quality time with Max and Elvire, I'd only been a visitor before—a fly-by tourist. Being their stepmother day in and day out—that would be different.

Breathe. Breathe. Breathe.

I thought back to the time I'd had with Max and Elvire in Chicago before the wedding. Jean-Luc had arranged to speak at an aerospace conference. While he rubbed shoulders with his cronies from the industry, I could show the kids the city in which I grew up.

For two days, I took them all over Chicago. We rented bikes and cruised down the lakefront, swam at the beach to cool off. We visited Millennium Park and played in the fountain, which featured "live" images of Chicagoans, the water pouring out of mouths in a well-timed electronic display. At the Museum of Science and Industry, they made their own mini-tornadoes, and at the Field Museum, they met Sue the dinosaur. We rode the Ferris wheel at Navy Pier and went on an architectural boat tour. We even went up to the top of the Sears Tower, where Max got over one of his fears.

I was standing on the famed glass floor, the city's streets more than one hundred floors below. Elvire stood beside me. Max stood back and shook his head. "*Je peux pas. J'ai le vertige.*"

I can't. I have vertigo.

Elvire rolled her eyes. "*T'es nul.*"

"Elvire, he's not a loser," I said, placing my hands on Max's thin shoulders, squeezing them lightly. "*Tu peux.*"

You can.

Max closed his eyes, took one step forward, then another. When he opened his eyes, he was standing next to me on the glass floor. He looked down and quickly jumped back onto more solid ground. His smile stretched as wide as from the Sears Tower to Oak Street Beach. "*Je l'ai fait.*"

I gave him a quick hug and said, "Yes, you did it."

But now, I'd be with Max and Elvire on a daily basis in France, not in a city I knew like the back of my hand. Surely, Max and Elvire wouldn't be polite little angels all of the time. When were they going to hit me with the "you're not my mom" sucker punch? Then again, *I* came from a blended family, and I had never said those hurtful words to my dad.

My biological father, Chuck, had abandoned my mother and me shortly after I was born. Didn't even leave a note. I was six months old, jaundiced and colicky. My mother was twenty-one years young, fearful of her future. Still, life went on for my mother and me—and it was a much better life. When I was six, she married the man I proudly call my dad, Tony. I wore my hair in Shirley Temple ringlets to their wedding. Chuck wasn't around to veto the judge's ruling, and Tony formally adopted me when I was eleven. He was the only father I'd ever known.

Cancer took the life of the mother of Jean-Luc's kids in 2006, one week before Max's seventh birthday. Max and Elvire had known their mother, Frédérique, but I wondered if perhaps now they would want to complete the family circle, as I had when I was young. Maybe it wouldn't be so hard for the kids to accept me into their daily lives, just as I'd done with Tony.

On the short plane ride from Paris to Toulouse, I sat in the aisle seat next to Max and Elvire—two tired kids with sleep in their eyes. Max dozed after takeoff, curling up against my shoulder. From across the aisle, Jean-Luc took my hand. "Ready to go home?"

"Ready as I'll ever be," I said.

I had love on my side. And, with love on my side, I could do anything. At least, that's what I told myself.

BIENVENUE EN FRANCE

D EVELOPED IN THE EARLY '60s, the town of Cugnaux supplied
homes for the workers in the growing aeronautics industry,
and today its thirteen thousand inhabitants mostly comprise retirees
or young families with kids. Quaint and quiet, the town has parks,
gardens, and an old manor that hosts musical festivals. And, as in any
French town, the center boasts the local church, complete with bells
that ring on the hour, a wonderful old clock, and a steeple reaching
into the sky. (If you ever get lost in a European village, head for
the church). On a brick paved road across the way stands our local
mairie, or mayor's office, where Jean-Luc and I first exchanged vows.
To my left is the kids' *école maternelle*, or primary school: Jean Jaurès.
Almost every French town has a school or a street named after the
French socialist leader, who was assassinated at the outbreak of
World War I and is considered by most to be a hero. The people
praise Jean Jaurès for his humanitarian efforts.

On the way home from the airport, we passed by one of the many
pharmacies, its crossed sign blinking green, which meant that it was
open, and made our way past Bar Eclipse, which I'd never visited
even though it was right at the end of the block. Not exactly my
scene—most of the patrons were older men forever drinking *pastis*,
the forty-proof anise-flavored liqueur, and chain-smoking cigarettes.
The taxi pulled up to a white town house with a green iron fence on
a tree-lined street.

The sky was clear and blue. The birds chirped out happy melodies as if they were welcoming us. Across the way, a group of young boys around Elvire's age played *pétanque*, France's version of bocce ball, which was invented in Jean-Luc's hometown of La Ciotat. They waved and said *bonjour* as we unloaded the bags out of the trunk before getting back to the game.

"Do you know them?" I asked Elvire.

She shrugged, but didn't look over. "*Non.*"

Jean-Luc fumbled with his keys. From inside the house, Bella, the ridiculously expensive Bengal cat we'd purchased last Christmas, mewed. Loudly. Adopting Bella had been my idea, a heart-felt scheme to get to know the kids prior to meeting them for the first time. Jean-Luc wanted to include me in their lives, ease me in. A friend of mine had posted a picture of her Bengal kitten, and the moment I saw him, I ran my idea by Jean-Luc. He suggested that I discuss my plan with Elvire via email. It didn't take much convincing, and the search for a spotted, cream-and-caramel-colored tiny leopard began. Elvire found a breeder in Bordeaux with female kittens, the sex she wanted, and we threw around names, me suggesting Bella, thanks to Elvire's love of the movie *Twilight*. Although she'd come with an exorbitant price tag, and Jean-Luc had joked that cats were free (you could find one on the street), through Bella, Elvire and I had created an initial bond. Our neighbors, Sylvie and Patrick, had been kind enough to look after the cat for the past few weeks while Jean-Luc and the kids were in California. I hadn't seen her panther-like spotted body and tiger-striped legs since May.

"Hurry up, Papa," said Elvire, and Max nodded.

The kids threw their bags on the floor in the foyer, and Elvire scooped up Bella in her arms. "Titi," she said. Titi or Titi-La-Titi was Bella's nickname. She and Max cuddled with the cat until Elvire screamed, "Something bit me!" and dropped the cat to the floor.

Bella scratched at her neck, her leg pumping briskly. Fleas jumped off her body, what looked like hundreds of them. Maybe thousands.

"*Sac à puces,*" said Max. Fleabag.

"Oh no," I said.

Elvire glared at me like it was my fault. I blamed her demeanor on being overtired. I was utterly exhausted, too. I glanced into the living room to find that fleas weren't our only problem. Instead of using her cat tree, Bella had shredded a corner of the grass-cloth wallpaper.

"I'll go to the pharmacy and the hardware store," said Jean-Luc with a sigh.

"I'll get to the market before it closes," I said. "You've been gone for five weeks. I'm sure there's no food."

Unlike in the U.S., where employers are not required to offer paid vacations, Jean-Luc had over fifty paid vacation days, including national holidays and when his company mandatorily closed its doors the first two weeks of August and one week at Christmas. Still, Jean-Luc worked long hours. On a typical day, he arrived at his office before seven in the morning, leaving before rush hour, and returning home at seven at night. Vacations, scientists have said, foster more productivity and far less burnout. Having formerly worked in advertising with only two weeks' vacation a year, I'd have to agree with that.

"Thankfully, all the bedroom doors upstairs are closed," said Jean-Luc. "But, just in case, we'll need to strip all the beds, washing everything in hot water. For now, put Bella outside."

I opened up the kitchen doors and ushered Bella onto the deck.

Blessed with an abundance of trees and beautiful plants—cherry, magnolia, mulberry, mimosa, two lilac bushes, roses, peonies, and lavender—in the spring, our backyard was amazing and private and magical. One of my favorite rosebushes climbed up a beam supporting the small tiled roof that shaded our kitchen. But today, with the hot weather and nobody around to water, the grass was the color of pale straw, scorched by the sun. Add in the overgrown weeds, and this was no paradise.

Uranus, a fat, black cat, scratched himself in the neighbor's yard. Just looking at him made me itch. Bella scurried up the wooden fence, leaping over it with grace, to join her flea-ridden best friend.

The idea of taking a shower to wash off a twenty-plus-hour travel day and potential army of fleas was tempting, but we needed food. I grabbed my straw basket. The kids were leaving for their maternal grandmother's home in Provence the following day, so I didn't have to buy much, putting off the big shop at Intermarché, our local grocery store, until Monday.

Usually, I loved going to the market—our Saturday routine when I had been just a visitor, and, surely, a weekly event now. But as I strolled through town, it was as if I were walking on another planet. Who were these people? What language were they speaking? *Blah-blah-blah, wonka, wonka, wonka*—that's what I heard. Even the air shimmered with a heat haze, making the streets feel all the more bizarre. I passed by a group of little old ladies wearing ballerina flats and dresses, chatting on the corner. I'd never seen women with hair colors of shocking chili-pepper red and pale violet, the hue similar to the macarons displayed in one of the patisserie's windows. Was this a mirage? Or was I just tired?

French women do tend to dress up when leaving the house— even just to grab a baguette. I stood on the corner of a pedestrian crosswalk, wearing yoga pants, a light cotton sweater, and Keds— comfortable travel clothes. Not one car stopped. In fact, the cars sped up as if threatening to run me down. Was my fashion sense so distasteful it was going to get me killed? Paranoia set in.

Finally, I made it across the street. The paved brick sidewalk narrowed, and I scurried along the side housing all the local businesses, my shoulder practically touching the walls, lest somebody shove me into traffic. I was fairly certain people stared at me because they knew I was a foreigner.

A young boy around four or five passed by with his mother. She wore jeans, black, strappy sandals, and a cute pink T-shirt with bows on the back, looking oh so effortlessly chic. I debated going home to change. The boy wore shorts and a New York baseball cap and a T-shirt from the Gap. American brands, especially Abercrombie, were extremely popular with French kids and teens. *There,* I thought, *something mildly familiar*—until the boy snatched his hand away from his mother's.

"*Putain,*" she said, speaking to her son. "*Tu m'as fait mal.*" You hurt me.

Putain, literally translated, meant "whore," and she'd said this word to her kid. And, oh, yes, he'd heard it, repeating it over and over again. "*Putain, putain, putain,*" he sang.

She laughed, but didn't correct him. My jaw dropped, although I shouldn't have been so shocked. After all, *putain* is probably the most widely used word in France. I've heard old ladies and men say it. And it's widely popular with teens. I've even used it. Depending on the tone, *putain* can express all sorts of emotions—pain, joy, surprise, disbelief, and more. Apparently, this woman was in pain. But, a "*gros mot,*" *putain* held the same connotation as my mother's least favorite word: the f-bomb. And, frankly, for me, using either of these words in front of impressionable kids was just plain wrong. There were politer words to express oneself in public to get your point across—like *mince,* which means "thin," or, oh, *purée.* An elderly gentleman walked by with a scruffy dog. By this point, I wouldn't have been surprised if either of them said *putain.*

Our market was big and lively, and there were seven or eight vegetable and fruit vendors, some selling organic produce, or "*bio.*" Jean-Luc and I usually shopped at one particular set-up, so I headed there. I grabbed some tomatoes, cucumbers, potatoes, bananas, carrots, lettuce, oranges, and whatever else tickled my fancy, throwing everything into my basket. Today, there were vegetables I'd never seen before—like the meteor-like *celeri-rave* (celery root), and Romanesco broccoli, which, with its chartreuse fractal peaks, reminded me of outer space and how I currently felt as though I were walking on the moon. Our vendor, a tall man with dark brown eyes and a head of unruly hair, smiled and motioned for my basket. I handed it over and, after he tallied everything up on his calculator, paid the twenty-eight euro.

"*Un peu de persil?*" he asked. They always gave away free parsley.
I nodded.

"*Les citrons?*"

"*Oui, merci. Je les veux bien,*" I said with a smile. Of course I wanted free lemons!

Beside me stood an elderly woman wearing a flowered dress and practical black shoes with a slight heel. She placed her goods into a caddy with wheels. Much more practical, I thought. I still had to get eggs, milk, yogurt, and *le goûter*, a snack, at the local 8 à Huit—our town's version of a 7-Eleven that was technically open from eight to eight, but that closed whenever the shopkeepers felt like it. At any rate, once I was finished with the market shop, I had to get the staples for my French family…or else! By this point, though, my basket was heavy and digging into my arm.

A French child's meal plan, like an American kid's, comprises breakfast, lunch, and dinner. But foraging in the cabinets or eating on the go (unless on a road trip) is strictly prohibited. Around four o'clock, children are allowed to have *le goûter*, usually a biscuit, muffin, or cookie. All meals and snacks must be consumed at the dining room table or breakfast counter—never in a bedroom or on the sofa.

Breakfast is simple. France is a nation of dunkers—meaning one dunks breakfast biscuits, croissants, or madeleines into milk warmed up in the microwave, for the kids, or hot tea, for Jean-Luc. Sometimes Max and Elvire ate cereal, also served in warm milk. Lunches and dinners are balanced—a protein, a vegetable, and a starch. A piece of fruit always follows a lunch and, unless it's a celebration or dinner party, a yogurt is served for dessert.

I'd read somewhere that French schools serve better lunches than American schools, the article making it sound like the kids eat gourmet meals in the cafeteria every day, and I asked the kids and Jean-Luc their thoughts.

"Ugh," said Elvire. "The food is disgusting. I only eat the salad."

"No," said Max. "It's eatable. And I never eat the salad."

Jean-Luc piped in. "Yes, but it is true that the meals are balanced—they might have a fish…"

"Fish sticks?" I asked.

"No, real fish," he said. I tried to imagine what would happen if American schools tried to serve *real* fish to picky students.

So, yes, there were some differences, and save for the fact that the French supermarket was closed on Sundays, when I liked to shop, I could get used to these new rules.

After such a long travel day, I really wasn't in the mood or mindset to cook anything from scratch. I made my way to the rotisserie truck, first picking up a succulent chicken for dinner, and then to the vendor that sold paella for a premade lunch.

The paella sizzled in a black speckled pan, filled with saffron-infused rice, black mussels, happy little clams, strips of succulent calamari, pink shrimp, and *langoustine*, crayfish. Not only was it a beautiful dish, it was delicious. I bought four portions, and lunch was set. The vendor, a stocky man with a square head and short-spiked gray hair, asked a question I didn't understand because he spoke so fast. I swore I heard the words "Bibbidi-Bobbidi-Boo."

But that couldn't have been right. He may have made a mean paella, but he wasn't my fairy godmother. And, sweating under the hot summer sun in my yoga pants and Keds, I was no Cinderella.

"*Pardon?*" I said.

"*Vous venez d'où?*" he repeated, this time slowly.

Oh, oh, oh! Where was I from? Got it. I answered, "Chicago and Los Angeles." And then I continued in French. "*Désolée. Je suis venue plus tôt. Et, maintenant, je suis super chaude et fatiguée.*"

His caterpillar-like eyebrows twisted in confusion, performing an acrobatic dance. The moment the words escaped my mouth, I knew I'd made a major error. The man choked back his laughter, his eyebrows now dancing the samba. His assistant clenched her teeth with surprise and fought back her giggles. Basically, I hadn't said, "I'm sorry, I've just arrived today, and now I'm super hot and tired," as I'd meant to. I'd said, "I came earlier and now I'm super horny and tired." I just stood there feeling like a fool until the man asked for his twenty euro.

Burning with embarrassment, I picked up the rest of the supplies at 8 à Huit, and shuffled the three blocks home, choosing to take the path behind the *mairie*, where there was no risk of somebody pushing this alien into traffic. In the back of the building, two bushy-eared donkeys with menacing eyes were tied to a cart. Our town had tons of events, including live music and puppet shows and circuses for the kids. But there were no flyers for a show in town. I wondered what on earth these donkeys were doing here. The only one way to get past them was to go around their rear ends, risking a kick. After my outing in town, I took my chances, chanting, "Nice donkey, nice donkey."

In a backyard along the path, a group of chickens squawked madly. These weren't cute, plump chickens, but scruffy, with elongated featherless necks and yellow, demonic eyes. They ran up to the fence and flapped their wings. Maybe they knew I'd just flown in from Los Angeles and thought I was casting the next *Jurassic Park*? Or maybe they just wanted to pluck my eyes out.

I walked faster, sweat pouring down my back, my basket so heavy I thought I'd have a heart attack. Finally, I made it back home, feeling as though the whole town, animals included, was out to get to me. It took me a few minutes to regain my composure. I chugged some water, deliberating whether I should open the bottle of wine I'd just picked up, and sat at the breakfast counter in the kitchen. Jean-Luc returned from the hardware store soon after, setting an arsenal of supplies on the counter.

"It's been so hot here, the whole town is plagued with fleas," he said. "I was lucky to get the last bombs."

"Great," I said.

"What's wrong?" he asked.

"This isn't the homecoming I expected," I said.

"Ah, it's just life, Sam. Nothing we could do. We'll get through it."

I straightened my shoulders and forced a smile. "I know. It's just such a pain." I didn't tell him about how disconnected and out of sorts I was really feeling. And the last thing I wanted was to be laughed at for my *faux pas* with the paella vendor. Instead, I asked, "Hungry?"

"Starved. I'm sure the kids are, too. They didn't eat much on the trip back home."

There was that word again. *Home.* Why didn't this feel like home? I set the table on the deck for lunch, and called *à table*, summoning them to the table the French way.

Elvire sat in her chair, looked at the dish, and smirked. "I hate *paella*."

I kept my internal scream deep inside.

Oh, *putain. Putain! Putain! Putain!*

THIS IS MY CIRCUS, AND THESE ARE MY FLEAS

I SUPPOSE JEAN-LUC AND I TECHNICALLY went on a honeymoon before our marriage, on the trip when we reconnected in August of 2009. I had called it the "rekindle the romance" tour, since I hadn't seen Jean-Luc in twenty years. The timing had been perfect. Max and Elvire were staying with their grandmother in Provence, so we could figure out if our connection was real without bringing his kids into the equation. I'd been nervous on the flight over, but told myself that if Jean-Luc and I connected in person the way we'd connected through letters, emails, and telephone calls, the adventure was worth the risk. We'd arranged beforehand that if I wasn't attracted to Jean-Luc on a physical level, I was supposed to kiss him on both cheeks, to *"faire la bise,"* the typical European greeting.

When he saw me, his beautiful bow-shaped lips curved into a sexy smile, and any worries I'd had vanished. He might not have had a full head of hair, but he worked the look well. And I loved the cleft in his chin, the square shape of his masculine jawline. He wore a blue and white striped shirt and jeans, undeniably French, and looked much better in person than in pictures. Our mutual attraction was instantaneous, just as it had been twenty years earlier.

For nine days, we traveled all over northern France, starting our trip in Chartres. From there it was off to the Loire Valley, where we visited castle after glorious castle, and then it was on to Dinan, a medieval town unique for its ramparts, in Bretagne. We visited the fortified city of Saint-Malo, complete with its pirate flags; enjoyed fresh oysters by the sea; and walked along the rugged beaches. We hiked through the ancient town of Mont Saint-Michel, which reminded me of a sand castle. We traversed the beaches of Normandy; the town of Deauville, known as the French Riviera of the North; and Bayeux, famed for its tapestry. We ate *moules frites* in the quaint seaside village of Étretat, known for the chalky cliffs Monet famously painted, and explored history, and drank fine French wines. We were a young(ish) couple falling head over heels in love and having the time of our lives. We spent our last two nights in Saint-Valéry-en-Caux, where the air was fresh and salty, clean—a promise of new beginnings.

At that time, I didn't realize that one year later, almost to the day, I'd be restarting my life in France. Yet here I was. The vacation fantasy was over. And real life was about to set in.

Max and Elvire were spending the remainder of the summer with their maternal grandmother, Meme, and we took the kids to the airport, waiting with them until a hostess gathered all the kids traveling without adults. Elvire listened to music. Max played a video game. Jean-Luc closed his eyes. I sat there, relishing the crisp air conditioning. A pretty flight attendant in a blue Air France suit came over, announcing the kids' flight to Marseille. Max and Elvire gave us quick kisses and scurried away.

"Call me when you land," said Jean-Luc.

"*Oui*," said Elvire with an eye roll.

We watched them pass through security and sat in the lobby until their plane took off. I was sad to see them go, but was looking forward to some alone time with Jean-Luc.

"Maybe, one day, we could take a trip to Paris?" I hinted, thinking it would be utterly romantic if we retraced the steps we had taken when we first met. Although he'd already taken me on the vacation of a lifetime, we never had made it to Paris. "Like a mini-honeymoon?"

"One day," said Jean-Luc. "But now we have a lot of work to do."

"I know," I said.

Instead of taking off on a romantic getaway, we were on a mission to de-flea the house. Bombs were ignited in all of the bedrooms. We washed the sheets, clothes, pillowcases, and blankets in hot water. And, much to Bella's delight, we combed her with a fine-toothed comb, wiping it off with a wet cloth, until there were no fleas in sight. The project took three days. When we weren't getting rid of the army of critters, Jean-Luc and I painted the bare walls in the stairwell a warm and rosy terra cotta to match the brickwork in the foyer.

My mother called, asking, "How's Bella?"

"Oh, she's better," I said. "She's playing with Uranus right now."

Uranus was the flea-ridden cat next door. And, phonetically, these words just came out so wrong we couldn't stop our laughter.

"And how are you?" asked my mom. "All unpacked?"

"I haven't even started yet. The suitcases are still in the hallway upstairs."

"You need to settle in."

I eyed my paint-splattered yoga pants, feet, and T-shirt. "Good idea," I said.

A nice breeze flowed in from the garden, a reprieve from the scorching weather. I opened the *volets* (shutters) off the kitchen and locked the heavy wooden doors into position with an iron latch. My favorite rosebush climbed up the wooden beams, its flowers nestling onto a small tiled roof. After a few days of watering, the bush was finally showing signs of life, its leaves no longer wilting. Perhaps it would bloom a second time? I needed to ground myself to this life, just like the rosebush.

Last Christmas, even before he'd proposed marriage, Jean-Luc had built me a closet on the balcony upstairs with pine floors and wood walls, and fitted it with shelves and bars from IKEA. It was time to unpack and make this house my home.

I hung up my clothes, folded my sweaters, and placed my shoes on the rack, setting all my kitchen tools and design elements to the side, thrilled that nothing had been damaged, especially the art I'd packed in Jean-Luc's suitcase. After jumping in the shower and scrubbing the paint off my body, I came to the conclusion that I probably shouldn't have painted barefoot. Clean and refreshed, I threw on a cute black cotton dress and toured my new digs, making mental notes on what we needed. Jean-Luc was utilitarian. If tape could fix something, he used it. For example: the bookshelf with the broken shelf mended with duct tape, and the scotch tape holding in place the wallpaper Bella had shredded. Thanks to a few family members and friends who had given us money for wedding gifts, we had some cash to spend.

I found Jean-Luc decompressing on the couch, watching the news on TV.

"Do you want to go to IKEA?" I asked.

. . . .

Jean-Luc went back to work the following week, coming home to share lunches with me when he could, and the kids stayed at Meme's home in Provence for two weeks, which meant I was left to my own devices for most of the day. Jean-Luc didn't like the color of the kitchen (he said the pale yellow reminded him of bile, and he hadn't had time to change it), so I painted the walls a warm, sunny orange. This time, I wore shoes.

Handy with a drill, I hung the art I'd brought from California on the walls—four pieces in the living room and two in the kitchen. I can't say that I'm a fan of putting furniture together, but I managed to assemble two bookcases and a desk without completely snapping. I just mumbled a lot of *putains*. Along with placing pictures of the family on top of the bookcase, I found a beautiful model of a wooden ship in the garage.

Jean-Luc regarded it with pride. "My father carved that, every detail, with his own two hands."

I ran my fingers across the delicate helm, then the mast. "It wasn't a kit?"

"*Non.*"

He shook the desk. It wobbled. "Did you use all the parts, Sam?"
"Yes?"

"Sam?"

He knew me so well. I grimaced and pulled out the rogue screw
I'd put in my pocket after I couldn't figure out where it should go.
"Maybe I should stick to decorating and gardening, not building?"

Jean-Luc shook his head.

The house was coming together one (hidden) screw at a time.
Add the green accent colors of throw pillows, blankets, candles, the
plants in the living room, and our tiny castle was bright and cheery.
Now that I'd put a little of my design stamp on it, I was feeling more
at home.

On Saturday, Jean-Luc and I went to the market together. I
blushed when I passed the paella vendor and kept my eyes down.
But with Jean-Luc by my side, everything wasn't so foreign. And, in
addition to carrying the heavy basket, he did all the talking.

"Do you want some olives?" asked Jean-Luc, stopping in front of
a vendor.

Wooden bowls overflowed with the plump beauties in shades of
black, green, and yellow, some seasoned with red peppers. "Yes," I
said. "And some spices, too."

"Which ones?" he asked, and I pointed.

My eyes darted to all the stalls, some with baskets filled with
fresh fruits and vegetables, explosions of color; some with plump
wild boar and pork sausages and wheels of beautiful, golden cheeses;
some with wine. There were so many local wines and cheeses to
choose from. Gaillac and Fronton! Corbières and Cahors! Real
Roquefort cheese from Roquefort! Cabécou, a mild goat cheese
from the Périgord! Tomme des Pyrénées, a rustic cheese from the
Ariège! And what a dream: Bordeaux and St. Émilion were only
two and a half hours away by car. My list of places to discover on the
weekends grew every day.

"What do you want for lunch?" asked Jean-Luc. "Paella?"

"No, we had that a few weeks ago," I said, shuffling my feet. "How about a nice salad? Like a niçoise? And a crusty baguette? I mean, we just bought those beautiful olives."

"Okay," he said. "Let's pick up a bottle of rosé, too?"

I smiled. He knew I never said no to wine.

Soon, my kitchen was stocked with everything I needed to cook French—including golden threads of saffron, two varieties of powdery paprika, whole peppercorns, garlic, *fleur de sel*, and *herbes de Provence*.

Back at home, Jean-Luc chilled the wine in the freezer and set the table while I prepared lunch, boiling potatoes and eggs, steaming green beans, making lemon vinaigrette, and chopping tomatoes. Twenty minutes later, we were about to sit down on the deck for the meal when our neighbors, Claude and Paulette, peered over the fence separating our property lines.

"*Coucou!*" said Paulette. Hey you!

"Oh, Jean-Luc and Sam," said Claude. "Welcome back home!"

Claude and Paulette were an older couple in their seventies. He was a burly man with a kind face and big brown eyes. Paulette, his wife, was a sparrow of a woman with a singsong voice and a perfectly coiffed curly head of hair. They were an adorable couple, continuously holding hands, and talking over one another.

"Do you want some tomatoes?" asked Claude.

I eyed Jean-Luc and mouthed, "We just picked up a ton at the market."

Before Jean-Luc could answer, Claude said, "We have too many and I'm bringing some over."

Thirty seconds later came the tap at the door. Hip for his age, Claude wore black track pants with a white stripe down the side, a white polo, and black sneakers. He held an enormous basket filled with tomatoes in every size and color imaginable—*coeur de boeuf*, cherry, and colorful heirlooms like Black Krims, Green Zebras, and Pineapples. Paulette stood next to Claude, wearing khaki pants, a light sweater, and a giant smile. She held three small jars and a plastic bag filled with something green and purple. More tomatoes? Jean-Luc ushered them into the house and we exchanged "*la bise.*"

"There's plenty of salad," said Jean-Luc. "Would you like to stay for lunch?"

"Oh no, but thank you," said Paulette. "I've already made our meal. We're waiting for Edith and Mark. They'll be over in an hour."

Edith was their daughter, and Mark was her husband. Both of them were legally deaf, but could read lips. Well, at least they could read Jean-Luc's lips. When I'd met them in the spring, I think my French led to some confusion in that department. They just smiled and shrugged.

"Well, at least stay for a glass of wine," said Jean-Luc.

"Maybe a little one," said Claude.

Paulette handed me one of the jars. "This is a *pâté*. Claude made it. Do you like *pâté*?"

I understood most everything so far. "I adore *pâté*."

"Me? I like making *confiture*. This one is peach, and this one is fig. Figs are in season now, and we've brought you some of those, too." She grinned while nodding, eyes wide, and handed me the remaining jars and, to my delight, the bag which was filled with glorious figs.

Jean-Luc uncorked the wine.

"Should I wash some figs and set out the *pâté* and a baguette?" I asked.

"Good idea," said Jean-Luc.

In France, time was never rushed, and company was always enjoyed, no matter if it was an impromptu get-together. When guests came over, the French way was to serve an *apéro*—an appetizer served with a cocktail, champagne, or wine. I washed the figs and sliced them, their insides bursting with colors of bright orange-pink. A couple of sliced tomatoes later and I set the goodies on the table with the *pâté* and a loaf of bread. While I was at it, I filled two bowls, one with olives and one with radishes, and made a quick dipping sauce with squeezed lemon and *fromage blanc*. We had the drinks. We had the food. And we had the company.

Even though I'd taken an intensive monthlong French course

the past spring, I was still having a difficult time with the language, especially when people like Claude and Paulette speed-talked with heavy southwestern-France accents. From what I could discern, they were talking about our wedding in California, the kids, and the hot summer weather.

Our conversation was a mélange of French (them and Jean-Luc), English (Jean-Luc and me), and broken French (me with everybody). Still, I was able to thank this kind couple for bestowing us with so many tomatoes. Paulette suggested that I make *tomates farcies* (stuffed tomatoes), a recipe she had given me a few months before, and which she'd had to write down because I couldn't understand her simple spoken instructions.

Rather than letting minor linguistic issues get me down, I immersed myself in learning to cook French. Served and prepared with love, food, for now, became my way of communicating. I had so many tomatoes that, along with the *tomates farcies*, I was able to make *tian Provençal* (a layered vegetable dish with tomatoes, eggplants, zucchini, and onions), *oeufs à la Provençal*, and ratatouille, recipes passed on to me from Jean-Luc and his family.

To my delight, tomatoes didn't need a translator.

WINGING IT

FOR THE FIRST COUPLE OF weeks, *ma vie française* with a touch of saffron and Spanish flavors was fantastic, filled with adventure and fun and discovering new foods. But when Jean-Luc went back to work, too busy to come home for lunches, and with the kids at their grandmother's, no matter how hard I tried to fight them, feelings of isolation crept in, crushing all optimism.

I pulled up all the employment sites, looking for anything related to graphic design or advertising in the Toulouse area. There was nothing. I pulled up the Airbus site, hoping to find a job opening in marketing. Nothing. To thwart a nervous breakdown, I started to blog, my posts struggling to convince others, and myself, that I loved my new life in France.

In my teens, I had wanted to be an actress or a singer and, in my junior year of high school, I attended the Chicago Academy for the Performing and Visual Arts, choosing theatre as my major and taking voice lessons once a week. But after a move to Boston at the age of sixteen, my dreams had metamorphosed, and art had become a big part of my life. Instead of singing "One" on Broadway, I ended up at Syracuse University, majoring in advertising design, my father's domain. Upon graduation, it didn't take long to understand this dream simply wasn't mine.

My first attempt to leave the advertising world came in 2002. I'd launched a handbag company, Samantha Kim, with a jewelry designer and very good friend, Susan Kim. After winning the Distinction in Design award at Marshall Field's department store in Chicago (now Macy's), we received an order of three hundred bags, which we had manufactured in China. Unfortunately, we didn't meet our manufacturers' minimum order and had to pay a premium for the bags as well as the shipping, plus meet the store's requirements of having general corporate liability insurance. Needless to say, we didn't make a dime. Still, I held on to the naïve hope this order would launch the company into Kate Spade fame.

A few weeks before the bags arrived from Hong Kong, I was checking the business email accounts for communications with the manufacturer and instead stumbled across a personal email. In it, Susan and a friend of hers had made a disparaging remark about my then-husband Chris, calling him a pretentious fop. They also questioned his involvement in our endeavor because he had never raised the money he'd promised. Chris forced me to choose where my loyalties lay: with Susan or with him. It got ugly. Very ugly. After a couple of rounds with an attorney, our friendship destroyed, Susan and I parted ways.

Three hundred bags were soon delivered to my apartment. There was a huge problem. The closure element, a hidden magnet, had slipped. I sewed every last magnet in by hand, through two layers of fake suede. My fingers were bloody and raw. I didn't eat. I couldn't sleep. The business for which I'd been so hopeful was going to fail—just like my marriage. So, it was back to advertising to pay the bills. Back to a marriage I no longer wanted to be in. Back to everything that didn't make me happy. Yet, I still hung in there.

In 2007, two years before I apologized to Jean-Luc via email and the seven-post blog, I discovered writing. Writing allowed me to do everything I dreamed of—sing on the page, act out scenes, and design new worlds. I wrote two middle-grade novels, one about two kids who play a role in saving the earth's creatures from extinction, the other about a sideshow attraction on a search for his identity. I even tried my hand at young adult fiction, penning a fantasy novel about a modern-day goddess.

In May of 2009, writing connected me to Jean-Luc. Later that summer, I also managed to rekindle my friendship with Susan, sending her a heartfelt apology via email. I also told her I'd left Chris. We Skyped later that day, and we cried and laughed and cried. Thanks to putting down words on a page, I really did have a second chance when it came to life and love.

Plus, writing didn't cost me a dime, only time. And one thing I had now was time. Until my French improved by Superman leaps and bounds, I couldn't just sit around the house having Words with Friends marathons with Nanny. Perhaps it was time for me to follow a new dream?

I had a new book concept in mind—a story based on my life, one that made me happy—the story of when I reconnected with Jean-Luc. I tapped at my keyboard all day long, my hair in a ponytail. But writing was a solitary task. Apart from Bella, during the day I was alone, disconnected. And the cat kept dropping lizard tails at my feet.

. . . .

At the end of August, when we picked up the kids at the airport, they were a bit quieter and more reserved than they had been before they left, most likely due the fact that Meme wasn't Jean-Luc's biggest fan. Jean-Luc had split up with Meme's daughter, Frédérique, in 2002, and in the midst of a midlife crisis, he took up with a younger woman he'd met while traveling for work—a relationship that was short-lived. He shared custody of the kids and visited them on the weekends until cancer took Frédérique's life in October 2006.

A few years later, in search of a balanced life, Jean-Luc had married a very, very young Russian physicist, Natasha, who, instead of love, showed only tolerance for his children. He'd thought the stability would change the strained relationship she'd had with the kids. It didn't. Their marriage didn't last long. And now he was married to me, a strange woman he'd met in Paris in 1989 and reconnected with on the Internet twenty years later—during his divorce from Natasha. It was up to me to prove to Meme and the kids that we were on our way to becoming a real family now.

When Max and Elvire walked into the house and saw the kitchen, now painted orange with two Italian paintings adorning once-bare walls and the big silver bowl filled with fruit on the breakfast bar, their smiles widened. Their eyes darted back and forth with glee when they saw the changes I'd made to the living room—the art on the walls and the bursts of color, thanks to the throw pillows, blankets, and plants. We headed upstairs, where pictures of the family adorned the bookcases. I retrieved an empty picture frame and handed it to Elvire. "*C'est pour la photo de ta mère.*"

I'd seen the photo of her mother, Frédérique, in her room. In it, Elvire sat on her lap, both of their hair covered in confetti. This was how I knew the kids had their mother's beautiful feline eyes.

"*Merci,*" Elvire said. "*Merci.*"

I knew I'd never replace their mom, and I certainly didn't want to compete with her memory, but I was now a part of their lives. And I was doing my best to fit in. We all had to get used to change. Especially me.

A few weeks later, I attended one of Max's rugby matches with Jean-Luc. The other parents were nice enough and introduced themselves. A never-ending round of *la bise* was exchanged. Everybody kissed everybody. The kids. The parents. And I was unsure of what to do. One of the fathers was about to go in for *la bise*, but I stuck out my hand to shake his. Awkward.

"Are you integrating well? Do you like it here?" people asked, and I'd smile and nod.

One of the moms came up to me. A blond, wearing jeans, she looked hip and cool, and I'd hoped to possibly strike up a friendship. "I hear you're American. I speak English."

She said all of this in French, and we had a polite but stiff conversation, which ended with, "Are you integrating well? Do you like it here?"

Max's rugby position was a winger. And I was the one winging it. "Uh, *oui*?"

As I stood awkwardly on the sidelines while Jean-Luc chatted with the dads, I wondered if it would ever be possible for me to make friends in Cugnaux. There was no welcome wagon, no invitations extended for a dinner. No acceptance. I was just there like a pest, an American fly buzzing around. I left at halftime and walked the three blocks home, loneliness creeping into my heart.

My mom called me every day, saying things like "You should find a job," or "You should make friends," or "You should teach English," and, putting the pressure on high, "You should have a baby!"

"I want to do all that. I do," I'd say with sigh. "But I think I need some more time to settle in."

Mothers really know how to twist the knife. Seriously, how could I have a baby when I felt exactly like one? I was the rawest version of myself, stripped down, bare and vulnerable, and, besides Jean-Luc, there was no safety net. Nobody had warned me that starting over would be so hard. And there were no guidebooks for starting over—not like this.

The only things keeping me sane were cooking, planning meals, writing, and Jean-Luc's love. I was happy in the kitchen and even happier when Jean-Luc came home from work. Plus, when I was cutting onions, I had an excuse for my watery eyes. I knew I needed to get the old, confident Sam back, but I didn't know how to do it, not when I wasn't comfortable in my own skin. I may have loved performing arts in high school, but I'd always thought that I was a horrible actress. Apparently not, because around Jean-Luc, I'd smile and laugh, playing the role of a lifetime: the good wife and stepmom. He had no idea how I was really feeling when I was alone.

Instead of sharing my feelings with Jean-Luc and my family and friends, as I should have been doing, I swallowed them down, trying to be the resilient woman everybody thought I was. But I'd packed a melon baller instead of a parachute and, instead of landing on my feet, I was splayed out on my back. I felt like a dog with severe separation anxiety, staring at the door and waiting for its owners to come home.

At least I could focus on food.

Eating in season is *de rigueur* for the French. You eat what's fresh and available at the market. In the U.S., it's not uncommon to find strawberries the size of baseballs year-round. In France, you'll only find strawberries at the market from May to early October depending on the variety. All goods—meat, fishes, vegetables, and cheeses— are marked with the country of origin, sometimes even the town. Jean-Luc always insisted I buy from la France when I could. While certain produce is available year-round at our colorful markets or grocery stores, either imported from neighboring countries like Spain, or from distant lands, I wouldn't find butternut squash in May or fava beans in September, unless they were packed up and frozen at Picard, a supermarket known for its packaged goods.

Mussels and oysters are best enjoyed in months with an r—September, October, November, December, January, February, March, and April. Once fall rolls around, wild mushrooms like *cèpes* (like porcini), *girolles* (chanterelles), and *pleurotes* (oyster), make mouths water with delight. Many French families take to foraging in the forests in the fall, bringing their bounty to the pharmacist to make sure their mushrooms aren't poisonous.

Lucky me, it was September. And I loved mussels to the point of being obsessed. So I didn't stop with *moules à la marinière*—not after I found the recipes for *moules* curry or *moules au Roquefort* or *moules à la plancha*, the latter of which were grilled on a platter with fresh garlic, parsley, shallots, and olive oil. The kids didn't mind, mostly because they were served with their favorite food group: French fries. Tonight, I was getting creative, adding slices of fennel and ginger to *moules à la marinière*. One word: delicious.

Max wasn't around the house as much as Elvire was. After school, he had rugby practice twice a week, and sometimes he went to a friend's house to play. I didn't understand why the girl was always home. When I was her age, I too, like Max, was always at a friend's house if I didn't have homework. After slicing up the ginger, I brought up Elvire's laundry to her room and tapped on her door, hoping maybe she'd talk to me, tell me about her day.

"*Quoi?*" she said, her tone harsh.

I set her clothes, which I'd neatly folded, on her dresser. "*Merci* would have been a politer response. The laundry doesn't do itself. Put your clothes away."

I stood in the doorway of her room. Clothes and school papers littered the floor. You couldn't even see her desk. One of my scarves was balled up in the corner. Apparently, she'd borrowed it without asking. That didn't bother me, but the fact it was on the floor did. I picked it up, brushing off the dust.

"How can you do homework in this hurricane?" I asked.

Elvire grumbled, then slammed her door, shutting me out. And I was hurt. More than hurt. All I wanted was a little acceptance. I brought up the subject of respecting our belongings over our meal of mussels. "Did you put your clothes away?" asked Jean-Luc, turning his attention to Elvire.

"*Non,*" she said.

"You do it right now," he said.

"After she clears the table," I said, hoping to establish one tiny ounce of authority.

"*Mais,* Papa," she said, batting her eyelashes. "I have homework."

"Maybe your homework would be finished if you didn't watch streaming videos all afternoon," I said, and Elvire's eyes narrowed into a glare. I didn't care if looks could kill. I was the one who was angry, and I had every right to be.

"Elvire," said Jean-Luc, his voice stern. "Is this true?"

Max fought back his giggles. It wasn't the first time I'd seen this kind of reaction from either of the kids. They seemed to get off when one or the other was in trouble. It was like a game to them. Jean-Luc was a good dad. Like most parents, he wanted his kids to be well behaved and get good grades. But I didn't always agree with his parenting style. Like most French parents, he didn't have a problem with threatening an occasional spanking, the dreaded *fessée*. On the other hand, he wasn't a helicopter parent; he didn't hover around making sure they did their homework or practiced the piano; he waited for their grades, and if they weren't good, all hell broke loose. But kids are kids, no matter where they are from. Jean-Luc could scream and yell if he wanted to, but I could tell his words would go in one ear and right out the other.

"Now," said Jean-Luc. "And hand over your cell phone and computer."

Elvire huffed while she slammed plates into the dishwasher.

During the day, I'd busy myself gardening, occasionally seeing Claude and Paulette in their yard, and I'd try to chat with them as best I could, doing everything I could to remain positive. Yet, I couldn't weed out my loneliness.

The honeymoon phase was definitely over, and a distressing stage of culture shock set in.

I'M AN IMMIGRANT?

L ONELINESS WASN'T THE ONLY THING troubling me during those first few months in France. My U.S. driver's license had reciprocity with the French government, which was a bonus. But if I couldn't exchange my license before it expired in October, I'd be up a very expensive creek without a paddle—namely the dilemma that would be French driving school and taking a test I would most likely fail.

Jean-Luc and I dashed over to the *préfecture* with all the required documents: my long-stay visa; my passport, which had said visa in it; my license; a certified translation of my license; two mug shots because it was *interdit* (prohibited) to smile for identification photos; proof of my address; and an affidavit from Jean-Luc stating that I lived with him. Because, come on, where else would I be living?

We spoke to a somewhat pleasant woman behind a plexiglass window, who told us to take a seat in the *salle d'attente* (waiting room). A few moments later, another woman—apparently the one in charge—came out of the back room and sauntered over, asking for my *carte de séjour* (green card). With Jean-Luc's help, I explained that the French consulate had told me my long-stay visa took the place of the *carte de séjour* for the first year.

The woman was quick to correct me. "*Non, non, non,*" she said, repeating the word three times, as the French often do for emphasis.

"You must get your *premier titre de séjour* from *L'Offi*, the French immigration service. After you pass your tests, they put a special stamp in your passport. But, unfortunately, it may take up to three months to get your appointment there."

I'd only been told to contact *L'Offi* within three months of my arrival; I wasn't told I'd actually had to go there. Now, I had to deal with my driver's license *and* immigration? At the same time? I was on the verge of tears.

The woman nodded with understanding. "This is not uncommon," she said. "I see that your license expires in one month. If you can get a statement from *L'Offi* that your appointment has been made"—the French are big on affidavits—"we can start the paperwork and I'll hold your license for you, rendering it when you have your *premier titre de séjour*."

Somebody in the French government was being nice, helpful, and understanding? After the woman at our local *mairie* had given us such a hard time, running us ragged on a never-ending paper trail for our marriage documents for our civil ceremony in France, this was most welcome news. I was tempted to hug the woman. Instead, Jean-Luc and I thanked her profusely.

The moment we got home, Jean-Luc called *L'Offi* on my behalf. He was able to get a man by the name of Didier on the phone, and he explained my situation. Although the first available appointment wasn't until November, after my license would expire, Didier agreed to send an affidavit to us via email. It arrived in Jean-Luc's inbox within ten minutes.

About two hours later, Didier emailed Jean-Luc again, alerting him that a *rendezvous* had opened up in early October. Would I like it? Jean-Luc set the appointment, which was followed by another email. Apparently, I had to fork out a three-hundred-euro tax that day, payable only with special stamps called *les timbres fiscaux* purchased at the local treasury, pass a medical exam (which was given at their offices), speak with an official so they could assess my French and employment skills, and sit through an hour-long cultural lecture on France. Once all these steps were completed, I would receive my *premier titre de séjour*.

My upper lip curled. "What kind of a medical exam is it? Why do I need X-rays?"

"They want to be sure you don't have tuberculosis," said Jean-Luc.

"Tuberculosis?"

"It's a problem from immigrants coming from northern Africa."

"But I'm from—"

"They won't change the rules for you. You're still an immigrant."

I'd been a "sandwich artist" in college and a telemarketer. I'd been a waitress, a salesgirl, a babysitter, an art director, and a handbag designer, not to mention a dog walker. I'd been married, and I'd been divorced, and I'd remarried. But I'd never been an immigrant. And I'd never been a parent. The words "instant immigrant stepmom" played on my lips, this new reality boggling my mind.

That night, I decided to introduce my French family to a new dish: tuna noodle casserole, accompanied by a salad. I was in the mood for a taste of "home"—one I hadn't had since I was a child. The kids set the table and we sat down to dinner. Jean-Luc poured some wine into my glass. It was only a centimeter deep, as usual, which really got under my craw. Whoever came up with the rumor that the French drank wine like there was no tomorrow, including the kids, well, they were dead wrong. I picked up the bottle of Gaillac and poured. "Tonight, I'm having an American-sized glass."

"You're only supposed to *taste* the wine," said Jean-Luc.

I took a sip and shot him a coy smile. "I *am* tasting it."

Elvire's upper lip curled. She pointed at our steaming meal. "*C'est quoi, ça? C'est dégueulasse.*"

"*C'est une casserole au thon,*" I said, serving her a heaping spoonful. "And it's not disgusting."

She grimaced and pushed her plate away. "*Non.*"

I shot Jean-Luc a look, my bottom lip quivering. It didn't matter that this meal came with a French twist, since I couldn't find cream of mushroom soup at the grocery store and had replaced it with a *velouté forestièr* (a mix of forest mushrooms) and a healthy dosing of *crème fraîche.*

"She hasn't even tried one bite. And all I'm doing is trying."

"*Mange-le,*" said Jean-Luc. Eat.

Elvire slammed her fork down and crossed her arms with defiance. Why was she being so insolent all of a sudden?

Isabelle, Jean-Luc's sister, had told me that Natasha, Jean-Luc's ex-wife, would glare at the kids and pout when they hugged their dad because she was competing with Max and Elvire for his attention. And the one time Natasha prepared a Russian meal for the kids, the kids refused to eat it. Natasha bolted upstairs to the bedroom, slammed the door, and cried, refusing to come out of the room for hours. She never tried her hand at cooking anything ever again, not one French meal, nothing.

Perhaps, I thought, Elvire was trying to keep me at arm's length, not wanting to get close. What if she thought I was going to leave too? Or had the novelty of having me as a stepmom simply worn off?

"*Elvire, mange ton repas,*" repeated Jean-Luc. Eat your dinner.

"*Non,*" said Elvire. "*C'est dégueulasse!*"

The French flew fast off Jean-Luc's lips, his voice deep. Max, of course, laughed. I put my head in my hands. I'd cooked over one hundred meals for the kids, and now this one casserole, which, admittedly, was not the prettiest of dishes, had caused a full-on war between father and daughter. Jean-Luc wasn't stupid. He knew Elvire was pushing her limits, testing me, testing him. Still, I knew I needed to defuse this bomb before it exploded, leaving smears of tuna noodle casserole on everybody's faces. It was important for Elvire to know that I wasn't a threat.

"Jean-Luc, I think I need to deal with this," I said, and he stopped his tirade about the starving children in Africa and how this wasn't a restaurant where she could order anything she wanted. In the best French I could muster up, I said, "Elvire, if there are some recipes of your grandmother's you'd like for me to cook, please ask her for them. It's hard planning meals all the time, especially since you and Max don't like the same things."

Although the kids' taste buds were accustomed to strange things like escargot, duck, and *foie gras*, in my experience French kids did *not* eat everything. One evening we had the *haricots* fiasco, in which Max refused to eat fresh steamed green beans and, thanks to Jean-Luc's prodding, ended up in tears. Since then, I'd made fresh green beans for Elvire, Jean-Luc, and me; canned for Max. Elvire didn't like the paella from the market; Max did. Max didn't like salads; Elvire did. When one kid liked mushrooms or spinach, the other didn't. The list went on and on. Both of the kids had one thing in common, though: they were hesitant to try anything new to them and stuck to meals they were accustomed to. But I was *not* a short-order cook. This madness had to stop.

I sighed. "So, you'll get me some recipes?"

She shook her head and said that they didn't exist on paper, that her grandmother had everything memorized. I told her to look up her favorites on Google when she had a chance, and then I sent her into the kitchen to make a sandwich. We both had tears in our eyes.

Max took another bite of the casserole. "*C'est pas mal. C'est mangeable.*"

Although eatable wasn't quite a compliment, I'd take it over *dégueulasse.*

"So should I make it again?" I asked. "Or should I stick with *moules frites?*"

"*Ou McDo,*" said Max, nodding with a wide smile.

I groaned. To think, the kids thought McDonald's was the best restaurant in the whole entire world, worthy of a Michelin two-star rating. I poured myself a second glass of wine and said, "Tomorrow night, I'm making a quiche Lorraine."

. . . .

I may have perfected the ideal quiche, and the many ways to make *les tartes salées* (savory tarts), which got the stamp of approval from the kids, but a few weeks later, I upset Max to the point of tears, accusing of him of lying when he said he set the table. He had, but I'd been so scatterbrained with stress that I'd forgotten. Thanks to the language barrier, it took a half hour of apologizing to set things right.

For a little family bonding time, we took the kids bowling. Elvire's thin arms looked like they were going break off as she whipped the ball down the alley. We had something in common that day—we were both terrible bowlers. The problem was Jean-Luc; he was good. And Max was competitive. Jean-Luc's score was reaching one-twenty. Max sat on the bench, pouting and stomping his feet. When it was his turn, he deliberately threw gutter balls. Elvire laughed at her brother. "It's only a game," she said.

"Shut up," Max said. And then he punched her in the arm.

He was a very sore loser. Jean-Luc took him to the side. I didn't know what to say, except that I really hated Max's reaction. "*Pourquoi est-ce que tu agis comme ça?*" I asked. Why are you acting like this?

Elvire repeated me, making fun of my pronunciation and bad grammar with an annoying, nasal-sounding French accent.

Wasn't this outing supposed to be fun?

Considering I came from a blended family, I'd thought I was prepared for instant motherhood. But I'd thought wrong. I was trying to put my best foot forward, but kept tripping. One issue and frustration at a time, the pressure kept building, so much in fact that I wondered if it was possible for people to spontaneously combust— surely probable when one locked up all of their feelings inside and threw the key over their shoulder.

My confidence was disappearing and I started to resent France, blaming the country for making me feel that whatever I did was wrong.

When I stopped by the local *boulangerie* simply to ask for a baguette, my words barely formed. I called this my "mouse voice" phase. It was kind of hard to communicate when people couldn't actually hear you. When the phone rang, I shuddered, eyeing it, but never answering unless caller ID displayed Jean-Luc's or my mother's numbers. When the doorbell rang, I hid upstairs and peeked through the curtains, trying to avoid les *Témoins de Jéhovah* (Jehovah's Witnesses), who apparently decided that I needed saving—even though they couldn't understand "mouse." The day the kind-hearted zealots caught me off guard, they shoved a brochure written in English in my hand and stood on my doorstep smiling. I let out an *eep* and a barely audible *merci*, right before I slammed the front door in their faces.

At night, sometimes I'd hole up in the master bedroom with my computer, checking out blogs, Facebook, or anything in English, just to avoid watching French television programs with my family— especially *Les Guignols*, a satirical show using puppets created to look like French political figures like Nicolas Sarkozy and Carla Bruni or François Hollande. Not only did I not understand the humor of the show, puppets scared the crap out of me.

Even simple tasks like going to the grocery store brought on severe frustrations. The grocer had a "world" section filled with Japanese products, but they didn't carry panko? How was I supposed to make my famed chicken Milanese with regular breadcrumbs? The yogurt aisle was overwhelming—there were too many choices. Why, oh why were milk, eggs, and cream not in the refrigerated section? And where, oh where was my beloved cottage cheese? I missed strange things I didn't even like or use. Yellow mustard. Peanut butter. Our pots and pans were warped on the bottom, and I wanted to purchase new ones, but, starting at thirty euro a pop, the prices for the quality were too high, and the pots weren't sold with lids. As I searched for one ounce of familiarity, always coming up empty-handed, homesickness set in. Plus, with an Indian summer upon us, it was ninety degrees outside, and the French version of air conditioning was to close the *volets*. I was sweating bullets.

I was close to tears when I talked to my mother on my forty-first birthday.

"Happy birthday to you," my mom howled off-key. "Did you get my ecard?"

"Yep, I did. Thanks."

"How's Jean-Luc?"

"Wonderful—as usual."

"And how are the kids?"

"They're great. They made me homemade cards." I paused. "Honestly, the kids are kind of driving me nuts. I had to break up a fight this morning. Elvire was teasing Max, so Max punched her on the arm, and then she went ballistic. I actually had to step in between them, separate them, and send them to their rooms."

"Good God, what did Jean-Luc do?"

"He wasn't here. He was at work." I bit down on my bottom lip—about to serve an American-sized glass of *whine* with my French cheese. I told my mom about my struggles, my feelings, ending my sorry monologue with: "Sometimes all this change is overwhelming—"

"New country? New man? The kids? I can imagine." She paused. "Sam, you've got to take some time and breathe."

"Uh-huh," I said, holding my breath. "But right now I have to get to French immigration."

When I came home from my second session—*la formation civique*—at *L'Offi*, Jean-Luc finally noticed the panicked look on my face. I couldn't hide it. The woman in charge of the session clearly hated her job. And immigrants. When an African man asked to use the facilities, she'd refused and then continued her lecture on how it was against the law to beat your wife when you live in France. Well, this life in France was beating me down one swift punch at a time.

"Are you not happy?" Jean-Luc asked, concerned.

"I'm happy with us," I said, "But—"

"But what?" he asked.

"I thought I could handle everything, all the change and adjustments, but everything kind of came at me at once," I said.

"Oney, you have to talk to me. We promised to keep no secrets from one another. You can't just ignore problems, hoping they'll go away. And you have to try harder to integrate."

"I know," I said. "But before I integrate, I really need to get my confidence back. Right now, it's shot."

"I understand," said Jean-Luc. "And I know you can do it. That's why I fell in love with you."

The question of the day was how could I do it? How could I rediscover the confident woman with whom Jean-Luc had fallen in love—the woman who took a risk and dared to follow her heart, the woman who changed everything in her world for him? Somewhere on this journey, I'd lost her.

PAULETTE'S *TOMATES FARCIES*

Prep time: 15 minutes

Cook time: 45 minutes

Serves: 4

Great for: a simple family meal

Wine suggestion: Bandol Rosé

- Extra virgin olive oil
- 8 large tomatoes*
- ¼ cup dry white wine
- 1¼ pounds ground meat, either hamburger or pork, or a mix of both
- 3 cloves garlic, peeled, de-germed, and finely minced
- 2 shallots, finely minced
- ½ cup flat parsley, finely minced, plus extra for garnish
- 3 healthy pinches *herbes de Provence*
- 1½ slices white bread, crusts cut off, torn into pieces
- 1 egg
- 1 handful breadcrumbs or panko (optional)
- 1 healthy pinch *fleur de sel* (or other coarse salt)
- Salt and freshly ground black pepper, to taste

Preheat the oven to 400°F. Lightly cover the bottom of a 9 x 12 baking dish with olive oil. Slice the caps off the tomatoes, and place them to the side. Hollow out the tomatoes with a knife and a spoon, without cutting through the bottom, so they resemble small bowls. Set the tomato pulp aside. Lightly salt the interior of each tomato, setting them upside down on a plate to drain. Coarsely chop the tomato pulp, place it in the baking dish, and pour the wine into the mixture.

For the *farcie* (stuffing), mix the ground meat in a large mixing bowl with the garlic, shallots, parsley, and *herbes de Provence*. Season with salt and pepper. Place the bread onto the mixture. Add the egg to the mixture, and mix all of the ingredients with your hands. Once the meat is well-combined with the herbs, use a spoon to fill the tomatoes to the top. Place the tomatoes in the baking dish, meat side up.** Drizzle with olive oil, and place a cap on each tomato. Sprinkle the entire dish with a bit of *fleur de sel*. Bake for 45 minutes. Serve with rice, spooning the sauce from the bottom of the baking dish on top. Garnish with chopped parsley.

* You can also stuff small squashes or zucchini, and mixing up your vegetables makes for a colorful, happy dish!

** If you'd like to sprinkle some breadcrumbs or panko on the farcie *(stuffing)*, now's the time to do it.

JEAN-LUC'S *MOULES À LA MARINIÈRE*

Prep time: 15 minutes

Cook time: 6 to 10 minutes

Serves: 4

Great for: lunch, family dinner, or a casual dinner party

Wine suggestion: Muscadet

- 2 tablespoons unsalted butter
- 1 tablespoon extra virgin olive oil
- 3 to 4 shallots, peeled and sliced
- 3 to 4 cloves garlic, peeled, de-germed, and sliced*
- 3 cups white wine (any white or rosé)**
- 3 healthy pinches *herbes de Provence*
- 1 healthy pinch *fleur de sel* (or 3 pinches salt)
- 4 pounds mussels, cleaned and de-bearded***
- ¼ cup flat parsley, chopped, plus extra for garnish

In a large pot, melt the butter with the olive oil. Add the shallots and garlic, and sauté for about 5 minutes, or until translucent. Pour in 2 cups of the wine, adding in the *fleur de sel* and *herbes de Provence*. Bring the liquid to a low boil. Add the mussels and the parsley to the pot, along with the remaining wine. Stir with a slotted spoon, and cover. Turn the mussels every few minutes, covering the pot in between turns. Once the mussels have opened (discard any that haven't), they are ready to serve with french fries. Garnish with parsley. For a change, try this recipe with one of the following sauces.

> * *A few delicious additions to the shallots and garlic are thin slices of fresh ginger, fennel, or a combo of both. Rounds of jalapeño peppers make for a spicy garnish.*
> ** *Instead of white wine, try experimenting with beer or cider!*
> *** *When cooking mussels, the general rule is one pound per person. Also, be sure to discard any mussels with broken shells.*

Moules Curry Sauce

Prep time: 15 minutes
Cook time: 6 to 10 minutes

- 2 cups unsweetened coconut milk
- 3 to 4 tablespoons curry powder
- 1 lime, juiced and zest removed, finely chopped
- 1 tablespoon grated ginger
- 1 lemongrass stalk, sliced into 2-inch long pieces (optional)
- ⅛ cup parsley, chopped (flat variety preferred), for garnish
- Salt and freshly ground black pepper, to taste

In a medium-sized pot, combine the coconut milk, curry powder, lime juice, lime zest, ginger, and lemongrass slices. Stir until well combined. Cook over medium heat for about 5 to 6 minutes until sauce is warm.

Once the mussels have opened, add two ladles of the wine broth they've been cooking in (about ¾ cup) to the curry sauce. Heat the sauce for another minute. Season with salt and pepper, remove the lemongrass, and discard. Using a slotted spoon, ladle sauce over the mussels, and garnish with parsley.

Moules Roquefort Sauce

Prep time: 15 minutes
Cook time: 6 to 10 minutes

- 1½ cups heavy cream
- 1 cup Roquefort or bleu cheese, crumbled, plus extra for garnish
- ⅛ cup parsley, chopped (flat variety preferred), for garnish
- Salt and freshly ground black pepper, to taste

In a medium-sized pot, combine the cream with the cheese. Cook over low heat for about 5 to 6 minutes until sauce is warm, stirring occasionally. Once the mussels have opened, add two ladles of the wine broth they've been cooking in (about ¾ cup) to the cream sauce. Heat the sauce for another minute. Season with salt and pepper. Using a slotted spoon, ladle sauce over the mussels, and garnish with parsley and a few morsels of Roquefort cheese.

MOULES À LA PLANCHA

Prep time: 10 minutes
Cook time: 10 to 15 minutes
Serves: 4 to 6
Great for: appetizer or light summer meal
Wine suggestion: Faugères

- Extra virgin olive oil
- 4 pounds mussels, washed and de-bearded*
- 1 red pepper, thinly sliced
- 3 to 4 shallots, peeled and sliced
- 3 to 4 cloves garlic, peeled, de-germed, and sliced
- ½ cup dry white wine
- 1 lemon, juiced
- 3 healthy pinches *herbes de Provence*
- ¼ cup parsley (flat variety preferred), chopped

Lightly oil the *plancha*, (a griddle or the flat portion of a grill) and set heat to medium-high.

In a large bowl, mix all ingredients, including the mussels, together. Once the grilling surface is hot, place the mussel mixture on it. Cook until the mussels open—about 4 to 6 minutes—occasionally stirring with a long grill spatula. Depending on the size of the surface, the mixture may have to be cooked in batches. When the mussels open, serve while hot. Discard any unopened mussels. Garnish with parsley, and serve with sautéed roasted rosemary potatoes (p. 246) and a crisp green salad.

* *Discard any mussels with broken shells. If adding other fruits of the sea, like squid, clams, or shrimp, cut the quantity of mussels in half.*

TUNA NOODLE CASSEROLE

Prep time: 5 minutes

Cook time: 35 to 40 minutes

Serves: 4 to 6

Great for: family meal

Wine suggestion: Anything goes—the bigger the pour, the better

- 5 cups fusilli pasta
- 3 tablespoons butter
- 2 cups fresh mushrooms, sliced (porcini, *cèpes*, white, or a combination)
- 1 (10.75-ounce) can *velouté forestièr* (creamy forest mushroom soup)
- 1 cup *crème fraîche* or sour cream
- 1½ cups peas, frozen
- 2 (6-ounce) cans tuna, drained
- ¾ cup cheese, shredded swiss or gruyère
- 3 healthy pinches *herbes de Provence*
- 4 to 5 tablespoons panko or breadcrumbs
- ⅛ cup parsley, chopped, for garnish
- Salt and freshly ground black pepper, to taste

Preheat the oven to 400°F. Cook the pasta according to package instructions. Melt 1 tablespoon of the butter in a pan. Cook the mushrooms in the butter until tender, about 4 to 5 minutes, and set aside. Once the pasta is cooked, drain. In an oven-safe 9 x 12 casserole dish, combine the pasta, soup, *crème fraîche*, peas, mushrooms, tuna, and noodles. Season with *herbes de Provence* and salt and pepper. Sprinkle the cheese on top. Bake for 20 minutes until hot and bubbling. In a small bowl, mix together the panko (or breadcrumbs) and the remaining butter. Sprinkle it onto the casserole, and bake for another 5 minutes. Garnish with parsley. Serve with a crisp green salad with balsamic vinaigrette.

JEAN-LUC'S QUICHE LORRAINE

Prep time: 15 minutes (if making a homemade crust, add 1 hour of rest time)

Cook time: 30 minutes (if making a homemade crust, add about 20 minutes)

Serves: 4 to 6

Great for: anytime

Wine suggestion: Pinot Blanc

I usually buy premade piecrusts, either *brisée* (thicker) or *feuilletée* (flakier), available at any French grocery store. Why reinvent the wheel? Search for premade crusts in the refrigerated (not frozen) section. If you prefer homemade crusts, a friend of mine, Chef DQ Flambé, has provided a stellar recipe, perfect for sweet or savory dishes.

FOR THE *PÂTE BRISÉE*

- 1½ cups unbleached flour, plus extra for dusting
- 1 pinch salt
- 1 tablespoon sugar
- 6 tablespoons cold butter, cut into small pieces
- 1 egg
- 3 tablespoons ice-cold water
- Parchment paper
- Baking weights

Sift the flour into a large mixing bowl. Add salt and sugar. Mix well with a whisk. Add butter, and use your fingertips to mix it quickly into fine sandlike crumbs. Fold the egg into the mixture until well combined. Add the water and mix the combination using your hands for 5 minutes. If the dough is sticky and moist, add 1 tablespoon of flour at a time until the dough is smooth. Form the dough into a ball with your hands and flatten into a disk. Wrap in plastic wrap, and place in the refrigerator for 1 hour.

Preheat oven to 350°F. Roll the dough out into a circle, about ⅛-inch thick, on a floured work surface. Press the dough into a parchment-lined 10- or 12-inch quiche dish or round, oven-safe baking dish. Poke the dough a few times with a fork to aerate. Cover the crust with parchment paper, then place the baking weights on the parchment paper. (A friend of mine, Oksana, uses garden rocks for weights!) Bake for 20 minutes. Let the weights cool before removing from the crust. Finally, fill the crust with quiche.

FOR THE QUICHE:

- 1 homemade *pâte brisée* (p. 60) or premade piecrust from the refrigerated (not frozen) section
- ½ cup milk
- ½ cup *crème fraîche* or sour cream
- 3 eggs
- ¼ cup cheese, Emmental or swiss, grated
- 1½ slices thick deli ham, cut into strips
- ¼ cup *lardons* or pancetta
- 1 tablespoon *herbes de Provence*
- 1 pinch grated nutmeg
- Salt and freshly ground black pepper, to taste

Preheat oven to 350°F. In a bowl combine the milk, *crème fraîche*, and eggs, whisking until creamy. Mix in the cheese. Pour the mixture into the piecrust, swirling the dish until coated. In a pan, cook the lardons or pancetta over the stove on medium-high heat until golden. Add the ham and *lardons* to the egg mixture, distributing evenly. Season with *herbes de Provence*, nutmeg, and salt and pepper. Bake for 25 to 30 minutes.

Ingredient Two

FRIENDSHIP

INTEGRATE OR DIE TRYING

P EOPLE HAVE SAID THAT SOME of life's most stress-inducing events include the loss of a job, a divorce, a new marriage, moving home, changing countries, and becoming a parent. One year prior to moving to France, I'd gone through a divorce right after I'd lost my job. And I'd survived. Surely, I could handle the rest of these changes.

Instead of letting everything hammer me down, I decided to chunk my life into bite-sized pieces. This system of "chunking" had worked for me before; it would work again. My relationship with Jean-Luc had moved at the speed of light. I needed to slow things down and breathe. Through open and honest communication, we had set a solid foundation. Now all we needed to do was build—one brick at a time, instead of piling all the bricks up at once.

It was time to "integrate" into my new French life or die—sometimes of embarrassment—trying. I knew I couldn't count solely on Jean-Luc for my happiness. I was determined to make la France more than an occasional tryst I flirted with, more than a *cinq-à-sept* (the two hours between five and seven, rumored to be when people have illicit affairs). Come hell or high water, this elusive country was going to love me back. But I had to commit to la France, too, give her my whole heart and dive into this life one hundred percent.

I knew I wasn't going to become fluent in parenthood overnight; building a true bond with the kids would take time. Mutual respect and trust were the foundation of any relationship, and it was time to set some boundaries with Max and Elvire by being more of a parental unit they couldn't make fun of or talk back to.

I wasn't a patsy. This was on.

I'd already taken over most of Jean-Luc's daily duties, since he left for work at six-thirty every morning, leaving me to make sure the kids ate breakfast, brushed their teeth, and made it to school on time. One morning, Elvire turned blue-in-the-face mad because I woke her up at five after seven, not seven on the nose as she'd requested. Instead of pretending that I didn't understand her when she talked back like I'd done over the past month, I said with a low growl, "*Comment oses-tu me parler comme ça?* How dare you speak to me like that?"

Elvire shuddered. So did I. I'd used the same words my mother had used with me when I was a hormonal teen with fire running through my veins. Still, the newness of parenting was no longer so intimidating, especially using the tried and true techniques I'd been raised with. Soon, when their dad wasn't around during the school week, I was the one Max and Elvire bargained with to watch TV or play video games on the Wii. Elvire learned that if she did what I asked, like putting her clothes away, there would be no telling Papa about the extra screen time. I could be fair—if the kids completed their homework and set and cleared the table without killing one another or mouthing off.

On weekends, sometimes we'd play Franco-English Scrabble or have *Just Dance* competitions in the living room. Elvire, Max, and I always laughed at some of Jean-Luc's bizarre moves, like the way he rolled his hips as if he was one of the long-lost members of the Village People. Oddly, *Papa* always undulated his way to the highest score, and it was our goal to beat him. My big man, it seemed, could bust a move. So could the kids.

At the end of October, Max turned eleven. I picked up a gourmet chocolate cake with a crunchy crust at the local *pâtisserie*, and sodas and juices from the grocery store. Six pint-sized rugby players with huge feet (Jean-Luc called them the platypus-foot generation) came over to celebrate. Max's main crew was Thomas, Clement, Willy, Oscar, and two Theos. After Max opened his presents, mostly manga books, Jean-Luc brought the cake outside, and the boys sang "*joyeux anniversaire*" at the top of their lungs. I snapped picture after picture, watching Max and his friends horse around. After a water-balloon fight in the backyard, the boys headed off to the park, armed with *pétanque*, rugby, and soccer balls.

Unlike Elvire, Max did everything I asked him to do when I asked him to do it. I supposed it was an age thing and the fact that the memories of his biological mother weren't as engraved in his head. He was more open to the idea of me. Elvire still tested me a bit—and I didn't blame her after the Natasha situation.

On another family bonding day, we went for a hike in the Pyrénées at a place called Plateau de Beille in the Ariège region, about an hour from our home. The kids sat quietly in the backseat on the drive. I watched the landscape change abruptly from flat and sprawling Toulouse to mountainous. Driving to beautiful places was one of the benefits of living in Cugnaux. We were spitting distance from the Pyrénées, the Mediterranean Sea, the Pays-Basque region of France on the Atlantic Ocean, as well as the wine regions of St. Émilion and Bordeaux, and the Catalan/Costa Brava region of Spain. There were so many wonderful places to visit—all within a two-hour drive. For this, I considered myself extremely lucky.

I had packed a picnic lunch of ham and cheese baguettes, potato chips, homemade chocolate chip cookies, and bottled water, which Jean-Luc carried in his backpack. We passed a herd of happy cows, complete with copper bells hanging on their necks, on one of the winding country roads. For the beginning of November, the weather was warm—almost summerlike. Even some of the wildflowers were still in bloom. Finally, we pulled into the parking lot. Jean-Luc, Max, and I jumped out of the car. Elvire, as usual, was a bit slower.

"Hurry up," said Max.

"Shut up," was Elvire's response. She packed up her iPod, put her shoes on, and eventually scrambled out of the car.

Jean-Luc, Max, and I were already headed to one of the trails.
"Shouldn't we wait?" I asked.

"No," said Jean-Luc. "She has to learn that the world doesn't
revolve around her."

When she caught up to us, Elvire hugged Jean-Luc, looked over
his shoulder, and met my eyes, her face reading: "He's mine."

In the not-so-distant past, Jean-Luc had told me that when
Elvire or Max would hug him, Natasha would glare at the kids, and
that she was in constant competition for his affection. Natasha even
made them put pictures of their mother away because she saw her
as a threat.

I crossed my arms over my chest, raised an eyebrow, and said,
"Elvire, I have no problem sharing him. And, maybe, just maybe, I
need a hug too."

Her jaw dropped and the distrust in her eyes melted away. She
smiled and approached me. We exchanged an awkward but love-
filled hug, Jean-Luc sandwiched in between us.

"Let's get Max," I said.

He overheard us and ran down a path, toward a bubbling river.
"Catch me if you can."

And so, Jean-Luc, Elvire, and I raced after him. We jumped over
a small riverbank and we ran and we laughed, finally catching the
tiny rugby player and dragged him to the ground. Once our laughter
died down, we had a picnic with the Pyrénées Mountains rising high
into the sky behind us.

Things were settling into place with the kids. But I still had
issues with my language skills. Part of the problem was that Jean-
Luc always spoke English with me, and then asked why was I not
speaking French?

Although I had three native speakers in the house, I couldn't get
by just on the words I picked up from the kids: *méga moche* (super
ugly) or *un nul* (a zero/loser) or *dégueulasse* (disgusting). I'd taken
French in high school (four years) and in college (two years), but after
a twenty-year hiatus I was far from fluent, even after my intensive

course at one of the universities, L'Institute Catholique de Toulouse, where I surprisingly tested into *Elementaire II* (right before intermediate), and where we paid close to 480 euros. *Ce n'était pas donné* (it wasn't cheap), so I had to get creative. Enter iTunes and the Internet. Why hadn't I discovered podcasts before?

Katia and Kyliemac's podcasts were hysterical and made learning French fun, instead of a chore. They taught colloquial expressions that one doesn't learn in school, like *avec ma bite et mon couteau*, which, translated literally, meant "with my dick and my knife," but actually meant "I'm making do with what I have." Which was exactly what I was doing.

The best part of all? Most of these resources were free. Well, that, and nobody corrected my conjugations.

A truly joyous moment arrived when I was playing around with the remote control for the television. Lo and behold, I discovered that most of the American and English series and video-on-demand movies could be accessed in VO (*version original*) with the press of a button. No longer did my favorite actresses speak in strange, high-pitched French. Hallelujah! I could actually *enjoy* my favorite shows!

Bouts of homesickness occasionally set in, but on a quick trip home for Thanksgiving to recharge my batteries, they were cured, and I stopped idealizing my former life so much. Plus, when I was home, thanks to a few friends, I picked up a few freelance gigs—a couple of logo designs and a website. My confidence was back on track.

No longer hiding underneath my covers, I'd leave the house with confidence, having finally figured out that staring, just like *la politesse* (politeness), was simply part of French culture. My fellow pedestrians weren't trying to push me off the sidewalk and into oncoming traffic because they knew I was a foreigner—the sidewalks were just much narrower, and you simply had to hold your ground. I even started to answer the phone. Did the telemarketers understand me when I told them we had *une ligne rouge* (unlisted number) and to take us off the list? Maybe. Maybe not. Who cared?

Formerly, in the throes of my mouse-voice phase and intimidated by the idea of speaking with anybody other than my French family, I'd attended only one of Max's rugby games. This situation was rectified with my new, positive attitude. If people laughed at my accent, so be it. I'd laugh right along with them. Hey, Joey from *Friends* always got a chuckle with his manner of speech ("How *you* doin'?"). My life, at times, felt just like a sitcom. Might as well play my part.

Adieu, mouse voice.

Under the clear cerulean sky, after exchanging pleasantries with the other parents, I whipped out my camera, taking shot after shot of my little man and his friends in their red and black uniforms, only pausing my clicks to cheer and clap and scream, especially when I captured a grand moment. Max scored *un essai* (a "try," or as I liked to say, a goal).

A fiercely proud rugby stepmom, I showed the pictures to Max and he grinned like crazy, but the green-eyed jealousy monster inched into Elvire. I could tell she wanted some picture love, too, especially after she invited me to watch her acrogym performance at school. I sat with the mothers of her friends, making small talk, and captured the spectacle—a combination of light gymnastics and cheerleader-like pyramids.

I was the keeper of their youth now.

This new outlook had me thinking: maybe it was finally time to try for a child of my own? Tightly wrapped in Jean-Luc's arms, I whispered, "I think it may be time to stop being so careful, if you know what I mean. Would that be okay with you?"

"'Oney, I want what you want," he said.

DRIVING FORWARD

E VER SINCE I'D RECEIVED MY temporary driver's license, Jean-Luc and I had taken the car out to refresh my memory, since I hadn't driven a car with a manual transmission in over twenty years. I didn't grind the gears of our silver Ford (too badly), and it all came back to me—like riding a bike (sort of). But our C-MAX had an electric brake, which meant I couldn't play around with it in case I was stuck on a hill with another car riding my tail. Jean-Luc teased me by placing his hands over his eyes when I panicked on a road with a small dip (minuscule, really), but I forged ahead, balancing the clutch and gas pedals while holding my breath and making a mental note to avoid any inclines—great or small—at all costs.

A postcard arrived in the mail, stating that my *permis de conduire* was ready for pick up. Jean-Luc, of course, offered to accompany me to the *préfecture*. I thanked him, but said no. Instead, I took the bus to the metro station that would get me to Toulouse, saying "*Bonjour*" to the driver when I got on and "*Merci, au 'voir,*" when I got off, just like everybody else.

At the *préfecture*, the helpful and understanding woman I'd met the first visit stepped out of the back office and handed over my license with a smile, which I returned with a hearty "*Merci mille fois!*" The *permis de conduire* was a pink piece of paper folded into thirds with my nonsmiling photo stapled into it. I could now legally drive in France. And, a few days later, I was the one taking Elvire shopping for clothes, not her dad. Let the adventure begin.

"I don't want to go to Portet," said Elvire. "I don't like the stores there. Can we go to the *centre commercial* in Blagnac?"

I shot Jean-Luc a nervous glance. The shopping center she wanted to go to was located about half an hour away, instead of the one ten minutes from our house. "Are there any hills on the way?"

"It's mostly highway—so the route is flat."

"Okay," I finally said, and Elvire smiled until I asked Jean-Luc what her shopping budget was.

We set out at nine in the morning. Elvire turned on the radio, loud. I turned it off, explaining I had to concentrate. "Should I plug in the GPS?" I asked. "Or do you know how to get there?"

"I know." Elvire blurted out directions. *Droit. Gauche. Droit.* Right. Left. Right. "*Tout droit,*" she said, and I made a right. "*Non, tout droit,*" she said, and I took another right. "*Noooooo. Tout droit! Tout droit!*"

"I am turning right!" I said, pulling the car over into a parking lot. "All rights!"

She pointed straight ahead. It was then that I figured out that *tout droit* didn't mean to take all rights; it meant to go straight. Exasperated, I yanked the GPS out of the console. Elvire pulled out her iPod and plugged in her earbuds. I could hear the bass thumping like a herd of wild horses—right in tune to my nervous heart. The voice on the GPS barked out instructions like an angry drill sergeant. At least I understood *her.*

On the highway, Elvire said, "*Tu conduis comme une grand-mère.*"

It was true. I was driving like a grandmother, about twenty kilometers under the speed limit. In fact, grandmothers were passing us on the route, a few of them glaring in our direction. But we made it to the shopping center alive.

My worst fear came true at the mall. There was no outside parking, no space I could just pull right up into. Nope, I had to wind up in one of those circular parking structures with another car riding my bumper. "*Merde, merde, merde,*" I said under my breath and white-knuckle gripped the steering wheel.

Elvire took out her earbuds. "*Y'a un problème?*"

"*Oui. Oui.*" Yes, there was a problem. As I held my breath, I tried to explain in between panicked gasps for air that I was petrified of rolling backward into another car. "Balance the clutch and the gas," I said over and over again as we circled up four levels until finally seeing a sign indicating free spaces. I pulled into a spot, with shaky, tired, and sweaty hands. It took a few minutes to regain my composure. I broke out into laughter. One tiny victory for immigrant kind! Elvire looked at me like I had three heads.

"*On y va?*" she asked.

"*Oui, on y va.*"

Let's go.

Shopping with Elvire was like shopping with my mother; the girl couldn't make up her mind. She knew she had a budget, and even if she liked something, she held off on the purchase just in case she loved something more. After visiting five stores two times over four hours, we ended up with three T-shirts, one blouse, and two pairs of jeans. We still had to buy her shoes. On the other hand, I loved the happiness lighting her eyes and the fact that she seriously considered each and every one of my opinions. There was nothing like shopping to bring a would-be stepmonster and stepdaughter closer together.

Finally connecting with Elvire was cause for celebration, and I believed it was important to celebrate all moments great and small, so I began planning my first dinner party for the following night, a pre-Christmas get-together—but not of the tuna-noodle-casserole variety. Along with the four of us, I asked Jean-Luc to invite Christian and Ghislaine, the witnesses at our wedding in France, their daughter, Anne, and her boyfriend, another Jean-Luc, who, at well over six foot five, we called Grand Jean-Luc. Christian had sparkling blue eyes and a huge smile, and like Jean-Luc, he came complete with an infectious laugh. Ghislaine, his wife, had a warm and cheerful face, cropped blond hair, and wore funky glasses with orange frames. Both of them, I guessed, were in their early sixties. They'd had us over for at least four meals and it was high time we returned the favor.

The night was going to be all about food—the French way, where course after course was served, starting with an *apéro* (appetizers and drinks), followed by an entrée (the small first plate), then the *plat principal* (main plate) with a side dish, which, *bien sûr*, was followed by a selection of cheeses or a salad, and a dessert, which, thankfully, Christian and Ghislaine had offered to bring along with a bottle of chilled champagne.

I had finally become familiar with the finer points of French cuisine. The kitchen was now my domain and would soon smell of France—sweet and salty, warm and delicious. I was queen of the quiche, a creator of crêpes. I could make *moules à la marinière* with my eyes closed. One day, I would even try my hand at flambéing—once I got over my fear of singeing my eyebrows off or burning down the house. True, there had been minor confusion at the butcher when I'd asked for a *tenderloin de porc*, thinking that pork tenderloin was the same in English with French pronunciations, which oftentimes worked. Nope, not this time. In France, when I wanted this cut of meat, one asked for a *filet mignon,* which had me wondering about steak. But no matter. Supplies in hand, I became a Tasmanian devil of a chef—chopping and slicing, whipping and whirling.

Elvire noticed how busy I was and offered to play sous-chef, helping me prepare the tomato and zucchini tarts for one of the appetizers and snapping the tips off the green beans.

"We must speak in English," she said. "I want to improve. One day, I'd like to live in another country."

"What about my French?"

"You're doing better."

"I am?"

She nodded. And then she mimicked my French accent, speckled with Chicago and a hint of Californian valley girl.

"I don't talk like that," I said with a laugh.

"Yes, you do." She glanced at her watch. "I have to go. I have a *rendezvous* at the aesthetician. And I'm late."

It is true. French women don't shave their legs or armpits; they either get lasered or waxed. And they start young. Ouch. Ouch. Ouch. It hurt just thinking about it. I cringed. All my spa experiences had been complete nightmares. The first time I got waxed, the woman ripped off my skin, bruising my entire bikini line in the process. The first time I had a massage, I swear the male therapist tea-bagged my head, muttering a guttural *oof* in the process. And the first time I had a facial, the aesthetician dislodged my contact lenses. Suffice it to say I wasn't a fan of being "serviced." But Elvire was a well-put-together French girly-girl. Sometimes, she even gave me makeup tips. *Bonjour*, cat eyes!

"Thanks for your help," I said.

I spent the entire day cooking, ironing our tablecloth and napkins, and setting the table, knowing that when Max and Elvire did it, they transposed the knives and the forks and knocked over glasses. I collected red berries and sprigs of rosemary from the garden to decorate the plates.

Our guests arrived. Jean-Luc popped a bottle of champagne open, and I brought out the appetizers. Phase one of the dinner was going swimmingly. The entrée, soup of roasted *potimarron*—a chestnut-flavored squash—was a hit, warm, sweet, and peppered. The pork roast was tender, bursting with French flavors of garlic, parsley, cream, and spicy mustard. I exhaled a sigh of relief. I was actually hosting a dinner party for real live French people. And, so far, they seemed to love it. Knives and forks clattered on plates.

Over dinner, the conversation turned to a recent trip I'd taken back home for the Thanksgiving holiday. I could handle the questions. On the return trip, I had packed my suitcase with solid deodorant, panko, hot sauce, Vigo black beans and rice, and red pepper flakes, as well as a reasonably priced set of pots and pans from Costco—ones that came with lids. I left all the emotional baggage behind me. I was equipped as I'd ever be. "*C'était super-bon. Et c'était moi qui a fait la dinde.*"

My statement was followed by laughter. What had I messed up now?

Jean-Luc nudged me in the ribs. "You just said you did the turkey."

"But the verb *faire* means to make or to do. So I made the turkey."

"*Ouf.* You should say you prepared the turkey. Unless you go around impersonating turkeys. *Glou, glou, glou,*" said Jean-Luc, clucking like a turkey the *French* way and flapping his arms.

Instead of letting embarrassment blush my cheeks and slinking lower into my chair, I said, "First of all, turkeys don't say *glou, glou, glou.* They say gobble, gobble," and then I told our guests about another *faux pas* I'd made, when the kids had asked me what was for dinner and I replied "*connard.*" *Connard* was slang for dickhead or asshole. And I'd meant to say *canard*, duck. For once, my humor translated and our laughter was boisterous, unrelenting. This former mouse voice of a girl smiled from ear to ear.

"*Qui veut du fromage?*" I asked. Who wants some cheese?

Before they left, Ghislaine took me to one side, thanking me for a lovely evening and letting me know how thrilled they were to see Jean-Luc and the kids so happy, how thrilled they were that I was a part of all their lives. "*Nous te considérons comme notre propre fille,*" she said, giving me the tightest of hugs.

I blinked back the tears in my eyes. They thought of me like a daughter? With my parents being so far away, being accepted into their family warmed me from the inside out. Whoever started the rumors about the French being rude, unfriendly, snobbish and hard to get know hadn't been embraced by the loving spirit of the south of France.

The more I settled *into* change instead of fighting it, the more positivity ruled my world.

I was on a roll, or rather, a baguette.

BRING ON THE MISTLETOE AND HOLLY

Our little town of Cugnaux had some serious Christmas spirit going on. One day, after dropping Max off at rugby practice, Jean-Luc and I rounded the corner to find a giant crane in the middle of the town square, with arms like an octopus. Dangling off the arms, seven drummers dressed as nutcrackers beat drums and one super limber aerial artist dressed in white spun around gracefully, twisting her body. The arms of the crane spun around like an amusement ride, dipping and falling in an orchestrated dance.

"What's going on?" I asked Jean-Luc.

"I guess they are practicing for tonight's holiday spectacle," he said.

"We're so going to the show."

That afternoon, as I wrapped Christmas presents, I played classic Christmas carols sung by Bing Crosby, Nat King Cole, and Dean Martin, eyeing the clock, waiting for six o'clock with great anticipation. Finally, Max returned home from rugby practice.

"*On y va*," said Jean-Luc.

"It's time to go," I repeated.

"I'm not going," said Elvire.

"Me neither," said Max.

My lips pinched together. "Why? What else do you have going on?"

"Ugh, *c'est nul*," said Elvire. "It's for kids."

They were at the age when everything was uncool. This didn't stop me. And parental bribery (and threats) can get you anywhere. "Well, whoever comes with us tonight will eat *tartiflette*"—a baked potato dish with onions, *lardons*, and melted Reblochon cheese, and one of the kids' favorite meals—"and whoever doesn't will eat tuna noodle casserole."

Max threw his sneakers on. "*Tartiflette?*"

"*Oui*," I said.

"*Deux secondes*," said Elvire. "I'm coming."

We waited ten more minutes for Elvire, and as a family we walked the three blocks to the show. It seemed the whole town was in attendance, including the mayor. What I hadn't seen in the practice earlier were the well-timed lights blinking on the drummer's uniforms. The aerialist sat on a swing and soon flew through the sky, and I had to catch my breath. This free show in the center of town rivaled the Cirque de Soleil and reminded me a bit of a living Alexander Calder mobile, the performers responding to the movement of the crane. When the drumbeats and chanting settled down, the kids said, "That was super cool."

Sometimes you just had to open your heart to the magic of Christmas.

This year, we were not going to have a Charlie Brown Christmas "branch" at our house, like the one I'd witnessed last year when I'd only been a visitor. Although it was clear Jean-Luc had tried to be festive, I couldn't handle a twig with four colored lights and a few pieces of multicolored garland thrown on it. Plus, this was our first Christmas together as a married family.

So this year we were getting into the spirit of the holidays—mistletoe and all. We dashed to the local hardware store to pick out the tree—a Normandy pine, about five feet tall—and added a couple of strands of lights to our purchase. After I weaved the lights in and out of the branches, we opened up a bottle of wine, put some classical music on, and watched the kids go at it. As the kids trimmed the tree, I hung the monogrammed emerald green and burgundy stockings my mother had given us the year before—not on the mantelpiece, because we didn't have a fireplace, but on the radiator in the entryway—with care. When Max and Elvire were finished, they smiled at their endeavor.

"*C'est super-beau,*" said Elvire.

"*Alors,*" I said. "It is beautiful, *mais, l'arbre manque de quelque chose.*"

The tree was missing something. I ran upstairs and grabbed a bag of starfish left over from our "garden by the sea" themed wedding. After tying one of the larger starfish to the top of the tree with silver, wire-rimmed ribbon, I took the strands of blue, silver, and red garland and draped them around the branches in order of the colors on the French flag. When you eyed the tree from the bottom to the top, it was American. I grinned. "Now, *c'est parfait.*"

The kids already knew what their big gifts were—their brand-new bikes were in the backyard, and I'd picked out a reasonably priced food processor for myself, along with an eggplant-glazed Emile Henry *cocotte* (Dutch oven) my mom insisted on sending to us from Amazon France. While the kids spent the last week of the winter break with their grandmother, Jean-Luc and I planned on freshening up their rooms with art for the walls (New York City for Elvire—a dream place of hers to visit; rugby for Max), new bedding, and whatever else I found within budget at IKEA. But there were still a few surprises to come.

The night before we drove the four and half hours to Provence to spend Christmas *chez* Isabelle and Richard—Jean Luc's sister and her partner—Jean-Luc suggested opening the boxes that had miraculously appeared under the tree, considering the car was going to be overloaded with suitcases, a case of champagne, gifts for Jean-Luc's sisters, his nephews, and a few smaller packages for Jean-Luc and the kids.

"Who are they for?" I asked.

"You. And it's better to leave them here. We won't have room in the car, so open them."

"But I already have my gifts," I said. "And I've already used them tonight."

"Sam, a food processor isn't for *you*. It's for the kitchen," he said, handing me two boxes. "This is from me."

I opened up the packages to find a docking speaker for my iPod (so I could listen to music in the kitchen and dance when I cooked!) and a bottle of Chanel's Coco Mademoiselle. I threw my arms around his neck and kissed him. "*Merci.*"

"*Donne-lui nos cadeaux,*" said Elvire. Give her our gifts.

"This is from Elvire and Max," said Jean-Luc, handing over a heavy box.

A large 10 x 14 eggplant-glazed Emile Henry casserole dish with fluted edges! The matching Emile Henry square 8 x 8 baking dish! I knew that Jean-Luc had picked the items out (and paid for them), but the light in the children's faces for the fact that they'd made me happy was priceless. I kissed the kids on both cheeks, and then wiped away the tears threatening to explode from my eyes. "*Merci! Merci! Je les aime beaucoup!*"

I loved them!

"You're spoiling me," I said, turning my teary-eyed smile to Jean-Luc.

"Not as much as you've been spoiling us. The meal smells incredible."

"Oh my God. I've got to check on it," I said, scrambling off the couch.

"*Attends*. Wait. We're not finished yet," said Jean-Luc, pulling me back down. "This is from the cat."

We all laughed when I opened up a small box to find a set of escargot serving trays, complete with tongs and tiny forks. No wonder Jean-Luc had suggested that we pick up the box of frozen snails loaded with garlic, parsley, and butter at our local Picard. "Who wants an appetizer before dinner?" I asked.

"*On mange quoi ce soir?*" asked Max. What are we eating tonight?

"*Une casserole au thon,*" I said, and Elvire's jaw dropped open in disgust.

"*Je te taquine.*" I'm teasing you. "*On va manger du boeuf bourguignon,*" I said, hoping it turned out okay. I'd combined three recipes, one of Julia Child's and two others I'd found on the Internet, along with my own additions. What could I say? I liked to get creative in the kitchen.

Elvire nodded with approval. Max licked his lips. Jean-Luc smiled. My heart soared.

Oh, and this experimental dinner was a hit. "I could eat this every night," said Max.

Yes, this recipe had scored *un essai.*

. . . .

Even months after moving to France, some of the cultural differences still came as a surprise, like the never-ending cycle of kissing. Kids kissed kids. Men kissed men. Women kissed women. Everybody was kissing everybody, when we said hello, and when we said good-bye. Every region had different customs, like how many times to swap cheeks. Two, three, or four kisses? Some people kissed from the left, some from the right. Jean-Luc told me to stick to one direction, so that there was no confusion—like accidentally meeting lips. Did I "*faire la bise*" with people I'd just met? If a friend or family member introduced me, the answer was yes. At parties, at social events, and even at Max's rugby games, everybody swapped *la bise*, no matter if there were ten people or over one hundred. Plus, at a party, one waited for every single guest to arrive before touching one appetizer or cocktail. That was *interdit* (prohibited). But *la bise* was a habit of mine now, which led to some very awkward moments when I was back in the States.

Even with some kissing confusion, I loved the French way of life, the long meals, the appreciation, and the discussions—especially when it included food and family. I also loved the fact my husband loved to cook and could do it very, very well (when I let him in the kitchen). Food is a reason to live and breathe in France. Jean-Luc's family was big, and meals were always an event. For Christmas Eve, Jean-Luc was in charge of the main course, preparing one of his specialties—*langoustes à l'armoricaine,* or crayfish flambéed in cognac and then simmered in a tomato base infused with shallots, garlic, and parsley.

All the usual suspects were at Isabelle and Richard's. In total, there were eighteen family members, including Jean-Luc's youngest sister Muriel and her husband Alain. Both of his sisters were gorgeous with long straight hair and beautiful smiles. That rumor about French women being effortlessly stylish was true; they had a certain *je ne sais quoi* about them. Whereas Isabelle had a penchant for designer brands like Burberry, Muriel's tastes gravitated toward rock-star chic. Fashion aside, everybody had his or her duty when it came to preparing this large feast.

Isabelle took charge of setting the fifteen-foot-long dining room table, her final decorating touches the sparkling, silver votive candles, which I'd given her, and confetti stars. Then she and Elvire arranged the thirteen desserts—a tradition in France representing Jesus Christ and the twelve apostles, always displayed and enjoyed until December 27—consisting of a combination of dried fruit, fresh fruit, nuts, and sweets, like *Calissons d'Aix,* a cookie made from almond paste and candied melon, and *fougasse à l'huile d'olive,* a Provençal cake made with olive oil. Richard, Isabelle's partner, brought out his homemade *foie gras* with a fig compote, proudly showing it off, and then he shucked oysters, the trick being to wear a glove and wiggle the knife. Muriel and Alain prepared a *verrine* of grapefruit, shrimp, and fennel for the *apéro.* I helped Jean-Luc, playing sous-chef, cutting up shallots and dicing the garlic. And since I was already chopping, I made a mignonette sauce for the oysters—red wine vinegar, sugar, and shallots. The kitchen was madness, a scene right out of a busy Michelin restaurant, but with laughter. And I loved it. Yes to all the chefs!

Isabelle and Richard had an insanely beautiful collection of *Santons de Provence. Santons,* or "little saints," were hand-painted terra cotta figurines depicting Provençal villagers. The setup was about five feet in width by eight feet in length, featuring three different sizes of the characters. Isabelle and Richard had well over one hundred of the beautiful figurines—the villagers on their way to visit Mary, Joseph, and Baby Jesus (who, per tradition, would be placed in the crèche by the head of the family at midnight on Christmas Eve). During our *apéro*, I was pretending to admire the nativity scene when Richard walked over.

"*T'aimes nos santons?*" he asked. You like our *santons*?

"*Oui*," I said, trying to hide my mischievous smile.

It took him a minute to notice the giant rooster from the larger *santons* terrorizing the villagers in the smaller setup. His laughter started out soft, then it boomed. He grasped his belly, his brown eyes watering. He poured some champagne into my glass and wrapped his other arm around me, squeezing me tight. "Jean-Luc, *ta femme est une vraie vilaine!*"

Your wife is a real villain!

Dinner started at nine o'clock, and we didn't leave the table for three hours. Then madness ensued. In France, or at least in this family, when the clock struck midnight, eighteen excited people ripped open packages, wrapping paper flying everywhere and floating down to the ground. Somebody had given Max a creepy plastic horse mask that covered his entire head, and he was running around, wearing it and a new sweatshirt, and holding the iPod Touch he had received from my parents.

Jean-Luc always told me that he thought Christmas gifts were for children, but his eyes lit up when I took him aside to give him the black cashmere sweater, new socks, and a bottle of Armani cologne from Max, Elvire, and me. The kids had pitched in twenty euros each and, thanks to a small freelance job designing a website, I'd had a couple of bucks to spend.

Per tradition, Richard, the head of the household, placed the baby Jesus in the crèche and Isabelle called everybody back to the table for dessert, because no French Christmas was complete without a *bûche de Noël*, a cake shaped like a log and made of sponge cake or ice cream. Our family gathering was so big we had three of them.

After dessert, I joined the traditional game of charades called

Time's Up, which we played girls against boys. Thankfully, I picked really easy words out of the jar: *ouvre-boite* (can opener) and *tendon d'Achille* (Achilles tendon). But Jean-Luc wasn't as lucky. He stood in front of us and brought his arms in front of his chest, extending them up and outward, and stretching them to his sides, his facial expression intense. He wiggled his fingers and undulated his body from side-to-side. Isabelle and Muriel spit out their laughter. Laura, the fiancé of Isabelle's son Steeve (yes, with an extra e) and I rolled off the couch onto our knees, clutching our stomachs. Finally, somebody yelled, "Time's up."

Nobody had guessed that Jean-Luc was a tree—a tree that, apparently, was sprouting and blowing in the wind. And nobody got his *Mona Lisa* either, when he indicated a frame, then tucked his hands under his chin, and blinked his eyelashes with a weird closed-mouth smile. I'd never laughed so hard in my life. Suffice it to say, the girls won the game and, at three-thirty in the morning, we set off for bed with laughter and love in our hearts.

It had taken some effort on my part, but I finally felt like I was fitting into this life.

. . . .

On Christmas day, we visited with Jean-Luc's parents, Marcelle and André, before dropping the kids off at their maternal grandmother's. Michel, Jean-Luc's brother, opened up the door to let us in, said hello and Merry Christmas, and then excused himself. He and Jean-Luc got along just fine, but Michel wasn't the most social of creatures, especially when compared to the rest of the family. Jean-Luc was a true *Marseillais*, a native of the area, known to be quite loquacious. Sometimes when Jean-Luc launched into blabbermouth mode, not giving anybody a moment to put a word in edgewise, Elvire, Max, and I would make talk signs with our hands, flapping our thumbs against our fingers, and then pretend to fall asleep. But, truthfully, we all loved his excitement for whatever subject about which he was expressing his ideas and thoughts so passionately. Michel? Well, he was the quiet, slinking-off-to-his room type.

Jean-Luc's father André—a kind man with a head of white downy hair, soulful brown eyes, and a mischievous smile—was his usual dapper self, but there was no mistaking that he was worn out. Upon seeing Jean-Luc's mother, we knew the reason why. We hadn't been expecting Marcelle to be in such bad shape. She was in a wheelchair, unable to move, her body bloated. An industrial hospital bed stood in her room. Still, her spirits were up, and she clapped her hands when she saw us and called us over for kisses. Unfortunately, she was also a bit confused and kept calling Jean-Luc by his brother's name. Worry flashed in Jean-Luc's eyes.

Since Marcelle and André hadn't been able to attend the wedding in California, I'd ordered a photo album with all the pictures of the family for them. I handed it over to her, trying to lighten the mood. She looked through a couple of pages, smiled, and then asked for her book on wolves. André stepped into the kitchen to grab some drinks.

Jean-Luc whispered in my ear. "Don't be offended. The older people get, the more they revert back to a childhood state."

André handed the kids their Christmas checks and we sat down on the couch for juice and colas. He picked up the photo album and went through every page.

"I wish we could have been there," André said with a quick nod to his wife. "But her health is getting worse every day."

Just then, Marcelle announced that she wasn't feeling well and wanted to rest. The kids' eyes widened. André wrung his hands. "I have to help her," he said, his face flushing with embarrassment.

"Papa," said Jean-Luc, "we'll come back to visit before we head back to Toulouse."

"Please do," he said, escorting us to the door. "I'm sorry."

Jean-Luc kissed his father on both cheeks. "There's nothing to be sorry about."

On the car ride over to drop the kids off at Meme's house, Jean-Luc gripped the steering wheel, huffing and puffing. "He has to put her in the retirement home or she's going to kill them both. He can't take care of her anymore."

I squeezed his hand, glancing quickly at Max and Elvire in the rearview mirror. Some conversations, I felt, weren't meant for children's ears.

Jean-Luc had no qualms about discussing sensitive issues in front of them, telling me on more than one occasion that he didn't want them to live with their heads in the sand, that they needed to experience life and come to their own conclusions. In a way, I agreed with him. But I didn't want the kids' heads to be filled with worry. Elvire was already paranoid enough with health issues because her mother had died of cancer.

"I'll give Ghislaine a call when we get home," said Jean-Luc.

Ghislaine was the director for a retirement home in Toulouse. In the past, family members had been required to provide for aging relatives, in accordance with French laws and their means. Plus, people were skeptical of nursing homes, and the majority of senior citizens wanted to remain independent as long as possible. But with the cost of living skyrocketing, it had become increasingly difficult for children to look after their parents under the same roof, and new benefits and financing programs had been put into place. The average cost of an assisted-living home is around two thousand two hundred euro per month, and seniors receive an average pension of twelve hundred euros, allowing family members to pay for the difference for the needed care, the homes staffed with round-the-clock doctors and nurses and all medicines and meals provided.

"Good idea," I said. "And I'm sorry. I know this is tough."

He cracked a withered smile. "It's just life. We have to take the bad with the good."

Thankfully, this season was capped off by something wonderful. I became Facebook friends with Cristina, the kids' maternal uncle Thierry's wife. She sent me a kind message, letting me know how Meme had noticed a huge difference in the kids' demeanor and how happy she was that I was in their lives.

10

A BAGUETTE
IN THE OVEN

U NFORTUNATELY, JEAN-LUC AND I HAD to cancel the romantic
dinner we'd planned to ring in the New Year. On the morning
of December 31, nausea hit. I ran to the bathroom dry heaving. Then,
I crawled back into bed with cramps, unusual and stronger than I
normally had before my period. My breasts stung to the touch, and
my nipples were raw. Jean-Luc had left the house early that morning
to pick up some papers he needed from his office. I called his cell.

"Hi, 'oney," he said. "I'm heading back soon. I made the mistake of
checking emails. There are over four hundred of them."

I blurted out, "My period is five days late and I think I'm pregnant."

"*Ah bon?*" he said with surprise. "Do you want me to grab a test
on the way back home?"

"No, I'm going to the pharmacy right now. What do I ask for?"

"*Un test de grossesse.*"

Although this was my first pregnancy possibility, I knew a test
would be the most reliable with the day's first stream. I had to
pee like a racehorse, but I held it in—galloping the three blocks
to the local pharmacy and then home. I could barely contain
myself, wiggling on the toilet, about to explode. I ripped open the
package, read the instructions, took the cap off of the unit, and got
'er done. I stared at the test. The results were supposed to appear
within five minutes.

Two pink lines became visible in less than ten seconds.

Two bright pink lines.

There was no mistaking the result. I let out a gasp. I was thrilled. But I was also thrown for a loop.

My friends had always asked when I planned on having children, right after they'd scared me to death about the horrors of childbirth. My nipples would turn large and brown, possibly dangle like tiny toes, they said. And I'd say with a petrified smile and confess one of my biggest insecurities, which my good friends already knew about: "Well, that shouldn't be a problem because my nipples are inverted."

"They'll come out," they'd say. "But you'll pass gas a lot and not at the most opportune times. Probably in yoga class while doing downward dog."

My friends continued their spiel. "Mommy weight" and morning sickness were issues I understood. But green discharge and incontinence? And none of my friends lived here—they were all back in the U.S., too far away to provide much comfort. I knew I could get over the things that would happen to my body. But my parents were thousands of miles away too; I wouldn't have my mother's help when I needed her. Not even Jean-Luc's sisters lived around the corner. Plus, no spring chicken, I was forty-one. What if the baby had birth defects?

The test shook in my hand. I sat on the toilet, staring at it for about ten minutes, until excitement took over. My heart skipped a beat. What would our child look like? Would he or she have my husband's perfect mouth? My eyes? I pulled up my pants, picked up the phone, and I called Jean-Luc. "Well, you're going to be a papa."

"Are you sure?"

I stared at the test. "Ninety-nine-point-one percent sure."

"That's great news." He paused. "But, until you see a doctor, let's not get too excited."

His reaction didn't surprise me. A scientist, he needed undeniable proof. My mom, on the other hand, flipped her lid, her screams of joy reaching decibels high enough to carry from my former home in California all the way to Toulouse. I was surprised, however, the following Monday when Jean-Luc pulled our car onto a dimly lit street on our way to the doctor appointment. "Uh, where are we?"

Jean-Luc motioned his hand toward a white house with brown wooden shutters. "In France, many doctors practice out of their homes."

"But—"

There were no buts.

Before I knew it, we were opening the front gate, where a yellow Labrador retriever puppy darted around the front yard like an escaped mental patient. He jumped onto my jeans, dirtying them with muddy paws. "I hope this isn't the doctor," I said, trying to make a joke to settle my live-wire nerves.

"Very funny, Sam." Jean-Luc took me by the hand. "There's nothing to worry about."

We sidestepped the puppy and entered the *salle d'attente*. Complete with year-old magazines in the racks, it was like any other waiting room I'd grown accustomed to, save for the fact that we were the only clients in it and there was no wait. A woman in her late sixties with short gray hair and a long charcoal skirt introduced herself in a perfunctory manner and led us into her office. Besides Jean-Luc helping with some translations, everything seemed to be routine until the doctor ushered me into the exam room, demanding that I undress and install myself on the table. I searched for the giant paper towel, a hospital gown, to no avail. She turned her back on me, but didn't leave the room.

Pants-less, and hoping I'd understood her correctly, I hopped up onto the exam table, making a mental note to find another doctor—one who spoke at least three words of English, and, after some probing and prodding, one who didn't scare my pants off. After telling me that women in France go through *rééducation périnéale* after childbirth, where a woman's vagina goes through physical therapy to strengthen the pelvic floor with an electric wand so you won't struggle with incontinence—and can soon have sex with your husband again (how French!)—and that the fifteen or so sessions would be covered by our insurance, she sent me on my way with two prescriptions, one for some blood work, and one for an ultrasound.

"I want to find another doctor," I said to Jean-Luc on the ride home. "That woman didn't have the greatest bedside manner."

"Doctors in France are serious," he said.

A few days later, the blood work confirmed the pregnancy, and there was no mistaking the tiny life displayed on the ultrasound monitor. According to the measurements, I was six weeks along, or *bien enceinte* (well pregnant), as the French said. With two grainy printouts of undeniable proof in hand, I called my mom.

"I saw the heartbeat today."

She couldn't contain herself. And so, the baby planning began, my mom emailing me pictures of furniture and toys every ten minutes. Dragonflies and butterflies for a girl, a jungle theme for a boy.

"Don't tell anyone, Mom. It's still early."

"I won't. But I'm so excited! I'm going to be a grandma!"

Her excitement was so palpable, I could practically feel it zapping me through the phone. I was doomed. She wouldn't be able to hold this kind of news in. Resigned to my fate, when we hung up, I called up the other two people I'd planned on telling—first Jessica, and then Tracey, the conversations nearly identical.

"Well, I've got some news—"

"You're pregnant."

"Yep."

A scream. "How did it happen?"

"Are you serious?" I asked.

"I meant when."

"By the dates, right when I got back from California. After Thanksgiving."

Apparently, absence not only made the heart grow fonder; it created a baby bump.

. . . .

Every day swelled with excitement. I couldn't wait to tell the kids our news of "Jack or Jill the Bean," but I was holding off for a bit—until I knew it was safe. I hoped this significant change in their worlds wouldn't be difficult for them. I hoped they wouldn't be jealous.

Most of our family discussions took place at the dinner table, where no subject went untouched, including sex and Jean-Luc's salary—two topics I'd never dare to discuss with my own father. I didn't know if it was the French way of communicating or just a "my family" thing. So I was surprised when, over a *raclette*—a machine that melts the cheese one pours over a variety of charcuterie and vegetables, a bit like fondue—and salad, Elvire announced, "I have my period."

But I was even more surprised with eleven-year-old Max's response. "*Ah bon?* Were you the first of your friends?"

Jean-Luc's held his hands up in mock surrender. "Sam, you'll have to help her."

"I'm a woman, and I've got this," I said with a smile. "*Félicitations*, Elvire! You're no longer a little girl. You're a little woman now! So, tampons are…"

Max grimaced. Jean-Luc looked panicked. Apparently, some subjects were taboo at the table after all. I picked up on all the looks, the hints.

"Okay. I'll take Elvire upstairs for a chat after dessert," I said.

Elvire smiled.

It was January 6, which came with the traditional dessert called a *galette des rois* (king's cake), a brioche flavored with *fleur d'oranger* (orange flower essence), to celebrate the Epiphany, when the baby Jesus was presented to the Three Wise Men. In the past, the cake was cut into portions, corresponding to the number of guests, plus one. This extra slice was known as the *part du pauvre* (the poor man's share), the slice given to the needy. Since the late seventeenth to early eighteenth century, under the reign of Louis the XIV, *une fève*, a small porcelain figurine depicting Mary or another nativity character, was hidden inside the cake. Whoever found the *fève* was crowned queen or king for the day, the paper crown supplied by the local *boulangerie*. Today, thanks to commercialization, we find cartoon characters like the minions or Bugs Bunny or *Les Lapins Crétins*. My rocket scientist may have not been a religious man, but he had faith, and he was fierce when it came to upholding French traditions. Important for any French family, these events were what people grew up with, no matter their beliefs. Traditions held families together, instilling values, a sense of comfort and belonging, and a way to celebrate, really celebrate, what mattered in life. Traditions also created memories, a time for reflection. Max poked his fingers into his slice. Elvire did too. Jean-Luc shrugged.

The *fève*—Minnie Mouse—was in my slice. The kids cheered, Jean-Luc placed the paper crown on my head, and I was queen for one day. With my recent pregnancy surprise, this had to be a positive sign. It just had to be. I was rich with love, and this moment would be etched into my memories forever.

. . . .

Day after day, my initial pregnancy fears turned into joy. When I wasn't ruling my royal realm with a velvet glove, I turned to my friend, the Internet, to track the pregnancy on TheBump.com. At eight weeks, the fetus was the size of a raspberry, or a small bean, the reason Jean-Luc nicknamed the life growing inside of me Jack the Bean. I combed through the site, absorbing as much information as I could. I avoided Bella as if the plague infected her—especially after she'd confused Max with a tree and climbed up his leg, scratching his behind. Most French women are immune to toxoplasmosis, but, as a foreigner in France, I was at high risk for the parasitic disease carried in the feces of cats. My doctor had given me a prescription for monthly blood screenings at the local laboratory. I peeled my tomatoes, cut out caffeine, and avoided undercooked meats. I did everything by the book.

I was on the website when Max came up the stairs. I closed out of the browser and quickly opened up an email just as he tapped me on the shoulder. A new fan of American sports, he was holding the baseball bat and glove my dad had purchased for him when we were in California. Jean-Luc and my dad had taken him to see the Angels play.

"You can play baseball with *moi*? *Dans le parc?*"

I pointed to my computer. "Later, Maxou," adding the *ou* like the French do, a sign of endearment.

"*S'il te plaît?*" he asked, looking at me with moony eyes.

The lyrics from Harry Chapin's "Cat's in the Cradle" ran through my head. By the time the chorus hit my brain, Max's smile had turned into the saddest of disappointed pouts. He walked into his room, head hung low. I was a goner. With Jean-Luc always working, it was up to me to throw the ball. I made a mental note to pitch underhand, so as not stress my body out. But first I checked Babybump.com to make sure light exercise was okay. It was.

"*D'accord*, Max," I said, tapping on his door. "*On y va.*"

Okay. Let's go.

That evening, we were all watching TV in the living room, save for Elvire. who was watching streaming videos, no doubt, in her room. Max wiggled his way over from Jean-Luc to my side of the couch and placed his head on my shoulder.

"*Merci pour aujourd'hui*," he said.

11

ONLINE (FRIEND) DATING

W HEN I WAS A PIGTAIL-SPORTING four-year-old wearing homemade flowered dresses, my mom used to bring me to the playground in front of Lincoln Park Zoo in Chicago. She'd sit on a bench and read a magazine, shooing me away to have fun with the other kids. But until somebody called out to me with a "Hey, you," I just stood on the sidelines with a creepy Cabbage Patch Kid smile, watching the children as they ran round and round, shoes kicking up dirt and sand, as they'd jump and spin gleefully on the merry-go-round. Sometimes the kids called out to me, and I joined in with their games. Sometimes they didn't.

As an expat living in a foreign land, starving for friendship, I couldn't be bashful or just sit around waiting for friends. If I was truly going to be happy in France and not torture my family with subjects they couldn't care less about or that made them cringe—like the latest romantic comedy or the weird, crunchy chin hair I had to keep plucking—I needed my own friends. And, honestly, I was tired of everybody correcting my French when I opened my mouth.

"It's for your own benefit," Jean-Luc would say when he corrected my pronunciation. Perhaps in the long run. But if I snapped, it wouldn't be good for anybody. I truly needed a break from conjugating. Enter the expat blog with a whole section dedicated to the Toulouse area. I put up an introductory post. A couple of hours later, I received a response.

Hi Samantha,

Nice to meet you—my name is Monique and I've just moved to Toulouse (from L.A. but via Paris after eight years). I'm in the center of town and don't know a soul. I am married to a Frenchman and have a 10-month-old little girl. I work from home, so socially I know it will be even more difficult to meet new people. If you're free one afternoon, would you like to meet for a coffee? Thanks and look forward to hearing from you.

Cheers!

It was so serendipitous! A girl from L.A.! Also married to a Frenchman! I emailed her back immediately and, after a round of rapid-fire exchanges, we made plans to get together. Shortly after this, Oksana from Canada contacted me too. She had also been in touch with Monique. And she was also involved with a Frenchman. It seemed I was on my way to making friends with women of similar backgrounds and interests. I was thrilled at the prospect. Of course, I deleted the messages from creepy men who wanted to get together for a drink and exchange "cultural" ideas.

It was the beginning of January when I finally had my Internet date with Monique, my Californian counterpoint, in Toulouse. Oksana, our Canadian neighbor, would be joining us, too. Since she lived in *centre ville*, Monique took charge. We agreed to meet in front of the Midica, a store that sold home and kitchen goods, right by the Esquirol station in Toulouse at half past twelve. For the love of cuisine, of course, I knew Midica!

Monique, Oksana, and I sent each other descriptions of what we looked like and what we'd be wearing. We all had blond hair and blue eyes. In Toulouse, the majority of French women had straight, chestnut brown hair with the occasional (and sometimes shocking) "Power Violet" or "Hot Chili Red" that seemed to be in fashion for *les femmes d'un certain âge.* It was going to be easy to spot my North American cronies.

Door to door, it took about twenty-five minutes to get from my home to *centre ville* via the bus and metro, the bus ride a harrowing journey. I hung onto my seat as the driver drove over, not around, the roundabouts. A petite blond paced in front of Midica like a caged nervous bird. I made my approach, hoping she wouldn't fly away. "Oksana?"

She eyed my brown boots. "Samantha?"

"*C'est moi.*"

She threw her arms around my neck and we quickly swapped *la bise.* "I'm so happy to meet you! You don't know how long I've been in France without any friends. I've been driving Philippe crazy."

"How long have you been here?"

"Two years," she said.

In five months, I'd nearly gone batty. How could she have waited so long? She answered my question before I could ask it.

"I met a few people on the expat blog when I first moved here," Oksana said. "But all they did was complain about France and how much they hated it. I couldn't stand it because I wanted to like it here and didn't want to surround myself with negativity. So, I took a little break from trying to connect with people." She paused. "Do you like living here?"

"It took some time to adjust, but I'm happy now."

"Thank God," she said. "And I know what you mean. It's overwhelming in the beginning."

Oksana spoke a mile a minute, her voice high and melodic. About five-foot-three, she had shoulder-length blond hair, and a cheerful smile as big her eyes. I loved her warmth, but I was confused; her accent wasn't Canadian. There was a slight hint of something else. With her name, I was thinking she was from Russia…perhaps even a spy for Jean-Luc's ex, Natasha? I couldn't stop the thought from popping into my head.

Since the finalization of their divorce, Natasha hadn't contacted

Jean-Luc or the kids. But I knew she was out there. Thanks to a program I'd installed on my blog called StatCounter, which listed the names of the cities and villages people visit from, as well as what posts they looked at, how long they stayed on my site, and what they'd downloaded, I knew Natasha stalked my page, visiting it for hours at a time. But she wasn't the only one with Mata Hari tendencies. With a little Google espionage, and more than just slight curiosity, I had discovered that Natasha had married another Frenchman (three months before Jean-Luc and I had tied the knot) and now lived in a village north of Toulouse.

"Do you know anybody named Natasha?" I asked.

Oksana squinted. "Who?"

"Never mind," I said, shaking off the paranoid thought. "Philippe is your husband?"

"Well, almost husband. We've been paxed for two years now." She paused. "We're going to get married soon, though. I just don't know when. There's been too much going on."

While preparing all the papers for my own French marriage, I'd done enough due-diligence to know that a "PACs" agreement— the *pacte civil de solidarité*—was a civil union between two adults— almost like a marriage, but not quite.

Another blond approached us with confidence in her stride. "Hey, ladies. I'm Monique." Introductions were made and—a never-ending cycle of kisses in the south of France—we exchanged *la bise* again. "Love your boots, Sam. I spotted them a mile away."

Oksana's gaze shot from my face to Monique's and back again. "Oh my God. You two look like you could be sisters."

It was true. Monique and I both had long, straight highlighted blond hair around the same length, and blue eyes. We were about the same height. And we were both wearing similar black coats and leather boots that hit just below the knee.

"What are you saying, Oksana? Girls from California all look alike?" asked Monique, crossing her arms over her chest.

"No, no, no," said Oksana with a little squeak. "I, uh, was that rude?"

"I'm just messing with you," said Monique. "Ready to head to lunch? I know a great place just around the corner."

"Wait," said Oksana. "I hope you don't mind, but another girl from the expat blog will be joining us."

"The more the merrier," said Monique.

A beautiful brunette joined the three blonds. Trupty introduced herself and another round of *bisous* was exchanged. Clearly, kisses were a habit for all of us now. The four of us walked down the cobbled street of Rue d'Alsace-Lorraine, the main shopping drag in Toulouse, heading over to Place St. Georges for lunch. Ten minutes later, we were chatting at a *salon de thé* as though we'd known each other for years. I told them my story of how I'd met Jean-Luc and how we'd reconnected, fallen in love, and married twenty years later, and in turn they shared their stories.

Monique, now forty-two, had moved to Paris ten years prior. She'd met her husband at a bar during the *canicule* (heat wave) of 2003. When she saw Jean-Christophe, better known as JC, a tall, handsome Frenchman, she pointed to him and said to her girlfriends, "That one is so gorgeous. He's mine." Eventually, JC, tired of being stared at by three cute girls, made his approach, and the rest was history. A few years after their initial flirtation, Monique and JC moved in together, and now they'd been married for eight years. They'd moved from Paris to Toulouse right when she'd contacted me on the expat blog. Like Jean-Luc, JC worked in the aerospace industry, while Monique worked for an American film distribution company, selling foreign rights for their films.

Oksana, like me, had been through a divorce, and her story was surprisingly similar to mine. When she was back in Canada, she'd set a goal for herself: learn French. She'd joined a pen pal site, which was how she met Philippe, who wanted to brush up on his English. After months of communicating through letters, Philippe flew to Canada to meet her in person as friends. But *le coup de foudre* struck, and they fell head over heels in love. For a while, she and Philippe had a tenuous long-distance relationship, flying back to Canada and

France, until Oksana took the leap, daring to follow her heart, finally settling in France two years prior. A nurse back in Canada, she was having problems finding a job because the French government didn't recognize her diploma as being equivalent to their own. She was in the process of applying to nursing schools in Toulouse with the hopes she'd qualify for one year of training instead of four. Until the pieces fell into place, she'd been flying back to Canada for six weeks at a time to work.

Thirty-four and hailing from Toronto, Trupty was a gorgeous, exotic beauty with dark almond-shaped eyes and flawless skin. A wealth of information on just about everything in the area, she'd been living and working in Toulouse for four years, after meeting and falling in love with a Frenchman. But we soon learned that Trupty and her boyfriend recently had a difficult breakup and she was currently having issues with renewing her *carte de séjour*—so much so, in fact, that she'd hired an attorney to help her with the fight to stay in France.

Soon, our conversation became very animated. We talked about sex, about having to repeat ourselves in both languages to make a point, and how men don't have the best listening skills—no matter what country they're from. I realized that the feelings of distress and alienation I'd felt the first month of living in France were completely normal. I wasn't crazy or neurotic. Along with becoming an instant stepmom to two teenaged French kids, I was simply going through the five stages of adapting to life an as expat: the honeymoon stage, culture shock, feelings of isolation, all leading up to stages I was now in—conquering acceptance and integration at the same time. We cheered Trupty on to fight for her right to stay in France, and laughed when I talked about my love of cooking and how—although she was capable of preparing simple meals—Monique got hives just thinking about turning on the oven.

"Thankfully, JC is a really good cook," said Monique.

"I think it's a requirement for men in France," I said.

Once we settled down, the waitress came over to take our order.

We all took the same thing—*le plat de jour*—a spinach quiche with a dessert of our choosing. The waitress responded to our French in English. I wasn't sure if she was trying to be polite or making a point, as if to say our French was so horrible that she'd rather die than hear us speak it again.

"Does it bother you when they do that?" I asked.

"What?" asked Monique.

"Respond in English when we're speaking French."

Monique lifted a brow. "After you've lived here as long as I have, you won't care."

"How's your French?" I asked.

"It should be better. Way better. But I manage." She blew out the air between her lips. *Pffftp.*

"Now, that's French," I said.

"It is, isn't it?" said Monique with a laugh, then she turned her attention to Oksana. "You have an accent. It doesn't sound Canadian. What's your story?"

Oksana's posture straightened. "My family moved from Belarus to Canada when I was a young teen. More or less, I grew up in Winnipeg." She shrugged. "I'm a mishmash. I have Polish roots, and, apparently, now I'm on my way to becoming French."

Monique laughed. "Ugh, God. We all are. What's up with these Frenchmen?"

Oksana's lips pinched into a sheepish grin. "It's so nice to finally have friends. I've really needed you guys. I've been dying for girl talk. In English."

"Me, too," said Monique. "I'm so glad I was able to find someone to look after Kissa today."

"What's Kissa?" asked Trupty.

"My daughter." Monique pulled out her iPhone and proudly displayed a picture of her mini-her—a little girl with fuzzy blond hair, dressed in pink. "She's one year old. And, yes, we made her name up."

Jean-Luc had told me about the naming laws in France, which

restricted the names that parents could legally give to their children to protect the child from being given an offensive or embarrassing name. Apparently, Kissa had made the grade.

"She's adorable," I said.

"She is." Monique smiled with fierce motherly pride. "JC and I tried for years. And after three rounds of IVF, we finally got our dream. So, I know you have two stepkids, but do you have kids of your own, Sam?"

Monique reached for the carafe of rosé and was about to pour when I stopped her. "Well, the thing is…"

"Oh my God. You're pregnant! How far along?"

"Eight and a half weeks," I said, thrilled to share the news.

"Did you see the heartbeat?"

"Two weeks ago."

"Oh, I hope you have a girl. I have tons of baby stuff I can give you."

Oksana's hands shot to her breasts. Her mouth dropped open. "I think I may be pregnant, too. My boobs, they are killing me. And my period is two weeks late."

Monique leaned forward. "Did you take a test?"

"No, not yet."

"You go buy one and take it tomorrow morning," I said.

"You need to know," said Trupty.

Oksana's lips pinched together. "Okay, fine. I'll do it."

Monique and I spoke in unison. "Email us the moment you find out."

The four of us exchanged an odd glance. And in that moment, we all knew we'd become forever friends. On the walk back to the Metro, we passed a bookstore. I noticed a cookbook in the window titled *Qu'est-ce qu'on mange ce soir?* What's for dinner? I nudged Monique in the arm. "Hey, I think that's the book for you."

"Is it a phone book listing delivery restaurants?" she replied, and we all burst out into laughter.

And that's how the first members of the Toulouse "Les Chicks" group came together. And how, with the little help of new friends who understood the triumphs and tribulations of being an expat, I began to carve out my own life in France.

. . . .

A few weeks later, on a blustery day in February, our core group of girls planned to meet up in front of the Midica. Oksana walked toward Monique and me, her head hanging low. There was no bounce in her step. She choked back a sob. "I just got back from the second ultrasound. There is no embryo. There is nothing. I have a blighted ovum. I'm empty." She pointed to her purse. "The doctor gave me pills to start a miscarriage. If they don't work, they'll have to operate."

We took our friend in our arms. Her tiny shoulders quivered, but she held back the tears. "Honey, honey," said Monique. "You could have canceled lunch."

Oksana looked up at us, her long eyelashes fluttering. "I know. I know. But I really needed to talk to you guys, to women. I'm not quite sure Philippe understands."

Before Trupty arrived, Monique took over the conversation, for which I was thankful. Oksana's news had me shaking in my boots. Monique noticed my discomfort. "Don't worry, Sam. You saw the heartbeat. The risk of anything going wrong goes down after that."

Oksana shook her head in agreement. "I'm praying for you. Because to go through this is hell."

I placed my hand on my stomach. Life was fragile. Anything could happen. Silently, I prayed everything would be all right.

12

LOVE DOESN'T JUST COME FROM DNA

A T THE ELEVEN-WEEK MARK, JEAN-LUC and I decided to share our two-armed, two-legged news with the kids. I'd been sleeping so much Max and Elvire thought I was sick. I'd burst into tears while watching Disney's *Tangled*, and the kids had looked at me like I was an escaped mental patient. I'd been extra cranky—not the usual, smiley me. Plus, they knew something was up since I hadn't touched one ounce of wine, unless it was to surreptitiously pour the glass meant to throw them off into Jean-Luc's glass.

February 2 was *La Chandeleur*. In addition to being a religious celebration for Catholics, it was also France's national crêpe day. Fortunately for us, we had a professional crêpe maker: Jean-Luc. In this house, any kind of crêpe was a hit, from ham and cheese to steak and spinach to chocolate. I'd tried them all, and I couldn't think of a better day to share the news, when life was looking pretty sweet. Tonight we were having both dessert crêpes and a savory dish, my mother's recipe of chicken and mushroom crêpes in a cream sauce. I sat in my chair, tapping my feet, nervous as to how they'd react to the news. Before dessert, I glanced at Jean-Luc. He winked.

"*J'ai des nouvelles*—" I began, my hands shooting to my stomach. Boy, did I have news.

Elvire's eyes went wide. She leaned forward and whispered, "*Tu es enceinte?*" Are you pregnant?

I shrugged and smiled. She gasped and clapped her hands over her mouth in delight. Max bounced up and down in his seat, nodding with a wide grin. I was floored by their happy reactions. But once the initial excitement died down, to my horror, the conversation turned to sex.

"I've heard to make a baby, couples need to make love once a month," said Elvire.

Max laughed. "Don't be stupid. It's once a week."

Instead of pretending that I didn't understand the French words flowing so eloquently from their lips (as I sometimes did when they mouthed off), I changed the subject. We threw around some names, Jean-Luc suggesting Salammbô, the heroine in a novel by Gustave Flaubert. The kids and I burst into hysterical laughter, me begging him to come up with something that didn't sound like salami. Chloé? Ah, no! That was a girl in Max's class. She was stupid. And weird. Sophie? Theo? Vincent? Ew. *Non*. Ugh. This scenario was repeated with every suggestion.

"Do you know if it's going to be a boy?" asked Max, a spark of hope lighting his eyes.

"Not yet," I said. "But we'll find out in a few more months."

Elvire jumped out of her chair and gave me a hug, which I returned, holding on to her. "I'm so 'appy for you," she said in her best English.

The following morning, though, the discussion turned from light-hearted and fun to serious. Apparently, Max was very concerned about three things. One: He wouldn't be able to understand his new brother or sister because I was American. Wouldn't the baby speak English? Two: He wanted to know where the baby would sleep. (Jean-Luc told him right in his arms, which didn't go over well.) And three: He was worried I'd love the baby more because it was *mine*.

Well, number three I could relate to.

Two months after my father, Tony, had officially adopted me, my mother gave birth to my baby sister, Jessica. I was eleven and I burst into tears. "Dad is going to love her more than he loves me. She's his real baby. And I'm not."

I was almost the exact same age as Max when my sister was born.

So just as my own dad had done with me, I told Max we were a family, that we were just adding one more person to our newly formed Franco-American mix. I assured Max that a baby wouldn't change anything, that I loved both him and his sister very much. Love didn't come from just DNA. When he told me they loved me, too, my heart almost burst.

Love aside—don't mess with a highly hormonal step-by-stepmom.

When Jean-Luc was at work, Max and Elvire got into another brawl over whose turn it was to set the table and clear it, Elvire taunting her brother until he slugged her in the arm. Their screams reached alien-like decibels. Once again, I had to physically separate them before they killed one another, sending them to their rooms, not caring who started the fight. And then I put a schedule on the refrigerator. Max would have Tuesdays, Thursdays, and Sundays. Elvire would have Wednesdays, Fridays, and Saturdays. On Mondays, they'd share.

. . . .

The day after Valentine's Day, I was to meet my new doctor for the twelve-week ultrasound. The new member coordinator at the Toulouse Women's International Group, or TWIG, a group Trupty had connected me to, highly recommended Doctor K when I'd asked for a referral for an English-speaking obstetrician. A man with kind eyes and a warm smile, Doctor K's English was impeccable. Plus, he ran his practice out of a private hospital, a *clinique*—not one puppy in sight. Upon my mother's insistence, I'd brought in a video camera to capture the moment. Jean-Luc had the camera pointed at the monitor. My eyes darted from the screen to the doctor's face. Just by the way his eyebrows furrowed, I knew something was wrong.

I let out a low, pain-filled wail. "Jean-Luc, turn the camera off. Right now. Please."

There was no fetal heartbeat.

The embryo had stopped growing at eight weeks.

I'd had what's called a missed miscarriage.

As Doctor K's words registered in my brain, the air was sucker-punched right out of me. I went numb, hoping Ashton Kutcher would pop out from behind the blue curtain, telling me that I'd been punk'd. That didn't happen. After trying his best to ease the shock, Doctor K scheduled the dilation and curettage for two days later.

Immediately after the ultrasound, the doctor sent me to the laboratory for blood work. Not usually one to cry in public, I tried to fight back the tears, but the moment the technician stuck the needle in my arm, the dam exploded. The poor woman thought she'd hurt me.

"*Non, non, ça va,*" I said, waving my hands. "*Je viens juste de recevoir de mauvaises nouvelles.*" I just received really bad news.

Jean-Luc and I left the hospital, passing by dozens of expectant mothers rubbing their bellies swollen with life. Averting my gaze, I stared down at the white-tiled floor and concentrated on putting one foot in front of the other—angry, jealous, and sad. Jean-Luc squeezed my hand. "It's just life, nature taking its course. There's nothing we could do."

I could only nod. On the ride home, I wondered how on earth was I going to tell the kids. I needed to be strong for them. It was hard, but I managed to sit them down to explain what happened. When I choked up, I pulled my turtleneck over my face.

"Don't be sad. You still have us," they said. "And Bella."

I snorted out a laugh. Unsure of how to respond to me, the kids let me have my space and they went up to their rooms. I emailed Monique, the only one of my new friends who had a child. She called me three seconds later, offering kind words and recounting the stories of her miscarriages while going through IVF in an attempt to make me feel better. Talking to Monique gave me the courage to do the impossible: tell my mom. I shut myself off in the master bedroom.

"I've been waiting for you to call!" she exclaimed. "How did it go today? Are you excited?"

"Mom," I said. "There is no baby."

"Sam, that's not funny," she said.

"I'm not joking. I wish I was."

I silently cried myself to an almost sleep, trying to hold back the sobs, my shoulders shaking. I didn't understand what had gone wrong. I had done everything you're supposed to do. Doctors in France were more lax with the rules. They said it was okay to have one glass of wine a week. They said it was okay to eat *foie gras, pâté*, but I'd done *none* of those things.

Jean-Luc wrapped his arms around me, pulling me close. "If we want it to, it will happen again," he said.

I wasn't so sure about that. For now, I was following doctor's orders; after the dilation and curettage, he was putting me on the Pill for two months. That night, I woke up with a nightmare so horrifying, I wondered if I'd ever be able to sleep again.

For three months, I'd woken up filled with joy and wonderment about the life growing inside me, my breath smooth and easy; now, it simply hurt to breathe. When I was alone in the house, I cried and I wailed and I shook my fist at the sky. I let myself feel all the feelings I needed to feel on the road to healing, such as the severe jealousy that overtook me at Doctor K's the day of the procedure, where I had to sit in the waiting room surrounded by women nearing their due dates. The happy smiles, the way they rubbed their bellies…everything about these women made my blood boil with anger. *Why them and why not me?* I questioned, avoiding their joy-filled eyes. Inside me, a life once alive with a heartbeat was now dead.

We were ushered into a private room, where I was to wait for Doctor K.

Most people think that health care is free in France. This is true for those who don't have jobs or can't afford it, but not true for all. Our family insurance policy cost around one thousand euro a month, half of which was paid by Jean-Luc's work, including additional coverage called the *mutuelle*. There are no deductibles, and all prescriptions, doctor's appointments, and hospitalizations are covered 100 percent. Even my contact lenses and glasses were "free."

I curled up on the bed with a book. Scared, sad, and nervous, I wasn't able to read. Jean-Luc pulled up a chair next to me and held my hand. I squeezed my eyes shut, trying to keep my tears at bay. I'd never been a crier. But after moving to France, the tears were constant. Part of it had to do with Jean-Luc; he'd opened up my heart. Part of it had to do with all of the ordeals I'd had to face. A nurse came in and put a wristband on my arm. I gulped. Doctor K had told us to arrive at noon. It was now three-thirty. I finally looked at the band on my arm. Maybe it would say what time the procedure was scheduled for?

"Who in the world is Svetlana?" I screamed. "What if she's here for a lobotomy?"

Jean-Luc's eyes went wide. "Wait. What? We're in the maternity ward."

"They put the freaking wrong name on me! And I, I, I—"

Jean-Luc raced into the hall and grabbed a nurse. "Sorry," she said, as if it happened all the time, and replaced my wristband.

Doctor K came into the room an hour later. He eyed his watch. "I thought I told you guys to be here at noon."

"We were here at noon," I said. "We've been waiting for hours."

He apologized profusely. "Heads will roll," he said. "Let's get you down to anesthesia."

Good idea. I wanted to numb out my sadness, my anger. I wanted to sleep. And, mostly, I wanted to get out of this damned hospital. On the one hand, I was blessed to have Doctor K. He wasn't cold and perfunctory like most French doctors, the type who treated everything—even miscarriage—lightly. On the other hand, I was still mad that they had screwed up my name. How could they have done that on a day like today?

A nurse rolled me down the corridor on a trolley to the elevator, and then ten minutes later—five, four, three, two, one—the anesthesiologist knocked me out. I woke up in my room, Jean-Luc by my side. The "procedure" was over. A few hours later, Doctor K released me from the hospital. We didn't get home until eight in the evening. I just crawled into bed. And I cried. And cried. And cried.

Jean-Luc was kind and supportive, but his scientific viewpoint offered little comfort. "It was a baby that just wasn't meant to be. It was just nature taking its course," he'd say. "There wasn't anything we could do."

Tracey was the only person who said the words I wanted and needed to hear. "When you're ready, and if you need to talk about it, I'm here if you need me. I won't say a word or offer advice. I'll just listen."

The others, my friends and family, offered condolences such as "It happens all the time," or "You can try again," or "It wasn't a baby yet; it was just a fetus." But, to me, the life I lost wasn't *just* a fetus. The pregnancy hormones still surging through my veins didn't help the fragile state of my emotions either: one moment I'd be laughing, and in the next, crying. I felt alone, like nobody really understood what I was going through. Miscarriage was a taboo subject. And nobody really wanted to talk about it. Especially me.

A few days after the "procedure," Elvire came home from school early and caught me gasping and wheezing, my back against the kitchen wall with my hands on my knees. Under my jeans, I was still wearing a car-sized sanitary napkin held in place with green mesh hospital panties. I felt like a freak. When Elvire sauntered into the room, I tried to pull myself together, quickly rubbing my runny nose with the back of my hand.

"*Ça va?*" she asked, her eyebrows knitted with worry.

"*Ça va*," I said. "*Juste un peu triste.*" I'm fine. Just a little sad.

"*A cause de la fausse couche?*" asked Elvire.

"*Oui*, because of the miscarriage," I said, then I found myself the recipient of the best hug ever. When she released me from her embrace, Elvire had tears in her eyes.

"*Merci*," I said. "I needed that."

"*Moi, aussi*," she said. Me too.

Prior to Jean-Luc, unless I was in an intimate relationship with somebody, I had protected my territory, avoiding close talkers, space invaders, and huggers. Friends and family members would recoil from my arms and say, "Well, that was awkward." But Jean-Luc had been the key, the one who had been able to open up my heart fully and completely. And I realized I had a lot of love to give—especially with two young children who needed the occasional hug. As Antoine de Saint-Exupéry wrote in *The Little Prince*, "It is only with the heart one can see rightly; what is essential is invisible to the eye." While love might be invisible, it was more than detectable. I could feel it radiating off both of us, a warm heat.

If I hadn't been the best of huggers before, I was one now.

SWINGING FROM (THE SUGAR HIGH OF) *LA CHANDELEUR*

· ·

INSTEAD OF LETTING LOSS GRIP me in a tight vice of pain, I knew I had to switch emotional gears and focus on gain, like how lucky I was to have Jean-Luc and the kids, my friends—old and new, and my family, even when flashes of grief threatened to bring me to my knees. Still, this miscarriage would always be an emotional notch on the belt of my life, and I needed to say good-bye on my *own* terms. Once the ground thawed in the spring, I planned on planting an orange rosebush in Jack or Jill the Bean's honor. Just the thought of performing this symbolic act eased my sorrow.

Jean-Luc came home from work. "If you're up to it, I was thinking to invite Christian and Ghislaine over for dinner this weekend."

I nodded. Cooking with love would provide the best of distractions. It was time to embrace my life again—and I desperately needed a huge American-sized glass of wine.

On Saturday, Elvire and I were dancing to Shakira's "Rabiosa" in the kitchen. She was dropping it like it was hot, showing off some sexy moves she shouldn't have known. I blamed music videos—not me or the fact I was channeling my inner Shakira. The song changed to JLo's "On the Floor." I wiggled my hips and poured a glass of wine. Like Julia Child, sometimes I liked to have a little nip while I cooked a big meal. Elvire eyed my glass and asked, "*Je peux?*" Can I?

"*Seulement un goûter.*" Only a taste, I said.

She took a sip. "*C'est bon.*"

That rumor about French kids drinking wine at every meal wasn't true. But they were allowed the occasional taste. Put it this way: French teens and young adults aren't drinking from kegs and doing beer bongs like Americans. I'd learned this when Steeve (still the one with an extra e), Isabelle's twenty-two-year-old son had people over one night during the Christmas season. He and his friends were watching a football (soccer) match while eating pizza and drinking sodas. And, no, the drinks weren't spiked. Just a different mentality here—not of the beer funnel kind.

"This weekend, can you look at my English paper?" asked Elvire, adding a "please" when I raised a brow.

Both of the kids took English at school, and Elvire insisted on practicing her growing language skills with me, pretty much everywhere. There I was, trying to blend into my French life like a chameleon, and she outed me as a foreigner at the grocery store, at the mall, and every opportunity she got. The upside? She was close to fluent in English. And I was improving my mangled French. I corrected her. She corrected me. There was a lot of repetition. It was a win-win.

"Of course," I said, throwing her a conspiratorial wink. Helping Elvire was a treat, especially when I compared her homework to the scientific papers Jean-Luc occasionally had me proof. Talk about speaking in another language…and reading the longest sentences ever known to man.

"Don't make it perfect," she said. "Or my teacher will think I cheat."

"Cheated," I corrected and turned the burner to low, the kitchen now smelling of cumin and ginger.

"By the way, I received my notes. My best mark was in English. I was the highest in my class," she said proudly.

"And what did you get?"

"Eighteen and a half!"

The French school system grades kids from one through twenty. A twenty is like getting an A plus—nearly impossible to achieve in

France, where the grading system is much stricter and isn't inflated simply to put a smile on a parent's or child's face. French sports, even in children's leagues, don't award trophies to losing teams for participation. You win, or you lose. And you work—or play—hard for achievements. I knew Elvire had been working extremely hard at learning English; she cornered me and asked questions whenever she could. Maybe I'd take her shopping? Or to lunch?

"I'm so proud of you," I said, giving her a huge hug. "What about math?"

Jean-Luc, like most French, believed that math and science were the keys to open every door in the future. He constantly made fun of the fact I had attended performing arts high school, calling it clown school. The French school system is divided into three areas of study: "S" (science), "ES" (economics and social), and "L" (literary/humanities). Jean-Luc was an "S" man, and often, we disagreed on the importance of the arts.

"Uh, my note in math is not so good. Papa is going to be mad." She paused, her eyes filled with fear. "Can you hide the paper for a week? I got a nine, and I want to go to a slumber party next weekend at Eva's."

I winked. "Your secret is safe with me. For one week."

In my defense, my mother would have done the same thing. A few times, I feigned an illness on exam days when I hadn't studied for a test. Miraculously, my malady would clear up around lunch. And my mother wasn't stupid; she was just a caring mom. She also liked having me around. I remembered the stressful days of being a teen. And what Jean-Luc didn't know for a week wouldn't kill him. Elvire and I both knew he would take away her cell phone and computer because of a poor grade in math.

Elvire blew out a sigh of relief. "Thank. You."

"Do you know what you want to do when you grow up?"

"I have no idea," she said.

"I think you should be a television journalist. You're so beautiful and well-spoken and you look great on film."

"On film?" Her face became brighter. I realized I didn't tell her often enough how smart and beautiful she was. As mentioned, I was the keeper of their youth now. I'd downloaded all the photos and videos from Jean-Luc's camera onto my computer and she was really photogenic. I'd also discovered something else.

"Yes, one video in particular. You were singing an American song into the camera. Boy meets girl, or something like that…"

"Ahhh! You saw that?" she questioned, her face flushing with embarrassment. "Please delete it!"

"No way. You'll love it when you're older." I laughed and turned the music up. "Now, it's time to dance."

We grabbed wooden spoons and belted out the lyrics to Shy'm's "*Et Alors.*" We danced and we sang and we laughed like nobody was watching. (Max was hiding upstairs in his bedroom with his headset on.)

Tonight's meal was a Moroccan chicken with preserved lemons, olives, apricots, and chickpeas. I'd picked up a tagine, a clay baking dish with a conical lid, on sale at the local Carrefour and wanted to put it to use. I'd serve the chicken over a lemon-infused couscous, along with braised asparagus seasoned with a shallot and a vinaigrette using Banyul, a regional vinegar, and a recipe I'd picked up from Ghislaine. A perfect meal for six. Yes, this dish was definitely cooked with an extra dash of love, the scents of cumin and garlic and pepper enveloping the kitchen. I was looking forward to sitting down with my family and friends. I was looking forward to laughter.

. . . .

After correcting Elvire's homework that Sunday, marking it up and explaining the errors she'd made, I called up Jess, telling her how much Elvire and I had been bonding woman to woman. "Do you think Elvire has a boyfriend?" she asked.

"No. She thinks all the boys in her class are *méga moche.*"

"*Méga moche?*"

"Not just ugly, but super ugly," I said, and Jess laughed. "Plus, they really don't date in France. You're either set up with somebody, and that person instantly becomes your boyfriend or girlfriend, or they go out in groups. And, typically, they never date more than one person at a time."

"That sounds nice," said Jess. "Because dating in the city sucks."

"Tell your big sis, what's going on?" I said, adding, "I promise I won't tell Mom."

"Please don't. She's giving me heart palpitations."

"I know what you mean," I said. "She keeps asking me when Jean-Luc and I are going try again." I sighed. "She's just being supportive. I guess."

Jess had recently suffered a miserable breakup with her boyfriend of four years. As any sister would, I wanted the best man for her, someone stable, and someone who wouldn't shatter her heart into tiny pieces. I wanted Jessica to have the same kind of love I had now.

Jessica sighed. "A few of my friends convinced me to sign up for one of those dating sites, and I've gone out with a few guys, but nobody special. I've been getting a lot of 'winks,' but I don't know." She spouted off her login info. "Please, help me decide. Anybody look good?"

I raced to my computer, pulled up the site, and flicked through her recent matches. "What about the thirty-seven-year-old? Viking5769. The guy with the really blue eyes? Some guys go gray early. He looks nice, has a good job, nice write-up. Anyway, I think he's handsome."

Plus, he was seven years older than she was. The exact age difference between Jean-Luc and me. Maybe I'd help my sister make an Internet love connection? The pitter-patter of hope raced in my heart.

"You think? I don't know. We've been exchanging messages and all he does is brag about how big his house is."

"Jess, it's just a date. It's not like you're marrying him. Be open to new possibilities."

As I'd been. And was.

Unfortunately, matchmaking wasn't in the cards for me. Jess called me a few days later. Along with an eye twitch, not only had Viking5769 lied about his age and height, over dinner he pretended to be a cat. A dying cat.

"I'm going to kill you," said Jess.

"What if I find you a sexy Frenchman?"

"Okay. I'm listening," she said.

. . . .

Like most French families, we traveled a lot on the weekends... in our own country. There was so much to see. It was important to Jean-Luc that the kids know the history of France. But it wasn't all an education. It was time for some fun. An even better benefit of living in France, and being married to a Frenchman, was the delightful fact that Jean-Luc's company supported cultural explorations and travel, offering discounted tickets to operas or plays and weekend jaunts, such as skiing in Luchon. I was a bargain shopper, and 30 percent off a cultural education was stellar.

Although it had snowed during my first winter in Toulouse, the weather typically averaged around thirty-four to forty degrees Fahrenheit. This season was gray and gloomy and rainy, not a winter wonderland. So of course I agreed when Jean-Luc proposed a ski trip. If the snowy mountains wouldn't come to us, we'd head for them.

There were just a few problems. Both of the kids were excellent skiers like Jean-Luc, all of them having hit the slopes since the age of six. And I was, well...terrible. The first time I attempted to ski in France was at a ski community in the Alps where Jean-Luc's childhood friend Gilles owned a ski *chalet*. Unfortunately, Jean-Luc had confused "I love to ski" with "I can ski," and he'd ignored my request to start off on the bunny hill with the little kids stuffed into their snowsuits. Panicked on a slope, I ended up falling down, smashing my head, and twisting my knee on a green run. Then I slid into an orange safety net. Jean-Luc stood over me. "You look like a little trapped bird," he'd said.

I was an angry and wounded bird.

But this winter I was committed to overcoming my fear of skiing. After a little research, I learned I could sign up for lessons with the ski school right at the station. Instead of torturing my family as I rolled down the mountain while screaming and falling down every two seconds or sinking into the snow with embarrassment, I opted to take a few private lessons with a ski monitor. Jean-Luc was in complete agreement. He booked me for two sessions that day.

Early on a Friday evening at the end of February, we approached the majestic snow-covered peaks of the Pyrénées and checked into a lovely snow-dusted hotel, a four-story historic château with wrought iron balconies and a very odd name: *Hôtel La Villa un Maillot Pour la Vie* (The Villa Hotel Jersey for Life), which didn't make sense until we saw the sport jerseys decorating our room. As usual, the four of us shared accommodations—two twin beds for the kids and a double bed for Jean-Luc and me, with one tiny bathroom.

"*J'ai faim*," said Max. I'm hungry.

"*Moi aussi*," said Elvire. Me too.

In the winter, and especially in ski villages like Luchon, the food was a bit heavier, consisting of hearty stews like a *pot-au-feu*, a *daube*, a *cassoulet*; *raclette*, the French version of fondue where you poured melted cheese over charcuterie, zucchini, and potatoes; or, the kids' favorite, *tartiflette*. We dropped off our bags and headed into the village for dinner. We passed by the Vaporarium, the one and only natural *hammam* (a spa with a steambath) in Europe, noting the sulfuric odor, and walked through the town with its boutiques and restaurants, making it an early night. Tomorrow was a big day.

The next morning, I woke up to find Elvire glaring at me.

"What?" I asked. "Why are you looking at me like that?"

"*J'ai dormi dans la salle de bain. T'as ronflé!*"

She'd slept in the bathroom because I'd snored. By the extent of her anger, I must have been making the sounds of a wood-chipper.

"Sorry," I said.

Jean-Luc laughed. "Now she knows how I feel."

"What?"

"Sleeping next to you is like sleeping on a farm, right next to all the barnyard animals."

"Not funny," I said, adding an *oink-oink* and pushing up my nose like a pig.

After Elvire shook off her irritation and we ate a continental breakfast of croissants, coffee, yogurt, and fruit, we jumped in the car, stopping quickly to pick up our rental gear at one of the local outfitters, and headed over to the Peyragudes ski station. The snow was coming down rather hard, and a flashing sign alerted drivers to pull over and put chains on the tires—obligatory in France even if your car had four-wheel drive. In the forest, we saw a beautiful buck with large antlers prancing in the snow. We all held our breath until he bounded off and then we squealed with excitement. Finally, we made it to the mountain in all its majestic glory. The flakes had subsided, and the sky was blue, dotted with puffy, white clouds.

Jean-Luc and the kids dropped me off at the ski school, and we set a meeting point for lunch. Then, I was left in the hands of my ski monitor, Jean-Jacques, who wore the required ESF (*École du Ski Français*) red jacket, and ski pants, and an orange wool jester cap. He only spoke two words of English, but my French was improving daily, and I'd manage.

Jean-Jaques asked for my level.

I adjusted my giant white helmet. "*Débutant*."

"*On y va?*" he asked.

Hello, bunny hill, here I come!

We made our way to the *tire-fesses*, which literally means "pull-butt," a lift comprising a disk you slip in between your legs, and three-year-olds raced by without their poles, navigating the hill like pros. If they could do this I could. Two hours later, I'd found my confidence and ski legs.

"Practice this afternoon," said Jean-Jacques. "Tomorrow, I think you'll be ready for a green run."

I smiled and nodded. *Take that, fear. I'm conquering you, France, and this mountain.*

I propped my skis outside the restaurant, then plopped on the ground and made a snow angel. When I opened my eyes, I found Max and Elvire splayed out beside me and Jean-Luc standing over us, smiling.

I *did* have love on my side, right next to me. And without fear holding me back, I could do anything I set my mind on. But as much as I loved this winter wonderland, I was really looking forward to spring—the season of renewal where everything grows and thrives.

JEAN-LUC'S *TARTIFLETTE*

Prep time: 15 minutes

Cook time: 45 minutes

Serves: 4 for a main course, 8 as a side dish

Great for: a winter meal or a side dish with poultry

Wine suggestion: Sauvignon Blanc

- 8 to 10 medium-sized red potatoes
- 1½ cups chopped *lardons* or pancetta, cubed
- 1 medium onion, sliced in rounds and halved
- 2 to 3 cloves garlic, de-germed and finely minced
- 3 healthy pinches *herbes de Provence*
- ⅛ teaspoon ground nutmeg
- ¾ cup *crème fraîche* or sour cream
- ½ cup dry white wine
- 1 round Reblochon cheese, or 1 round brie as a substitution*
- Extra virgin olive oil
- Salt and freshly ground black pepper, to taste

Preheat oven to 350°F. Bring a large pot of lightly salted water to a boil. Peel potatoes, if preferred. Boil for 12 to 16 minutes until the potatoes are soft enough to be pierced with a fork, but not cooked through. Drain, set aside, and let cool. In a pan, cook *lardons* until golden, around 4 minutes. Add the onion and garlic to the pan, cooking for another 5 minutes. Set aside. Once cool enough to handle, slice the potatoes in ½-inch-thick rounds. Place the potatoes in a lightly oiled

9 x 12-inch baking dish. Mix the *lardons*, onion, and garlic mixture into the potatoes, followed by the *crème fraîche* and wine. Add the *herbes de Provence* and the nutmeg, and season with salt and pepper. Mix well. Slice the cheese round in half crosswise, so it ends up in 2 rounds. Cut each round into 4 pieces, totaling 8 pieces of cheese. Place the slices of cheese on the potato mixture, skin side up. Bake for 25 minutes. Season with salt and pepper. Serve with a crispy endive salad with lemon vinaigrette.

*   *A true tartiflette uses Reblochon cheese, but it might be hard to find outside of France. If using brie, add an additional ¼ cup dry white wine, 1 tablespoon ground mustard seed, and more freshly ground black pepper to the potato mixture.*

How to Host a French Dinner Party

Every formal French meal starts with an *apéro*—appetizers served with champagne or a cocktail. This is followed by an *entrée* such as a soup or a salad with a few grilled scallops, the main course (*plat principal*), a cheese interlude (or salad), and then dessert. A standard *apéro* usually includes a small bowl of olives, green or black; potato chips (if children are in attendance); a bowl of cherry tomatoes or a crudité with a dip; plus one or two homemade dishes and a protein like *foie gras* on toast, a platter of charcuterie (meats), or sliced sausages. *Verrines*—small bites served in glasses ranging in size from shots to juice—are very popular. Basically, the options are endless for bite-sized nibbles—also the makings for an *apéro-dinatoire* (a tapas-style meal).

Appetizers

INDIVIDUAL TOMATO AND ZUCCHINI TARTS

Prep time: 10 minutes
Cook time: 25 minutes
Serves: 12 to 14
Great for: *apéro*
Wine suggestion: Champagne

- 1 homemade (p. 60) or premade piecrust from the refrigerated (not frozen) section
- ½ cup *crème fraîche*

- 1 tablespoon Dijon mustard
- 2 medium tomatoes, sliced
- ½ to ¾ zucchini, skin on, sliced
- Salt and freshly ground black pepper, to taste
- 1 healthy pinch *herbes de Provence*

Preheat oven to 350°F. On a floured work surface, roll out your piecrust, and use a 2-inch circle tool or a juice glass to cut the piecrust into small rounds. Roll out any leftover dough, cut again. Place the rounds on a parchment lined baking sheet. Brush the dough with a layer of *crème fraîche* and the mustard. Top each round with alternating tomatoes and zucchini, or a combo of both. Season with *herbes de Provence* and salt and pepper. Bake for 25 minutes. Serve warm or at room temperature.

ALAIN AND MURIEL'S GRAPEFRUIT, SHRIMP, AND FENNEL *VERRINE*

Prep time: 15 minutes

Cook time: 30 minutes (to chill in refrigerator)

Serves: 6 (juice-glass-sized *verrines*), 12 (shot-glass-sized *verrines*), or 24 (Chinese soup spoons)

Great for: an entrée or an *apéro*

Wine suggestion: Champagne, baby!

- 2 cups shrimp, precooked, or prawns, crayfish, or crab, roughly chopped into bite-size pieces
- 1 grapefruit, pulped
- 2 avocados, peeled and cubed
- 2 tomatoes, diced
- 1 fennel bulb, chopped into bite-size pieces
- ¼ cup chives, chopped, plus extra for garnish

- ½ lemon, juiced
- *Crème fraîche* or Greek yogurt, for garnish
- Salt and freshly ground black pepper, to taste

Combine the first 7 ingredients in a bowl. Salt and pepper. Chill in the refrigerator for 30 minutes, or until ready to serve. Serve in *verrines* or Chinese soup spoons. Garnish with a dollop of *crème fraîche*, chives, and a pinch of pepper.

Entrées

ROASTED *POTIMARRON* (HOKKAIDO SQUASH) SOUP

Prep time: 15 minutes

Cook time: 45 minutes to 1 hour

Serves: 4 to 6

Great for: entrée, main course, or served in *verrines* as an *apéro*

Wine suggestion: Alsace

- 1 medium leek
- 2 tablespoons extra virgin olive oil
- 1 onion, peeled and diced
- 2 carrots, peeled and diced
- 2 stalks celery, diced
- 1 garlic clove, peeled, de-germed, and finely minced
- 4 cups chicken broth or vegetable stock
- 3 healthy pinches *herbes de Provence*
- 4 teaspoons ground cinnamon
- 1 teaspoon ground cumin
- 1 *potimarron* (Hokkaido squash) or 1 medium-sized butternut squash
- ½ lemon, juiced (optional)

- ¼ cup chives, chopped, for garnish
- *Crème fraîche* or sour cream or Greek yogurt, for garnish
- Salt and freshly ground black pepper, to taste

To clean the leek, slice off the dark green end, trimming to the pale green or white end. Cut off the roots. Slice the stalk lengthwise, and run under cold water. Set aside until ready to chop and use.

Preheat oven to 400°F. Heat the oil in a large pot over medium-high heat. Add the leek, onion, carrots, celery, and garlic, cooking until vegetables are soft, about 10 minutes. Add the chicken broth or vegetable stock, 2 teaspoons of the cinnamon, cumin, and 2 pinches of the *herbes de Provence*. Bring to a boil, cover, and reduce heat to a simmer.

Remove the ends (top and bottom) of the squash using a sharp knife, then cut it in half from the top (the neck) to the bottom (the tail). Remove the seeds with a spoon. Cut the squash into large chunks, and place on a baking tray, skin side down. Drizzle with olive oil. Sprinkle with salt, a pinch of *herbes de Provence*, and the remaining cinnamon. Place on the center rack of the oven and roast for 25 minutes until soft. Let cool, then discard the skin, and chop into 1-inch or 2-inch cubes. Add to the pot of vegetables and broth. Simmer for another 15 to 20 minutes. Purée in batches with a food processor, or all at once with an immersion blender, until creamy. Season with salt and pepper. If the soup needs an acidic flavor boost, add the lemon juice. Serve in bowls, and garnish with chives and a dollop of cream.

Plat Principal

BALSAMIC GLAZED PORK TENDERLOIN WITH MUSTARD CREAM SAUCE

Prep time: 20 minutes

Cooking time: 50 minutes

Serves: 6

Great for: a dinner party or a family meal

Wine suggestion: Bourgogne

FOR THE PORK:

- 2 pork tenderloins (about 2½ pounds total)
- ¼ cup balsamic vinegar
- 2 to 3 tablespoons brown sugar
- 1 to 2 tablespoons Dijon mustard
- Freshly ground black pepper, to taste
- 2 to 4 sprigs fresh rosemary, or 2 tablespoons dried

FOR THE SAUCE:

- 1½-inch fresh ginger root, peeled
- 3 cloves garlic, peeled
- 2 shallots, peeled
- 1 red onion, peeled
- ½ cup *crème fraîche* or sour cream
- 3 tablespoons Dijon mustard
- ¼ cup flat parsley, plus extra for garnish
- ¼ cup fresh tarragon, plus extra for garnish
- 1 cup dry white wine
- Salt and freshly ground black pepper, to taste

Preheat oven to 375°F. Season the pork with salt and pepper, and place it in a large skillet over medium heat, searing all sides until golden, about 5 minutes. Transfer the pork to a plate, keeping the burner on. Rub the pork down with the mustard. In the same pan, pour in the balsamic vinegar, and add in the sugar, stirring with a wooden spoon. Place the pork back into the pan. Glaze by turning the pork into the mixture several times, until fully coated. Remove the pork from heat, and place it in a baking dish. Place the rosemary on top. Bake for 30 minutes; the thickest part of the pork should register 145°F. While the pork is baking, prepare the sauce.

In a food processor, mince the ginger until it's shredded. Add in the garlic. Mince. Then add the onion and shallots, and mince again. Add in the remaining ingredients, and pulse until smooth. Transfer the mixture to a pot, and heat on medium low, stirring occasionally until the pork is ready and the sauce is warm.

Transfer the pork to a cutting board. Let stand 10 minutes. Whisk the sauce, and pour it into a gravy boat. Slice the pork, garnish with tarragon and parsley, and serve with the sauce, rosemary potatoes (p. 246), and steamed asparagus with a lemon mustard vinaigrette (p. 135).

BOEUF BOURGUIGNON

Prep time: 40 minutes

Cook time: 3½ hours in a Dutch oven, or 1¾ hours in a pressure cooker

Serves: 6

Great for: family meals, holiday parties, and any other winter dinner

Wine Suggestion: Bordeaux or St. Émilion

- 3 to 4 pounds lean stewing beef, cut into 2-inch chunks
- 4 tablespoons all-purpose flour
- 1 cup *lardons* or pancetta, cut in cubes
- 4 cloves garlic, peeled, de-germed, and finely minced
- 6 tablespoons butter
- 16 to 20 pearl onions, fresh or frozen
- 2 to 3 large carrots, peeled and cut into 2- to 3-inch chunks
- 4 shallots, peeled and sliced
- 1 bottle red wine (a hearty, but not expensive, Bordeaux)
- 1½ cups beef stock
- 2 tablespoons tomato paste
- ½ cup brandy, Armagnac, or Cognac
- 6 cloves
- 1 bouquet garni*
- ½ pound fresh mushrooms, (*cèpes*, chanterelles, or white) sliced
- 1 (12- or 14.5-ounce) can button mushrooms
- 3 bay leaves
- ¼ cup parsley, chopped (flat variety preferred), for garnish
- 6 medium-sized red potatoes, halved and skin on (optional)**
- Salt and freshly ground black pepper, to taste

Using 1 tablespoon of the flour, coat the beef and toss to cover, and then season with salt and pepper. Blanch the onions in a pot of lightly salted water, drain, and set aside. In a Dutch oven, cook the *lardons* until brown and crispy, about 7 minutes. Add in the garlic, and cook for another 4 minutes. Remove the *lardons* with a slotted spoon, and set aside on a paper towel. Brown the beef in the same pot on medium-high heat, searing all sides until golden. Add carrots and shallots to the beef. Return the *lardons* to your pot. Add the beef stock to the pot, and then add enough wine to cover the beef. Add the bouquet garni, cloves, and bay leaves. Pour in the brandy, and add the tomato paste. Let simmer on low heat, covered, for about 2½ hours, stirring occasionally. If you notice the sauce is boiling down too much, add more wine.

Half an hour before serving, peel the pearl onions, and drain the button mushrooms. In a pan, melt 2 tablespoons of the butter and sauté the onions and all the mushrooms. Add them to the main pot, stirring them in with the wooden spoon. If using potatoes, now is the time to add them. Simmer, covered, for half an hour.

In a small bowl, mix the remaining 3 tablespoons of flour with 2 tablespoons of the butter with your fingers until it forms a paste. This is a *beurre manié*, which thickens the sauce. Fold it into the sauce about 10 minutes before serving. Season with salt and pepper. Remove the bouquet garni and the bay leaves, and garnish with parsley. Serve with an endive salad and a baguette.

If using a pressure cooker, prepare all ingredients as indicated—blanching the onions, sautéing the mushrooms, and preparing the beef and *lardons*. Place everything in the pot all at once except for the *beurre manié* (see above). Cook for 1½ hours. Release the steam. Add the *beurre manié* to thicken the sauce. Stir, and simmer for an additional 10 minutes.

---

* *Can't find bouquet garni? Make your own—it's easy! Using kitchen string, tie together these ingredients: 3 bay leaves, 6 sprigs of dried thyme, and 1 sprig of rosemary.*

** *This dish can be served with potatoes cooked into the recipe, or it can be served over an egg-based pasta, like tagliatelle.*

JEAN-LUC'S *LANGOUSTES*
À L'ARMORICAINE

Prep time: 20 minutes

Cook time: 45 minutes

Serves: 4 to 6

Great for: dinner parties or holiday meals

Wine Suggestion: Bandol Blanc or Cassis Blanc

FOR THE SAUCE:

- 2 tablespoons butter
- 1 tablespoon extra virgin olive oil
- 1 red onion, peeled and roughly minced
- 3 shallots, peeled and roughly minced
- 3 cloves garlic, peeled, de-germed, and finely minced
- 2 medium carrots, peeled, and shredded or sliced
- 1 cup tomato purée
- ½ cup tomatoes, diced
- 1 teaspoon tomato paste
- 5 cloves
- 2 sprigs thyme, leaves only
- 5 peppercorns
- 1½ cups dry white wine
- 2 bay leaves
- ½ cup flat parsley, finely chopped, plus extra for garnish
- 1 tablespoon madras curry powder
- ½ cup Cognac, Armagnac, or brandy
- Salt and freshly ground black pepper, to taste

FOR THE LOBSTER:

- 1 lobster tail per person, thawed if frozen*
- 1 tablespoon butter
- 1 tablespoon extra virgin olive oil
- ¼ cup Cognac, Armagnac, or brandy

First, prepare the sauce.** In a large pot, melt the butter and add the olive oil. Add the onion, shallots, and garlic, cooking until soft and translucent, about 5 minutes. Add the carrots. Cook for 3 to 5 minutes. Add the tomato purée, tomatoes, tomato paste, cloves, thyme, and peppercorns. Stir. Add the wine. Add the bay leaves, parsley, and curry powder. Stir. Season sauce with salt and pepper. Let simmer for 10 minutes while preparing the lobsters.

In a large pot (or two, if needed), melt the butter with the olive oil. Place the lobster tails in the pot, turning them occasionally. Once the shells are a red or orange color, add the Cognac, light a long kitchen match, and flambé—keep a lid handy in case the flames rise too high and you need to snuff the fire out.*** Once the flame settles down, add the lobster tails to the sauce. Simmer for half an hour on a low flame, seasoning with salt, pepper, and a dash of Cognac, to taste. Remove bay leaves. Garnish with parsley, and serve with steamed rice.

---

*   *A cheaper alternative to lobster is monkfish or extra-large shrimp, which can be used for cooking large quantities for a smaller price tag.*

** *If you are serving more than 6 portions—do not double the ingredients for the sauce. Add about an eighth more of each ingredient per serving. And don't throw the leftover sauce out; it's amazing on pasta.*

*** *Flambé at your own risk. Please be careful—we're talking fire here.*

The Salad or Cheese Course

For the cheese course, I normally pick out a goat cheese, a Roquefort, a Tomme, and a Brie—a variety. For the salads, here are two of my go-to dressings to serve on a crisp, green salad with veggies.

LEMON MUSTARD VINAIGRETTE

Prep time: 5 minutes

- ½ lemon, juiced
- 1 tablespoon Dijon mustard
- ¼ cup extra virgin olive oil
- 1 teaspoon finely minced garlic
- 1 healthy pinch *herbes de Provence*
- Salt and freshly ground black pepper, to taste

Whisk all the ingredients together in a bowl until creamy. Serve on a salad or steamed veggies.

CREAMY BALSAMIC VINAIGRETTE

Prep time: 5 minutes

- ½ cup aged balsamic vinegar
- 1 tablespoon Dijon mustard
- ⅛ cup extra virgin olive oil
- 1 healthy pinch *herbes de Provence*
- Salt and freshly ground black pepper, to taste

Whisk all the ingredients together in a bowl until creamy. Serve on a salad or steamed veggies.

Ingredient Three

ADVENTURE

14

A SPRING IN MY STEP

M AY FIRST IS A CELEBRATION of spring, new beginnings, and also a national holiday established when the eight-hour workday was introduced into France, much like Labor Day in the U.S. My neighbor, Claude, came over to the house and handed me a small bouquet of lily of the valley, known here as *muguet*, wrapped with a pink satin ribbon. This, I learned, was another wonderful French tradition, the flowers given to those you love to wish them happiness and good fortune for the upcoming year. Claude also handed me six tall bamboo rods to support the tomato plants we'd just planted in our garden, a thank-you to Jean-Luc for helping him with his taxes. I asked if he and his wife would like to join us for an *apéritif*. He pointed to his heart. "*Merci, c'est gentil, mais je peux pas. Demain, j'irai à la clinique pour un acte chirurgical.*"

Thank you, that's nice, but I can't. Tomorrow, I'm going to the clinic for a surgery.

"*C'est grave?*" Is it serious?

"*Non, pas de tout,*" he said, but his kind blue eyes and mouth crumpled. He French *pfftp*ed and knocked his chest twice. "*Mon cœur est fort.*" He kissed my cheek. "*Ne t'inquiète pas.*"

Don't worry.

The next day, Paulette waved in between the bushes that separated our property lines. "*Coucou!*" Hey you, she said, stepping around the corner, speaking a mile a minute, waving her hands, explaining how they would be traveling back and forth from their house in Narbonne and only coming back here for quick visits to the doctor to check up on Claude and his heart, and how they were getting old and had to watch their health, how Jean-Luc and I, the young kids that we were, needed to watch our hearts, too. And I was listening and nodding and it dawned on me: I understood sixty-five, maybe seventy percent of what she'd said.

It really was a new beginning.

As the sun set that night, I sat in the teak chair in our backyard listening to Florence and the Machine, thankful for so many things, including Claude's clean bill of health. I may not have had hummingbirds, but I loved watching the bats—*les chauve-souris*—and barn swallows—*les hirondelles*—at dusk. They swooped and glided in the air, eating the mosquitoes in an orchestrated dance. And it was beautiful. Well, if I ignored the lizard tails the cat kept dropping on the kitchen floor and the army of snails on my back deck clinging to the kitchen window when it rained. Snails aside (which I loved to eat when purchased frozen from the local Picard and doused in garlic, butter, and parsley), this was the life.

That's when I heard it. At first, I thought somebody was whistling. Maybe Max? But Max was in his room and his windows were closed. And if it was Max, Elvire would be screaming, "*Arrête de siffler!*" (stop whistling) and doors would slam and either Jean-Luc or I would have to break up another fight. The noise got louder and more frequent, like a beep, and it wasn't coming from inside of the house. What the hell? I called out to Jean-Luc. "Oh my God! What is this annoying sound?"

He stepped out into the yard. "What sound?"

"Beep, beep, beep. Whistle. Beep, beep, beep. Don't you hear it?"

Whatever it was got even louder. Jean-Luc shrugged. "I don't know. Some kind of an animal?"

What kind of an animal beeps incessantly? At dusk? I bolted into the house and fired up my computer. Google would come to the rescue. There was my answer: it was an owl—a very loud owl, maybe two of them, or so I thought. For the next week, from sundown to sunup, the beeping continued. But there was no sign of an owl, not one feather. Isabelle and Richard came to stay with us for a few days. Isabelle was helping me set the table on the deck when her eyes went wide. "Ah, *c'est horrible.*"

"It does that all night," I said. "I think it's an owl."

"It's not an owl. It's a frog," she said.

I had to curb my laugh. After everything I'd been through, now a frog was my biggest problem in life? Like cleaning up the rose petals the morning after our wedding, this was not a crisis. I could live with Beepy the Frog. In a way, his noise was soothing. This was nature, glorious nature. Our garden was blooming. And sometimes I called Jean-Luc my frog.

Isabelle shrugged and then asked me to keep dinner light, as Richard was on a diet. It was too late, though. Anticipating their arrival, I'd already made my famed chicken Milanese breaded in panko and it was warming in the oven, to be served with a mango-avocado slaw, steamed rice, a hearts-of-palm salad, and an apple crumble for dessert. As I brought the dishes out, Richard's eyes lit up and he licked his lips.

"*C'est trop,*" said Isabelle. It's too much.

By now, instead of being insulted, I was used to how the French voiced their opinions. In fact, compared to the way some Americans hid behind false compliments, it was kind of refreshing. Sort of. I'd learned my lesson to never ask if something needed more salt or sugar, especially with family members who were more honest. And if I asked somebody if my jeans made me look fat, I didn't necessarily want a truthful answer. Perhaps this was the reason French women were rumored to be more reserved when it came to opening up in the quest for new friendships.

"What are we doing this weekend?" asked Richard as he served up seconds of the chicken.

Isabelle shook her head, glaring at Richard. He shrugged, pulled out his iPhone, and sang an Elvis song. In English.

Quelle surprise! I wondered if Richard actually knew what he was singing. On more than one occasion, Elvire had randomly blurted out lyrics to American songs—songs whose meanings she didn't know, along with a few mispronunciations. Case in point: Katy Perry's "Peacock." One day, I swore she was singing "I wanna see your big cock" instead of "peacock" and I nearly died—even though *coq* in French is a rooster. I quickly corrected her.

But to answer Richard's question: What were we doing this weekend? His question should have been: What aren't we doing this weekend?

It was Isabelle and Richard's first trip to the area, and they wanted to see more of it. Alas, Jean-Luc, the good brother, had planned a non-stop itinerary—our first visit, the sweeping village of Rocamadour, built into the cliffs and overlooking a tributary of the Dordogne River in the Lot district, about a two-hour drive from Toulouse. I'd heard of Rocamadour at our local market. Jean-Luc, knowing my love for goat cheese, especially those from the neighboring department of Dordogne known as *cabécou*, ordered a package of the small, round creamy goodness called Rocamodour (after the village) from the vendor and placed it in our basket. Rocamodour cheese may have been amazing, but the town blew my mind. Breathtakingly beautiful, dramatic, and utterly impressive with its houses and churches, the whole village clung to the rocks, surrounded by greenery.

A UNESCO world heritage site, Rocamadour has been a popular stop on the pilgrimage route of Saint-Jacques-de-Compostole (Camino de Santiago or the Way of Saint James) for over a thousand years and, even in early May, was crowded with tourists. Most of the million visitors who visited Rocamadour every year didn't come to worship its wonderful cheese, but rather the black wooden Madonna, or Black Virgin, housed in the Chapelle Notre Dame and presumably carved by Saint Amadour/Saint Amator, a saint who was supposedly a myth or a legend. Thankfully, we arrived early enough to find parking. We passed through a stone-fortified gateway, leading to a stone-paved street, and climbed 216 steps, which the pilgrims used to mount on their knees, to visit the town and the chapel.

After Rocomadour, we visited Pech-Merle, a cave with prehistoric paintings of woolly mammoths, reindeers, spotted horses, and human handprints, some dating back to 25,000 BC. Then it was on to the charming village of Saint-Cirq-Lapopie, a small village overlooking a river with winding, cobbled streets, and considered to be one of the most beautiful destinations in France. In fact, southwestern France lays claim to the majority of *les plus beaux* (the most beautiful) *villages de France*.

And it was time to see one more.

It was the charming medieval village of Cordes-sur-Ciel, built in the 1200s, that captured my heart. We traversed the cobbled streets, ate crêpes, and took in sweeping views of pristine vineyards dotted with beautiful rustic farmhouses. Jean-Luc stood behind me, taking in the scent of Valentina by Valentino, the bottle of which he'd randomly surprised me with. The children darted off to pet a gray cat while Isabelle and Richard sauntered into one of the art galleries.

Famed author Albert Camus once said, "In Cordes, everything is beautiful, even regret."

"You smell so wonderful," Jean-Luc said, nuzzling my hair.

All I could think was: I have no regrets, no, not anymore. But there was still one thing missing for me, something whose possibility I wanted to explore more—a child of our own, a celebration of spring and of summer, of our love, of everything beautiful. I knew I'd regret not giving the thought another chance. "I'd like to try again," I said, and quickly corrected myself. "But I don't want to be one of those women who plans sex with the only goal of having a baby."

Jean-Luc popped his lips. "*Pffffp*. What's to plan? We make love every night. If it happens, it happens."

I pinched my lips together. "Maybe it will?" I whispered under my breath.

Exhausted from a full day of touring the French countryside, we had another not-so-light-but-already-planned dinner back at home—a French-Creole gumbo. Thanks to Trupty, I'd discovered the local Asian market near our house. When I'd shopped there, I was surprised to find fresh okra. I picked up a sackful, thinking back to my mom's southern roots and my spicy tastes. Gumbo was always better a day or two later, when all the flavors meshed together. Although I couldn't find Andouille sausage, *saucisse de Toulouse*, a local specialty, was a tasty substitution, along with poached and shredded chicken. Color me happy! All I had to do was heat the meal up, add in the okra and the shrimp—BAM! We were set. Richard patted his belly, his eyes lighting up with glee when I brought out dessert—a *gâteau fondant à l'orange*, a recipe I'd picked up from Isabelle and added my own touches to—caramelized pineapple slices and mandarin oranges.

. . . .

On a misty Sunday morning, it was time to leap back in time to the medieval village of Carcassonne, famed for its numerous watchtowers and fortifications, in the Aude region, followed by Château de Montségur, a ruined fortress. We were in Cathar country, an area with a turbulent history of the Albigensian Crusade spearheaded by Pope Innocent III in 1208—a holy war oftentimes described as the first act of genocide in Europe. Although the origins of the Cathar religion were believed to come from Persia or the Byzantine Empire, its exact origins would always remain a mystery. The route of the Cathars extended from the north of Toulouse, in Albi, then to the south toward Perpignan, near the Spanish border.

The village of Carcassonne was easy to explore. The four-thousand-foot hike up to Montségur took a bit more energy, the mist transforming into a light rain. We scurried up the steep path, careful not to slide down the moss-covered rocks or crush the colorful snails. I grabbed one of the yellow and brown swirled suckers from the ground, handing it over to Elvire.

"I'm taking a picture. Pretend to eat it," I said, and she did.

We both laughed. She knew I'd post the photo on Facebook, along with the caption *Yes, the French really do eat snails.*

Once we reached the top, inside the crumbling walls of the fortress, history came alive. One could almost hear the battle cries, the sounds of swords clanging against one another, the hooves of galloping horses.

On the way back to Cugnaux, we stopped by Château de Puivert, a twelfth-century castle set over a pastoral countryside dotted with wildflowers—favorites like *les coquelicots* (red poppies)—and sleek, happy horses roaming the land. A couple of beautiful wolves greeted us like dogs, closely guarded by the keeper of the castle. I didn't know why they were there. Jean-Luc made up a story about a haunting. The wolves kept away *la dame blanche*, the white lady, a ghost rumored to roam the lands. I googled that later. Jean-Luc's story, although convincing, save for the legend of *la dame blanche*, wasn't true.

We arrived home at about 7:30 p.m., and, again, Isabelle insisted on a light dinner. "I'd just like a green salad," she said.

"*Comme tu veux.*" As you wish. "But I'm putting some tomatoes, avocado, hard-boiled eggs, and hearts of palm on the side. Maybe some roasted peppers, a couple of potatoes, some Feta cheese…and some tuna for the kids."

For me, a salad wasn't a meal unless it had some tasty stuff in it. Richard raised his hands to the heavens in thanks.

15

SALMONLUHJAH!

ONE WEEK LATER IT WAS our first anniversary—for the wedding that technically counted, when we legally got married in France. *Le 7 mai.* Jean-Luc was taking me to the symphony in Toulouse. I decided to cook up some salmon fillets seasoned with lemon and butter before setting off. The filets slid off my fingers and into the pan. The odor was pungent, filling the entire kitchen. I refrained from gagging, barely making it through dinner, and choking down the fish with rice.

We made it to the theater and took our seats. They were uncomfortable, straight-backed and small. There was no air conditioning. Sweat pooled in my cleavage. And, here I was, in high heels and a tight black skirt, trying to look nice, maybe a little sexy. The conductor came out. I clapped my hands. They smelled of salmon, the oil of which had seeped into my skin, and I instantly fought back the urge to puke over the side of the balcony onto the unsuspecting music aficionados below. My mouth filled with a sour, putrid taste. The symphony began to play. Wagner? Bach? I couldn't have cared less at that point. My head was reeling, but I fought through it, making it through the first half. When it ended, I clapped, the scent of salmon infiltrating my nostrils. I tucked my hands under my thighs.

Jean-Luc turned to me during intermission. "Do you want a drink? Some champagne?"

"Water," I said.

He knew I never said no to champagne. Regardless, it didn't matter; there was no bar, no water or champagne to be found. The second act was torture, a cacophony playing in my stomach, on my taste buds, in my mouth. Salmonluhjah. Salmon! Salmon! When we left the theater I gulped in the fresh air like a fish lying on the sandy banks in the sun. A salmon?

"Oney, did you not enjoy the music?"

The only words I could form were, "I think I'm pregnant."

And, according to the test I took the following morning, indeed, I was. Jean-Luc met me at the *clinique*. We sat in the waiting room, waiting, waiting, and waiting. Doctor K was running late. It was sheer and utter torture. People going in. People going out. Finally, the good doc smiled at us, and waved us into his office, apologizing profusely.

"I'm glad to see you again, Samantha and Jean-Luc." His face was aglow. "So, let's see how things are progressing. But, first, Samantha, we have to update your chart. How much do you weigh?"

"I have no idea."

"Hop up on that scale."

And so I did. He marked down the number. "Sixty-eight kilos."

It couldn't be. I weighed fifty-seven kilos when I'd moved to France. I knew I'd gained a little weight, but close to twenty-five pounds? "What? Are you kidding me? Sixty-eight kilos?"

Jean-Luc sucked in his breath, raised an *I-told-you-so* eyebrow.

"How much did you think you weighed?" asked Doctor K.

"Um, a whole lot less than that. It must be the pregnancies."

No wonder my clothes don't fit anymore; and I'd thought they'd just shrunk. Yes, Jean-Luc had been dropping little hints like "Sam, you're cooking too much food," or "Honey, I think you've had enough bread," or "Maybe one slice of tart will suffice," but damn it if he ever said, "Darling, my *crème fraîche* puff, you're kind of getting fat."

Doctor K's face was unreadable. "Well, on that, my dear, let's see how things are progressing. Hop up onto the table." He squirted the blue liquid onto my belly, rubbed the magic wand. His lips pinched.

I held my breath. "Am I pregnant?"

"Oh, you're pregnant." He pulled out a wheel that calculated the dates. "But according to the timing of your last menstrual cycle, you're supposed to be seven or eight weeks along." He scratched his chin. "You might ovulate late."

"I don't understand."

"Well, you're measuring at about four and a half weeks now. And I don't see a fetal pole, only the gestational sac."

Oksana's experience slammed into my memories, making me tremble. "It's a blighted ovum?"

"It's too early to tell. I'd like to see you again in one week." He smiled. "And, please, don't worry. The only thing we can do is hope for the best."

Right. The best.

We set the appointment for the following week. Before we left his office, Doctor K said, "Don't even think about changing your diet right now. Eat healthy."

Jean-Luc took me by the hand. "'Oney, it will be okay."

I nodded. But something didn't feel right. At home, I combed through all the baby sites, looking for information similar to mine. What I found out wasn't good and brought me to tears. Jean-Luc had to pry me away from the computer. But I was a woman obsessed. I used my iPod Touch in the bathroom.

Over the weekend at a dinner *chez* Christian and Ghislaine's, I learned that Anne, their twenty-nine-year-old daughter, was pregnant and a healthy twelve weeks along. We were trying to keep my news quiet, especially with what had happened the last time. But I spilled the beans. Ghislaine squeezed my arm. "*Ne t'inquiète pas.*"

Don't worry? Easier said than done. I couldn't stop myself from worrying, and I was a freaked-out, shaky mess the next time I entered Doctor K's office. He ushered me onto the exam table, rubbed in the blue gel, and placed the scanner on my belly. I closed my eyes, praying and hoping for the best. I was back to my old self, holding my breath.

Breathe. Breathe. Breathe.

"Well, well, well," said Doctor K, his voice knocking me back into the present, "what do we have here? There it is, the fetal pole. You're measuring five weeks and two days." He turned a knob on the ultrasound machine. Thump, thump. Boom. "What you're listening to right now is the fetal heartbeat."

To keep myself from bursting into tears, I bit down on my bottom lip so hard I almost drew blood. "What is it?"

"121 beats per minute."

Not that strong, but it was still early. I'd take it.

I called my mother, Tracey, and Jessica, swearing them to secrecy. Jean-Luc and I did not share the news with Max and Elvire, although he did tell his sisters, and Christian and Ghislaine were already in the know. Everybody promised to keep quiet until I was out of the woods and well on my way through this pregnancy.

. . . .

Sunday, May 29, was Mother's Day in France.

I entered Elvire's bedroom to find her carving *Je t'aime, Maman* onto her wooden dresser, tears streaming down her face. I gave her a hug, told her I understood. In the frame I'd given her, a picture of Frédérique, the children's mother, rested on Elvire's desk. Dangling off the frame was the keepsake I'd given to guests—seven Tibetan charms symbolizing our union, like a fleur-de-lis and a dragonfly tied to a satin ribbon that hung from a starfish—at our wedding. I squeezed her shoulders and closed the door behind me, leaving her to settle all the conflicting emotions down. I was feeling a bit conflicted, too. I shut myself in the bathroom downstairs, crying silently.

Jean-Luc tapped on the door. "Are you okay, 'oney?"

I opened the door.

"What's wrong?" he asked, noting the tears on my face.

"Nothing."

"Sam?"

"God, Jean-Luc. Do I have to draw you a picture? I can't even believe I have to tell you this. I thought you would do something on your own accord."

"What are you talking about?"

"It's *Mother's Day.*"

He pointed at my stomach. "Is this because of Jack the Bean?"

"No. And yes. And also the fact I take care of your kids. So much in fact they're like mine now. I'm the one who cooks all their meals. I'm the one giving them *bisous* before sending them off to school. I'm the one who dries their tears when you're not around. God, I just want one ounce of appreciation." I sobbed. "Just one ounce on one measly day."

He drew me into his arms. "Of course you're appreciated. I love you. We all do."

I looked into his eyes. "I just went to the bathroom and when I wiped there was some blood."

He bit down on his lip. "Sam, it's probably nothing. But just to be sure—"

I was at Doctor K's again, Jean-Luc by my side, on the table, same old, same old, squeezing my eyes shut as he delivered the news. "I'm sorry, but Samantha is in the process of miscarrying. There is no fetal heartbeat. I'm afraid this isn't a viable pregnancy."

Bang. Bang. Bang. I was dead. I was mad at Doctor K. I was mad at Jean-Luc. I was mad at France. In that moment, I was mad at everybody, the entire world. I, a woman who would give her heart and soul to a child, had to go through this. It wasn't fair. A knot of pain twisted in my stomach. I couldn't breathe, couldn't speak.

"Was it something that could have been prevented?" asked Jean-Luc.

"If you're asking if the miscarriage was caused by something else, an outside influence, the answer is no. She doesn't do drugs, doesn't smoke, eats healthy. She *is* healthy. Most likely, it's a chromosomal anomaly. Sadly, it's nearly impossible to pinpoint a reason."

"Is there anything we can do to stop this from happening again?"

"Perhaps," said Doctor K. "It could have something to do with

the oxygen levels in her blood, but anything we try has no guaran-
tees. She'd have to go in for a series of tests. For now, we'll just check
all her hormone levels."

"Will she have to have surgery?"

"No, it's not far enough along for risking another D&C. The
material will have to pass naturally. It will be like a heavier period." I
tuned out Doctor K as he told us not give up hope, to try again, that
we were both still young.

But that was a lie. I wasn't young. A high-risk case, I was turning
forty-two that year.

Words echoed in my head, pulsing and throbbing. I just wanted
to go home and crawl into bed. Maybe forever. Jean-Luc wrapped
his arms around me. "Sam, I'm feeling this sadness too."

One week later my body convulsed in extraordinary pain. The
doctor had said the loss would be like a heavy period. It wasn't.
Along with severe physical torture, I couldn't blame the tears I had
to hide from Max and Elvire on PMS, so I came up with a little
white lie to explain my zombie-like state: I had a debilitating (and
very contagious) stomach flu. The kids steered clear of me. On the
many trips to the bathroom, I tried to find something, anything,
resembling a fetus. There was nothing, only blood, and strange alien
material covering my hands. I bled for a week.

And then I was empty.

This time, I let Jean-Luc's scientific reasoning offer comfort:
nature had other plans for the little life once growing inside me,
the bean that could've been a beanstalk, but didn't quite reach the
sky. His words prompted me into action, and I soon found myself
digging up the earth in the backyard with my bare hands, digging
like a wild dog searching for a long-forgotten bone, throwing rocks
to the side. I was now planting two rosebushes, one orange and one
hot pink—my favorite colors—in remembrance of two angel babies.

Jean-Luc came home from work to find me in the garden panting,
which is what happens when your garden is located over a former
riverbed filled with rocks. It wasn't easy, but I did it. Dirt covered

my entire body, mud splattering my arms and my face, everywhere. Blood tinged my fingernails. I may have looked certifiably insane, but my heart was in a lot less pain. I was angry and sad, but I hadn't given up on hope.

"When we can, we'll give this pregnancy thing one more shot," I said. "But if the third time isn't the charm, I won't be able to 'try without trying' anymore. I just can't do it."

16

WEIGHT NOT, WANT NOT

I T WAS THE END OF June, and Elvire had planned a slumber party with five of her friends for her fourteenth birthday. I needed to get back with the step-by-stepmom program. Although this second loss had shaken my nerves, the children's happiness was more important than my own. Thankfully, Elvire wanted to order in goat-cheese-and-honey pizzas, and Jean-Luc was picking up a chocolate mousse cake along with two *barquettes* of delicious, fresh strawberries, so all I had to do was set the table and shake off any sadness that might creep up. As I watched Elvire greet her closest *amies* with the required *bisous* and yelps of delight, it became easier to smile.

Elvire bounced into the kitchen. "Can we steal your shoes? *Les talons?*"

At five-foot-seven, Elvire was now taller than me, but we had the same size feet. I had let her borrow my favorite short, black motorcycle boots once. Now, when they went missing, I knew where they were: on her. Unless Jean-Luc and I went out on one of our rare date nights for a birthday or anniversary, I never wore heels. They were dangerous in my small town with its brick-paved streets.

"*Bien sûr,*" I said. Of course.

"*Et, aussi,*" said Elvire. "*Puis-je emprunter le kit maquillage? Celui avec toutes les couleurs de fard à paupières?*"

"You can keep the makeup kit," I said. I didn't wear colored eye shadows anymore—just black eyeliner, mascara, foundation, and blush, maybe a little lipstick.

Her eyes widened with surprise. "Really?"

"It's yours. It's in the drawer upstairs in the bathroom."

Elvire gave me a quick hug and bolted back to her room. If a used makeup kit made her screech with joy, just wait until she saw the silver necklace with a heart charm and tiny butterfly studs we'd purchased for her birthday gift. I set the table, listening to the giggles coming from upstairs with an ear-to-ear grin stretching across my face. Planting the two rosebushes had settled my nerves. The happiness lighting Elvire's eyes eased the stabs of pain.

Life, indeed, does goes on.

A few moments later, Max sauntered down the stairs with a grimace on his face. "*Elles sont tellement bizarres. Une des amies d'Elvire ressemble à un chat. Avec les moustaches!*"

They are so weird. One of Elvire's friends looks like a cat. With whiskers!

I noted that Max had used the word for *cat* in the masculine form, not saying *une chatte*. And I knew why. One day I made the mistake of asking our neighbor Claude if he'd seen my cat—"*Est-ce que t'as vu ma chatte?*" First, his jaw dropped and then he laughed so hard he almost fell down. Basically, I'd asked him if he'd seen my *pussy*. So, unless used in dirty pillow talk, using "cat" in the feminine form was another exception to French grammar rules. This rule also applied to saying that you were excited in French. One never said *je suis très excitée*. To say you were very excited also carried a strong sexual connotation. And so did saying *je suis chaude* (I'm horny) to the paella vendor.

Every day was an education. And I was definitely learning—mostly that I had foot-in-mouth syndrome in not one but two languages.

Apparently, the girls were getting creative with the makeup kit, doing the whole girly-girl thing. To my knowledge, Elvire and her girlfriends were still innocent. They didn't drink, smoke, or swear, although they did rat their hair (and were probably doing it right at that moment). There was no boy drama. Yet. Oftentimes, I liked to tease Jean-Luc, telling him that she'd probably fall in love with a guy who was just like him, and Jean-Luc would cringe with fear. He remembered what he was like at her age. And he'd told me all about it.

"In the summers of my youth, girls from all over Europe would come to La Ciotat. We especially looked forward to the Swedes…"

At this point, I'd laugh and call him a player.

Upstairs, the music and laughter reached new decibels. The girls sang Rihanna's "Only Girl (In the World)" off key and at the top of their lungs, their heeled foot-stomping putting Michael Flatley's *Riverdance* to shame. *Click, click, boom. Click, click, boom.*

Jean-Luc came home from work, cake and strawberries in hand. "What's all that noise? It sounds like a bunch of elephants are running around the house."

Max shook his head. "I wouldn't go up there."

I handed Jean-Luc a glass of wine. "Here. You'll need this."

He settled onto the couch, sighed. "I think I need something stronger."

This coming from a man who only *tasted* his wine.

. . . .

"Don't you ever call me Fantasia again," I said to Jean-Luc, stopping my cooking dance in the kitchen. He was referring to the dancing hippos in the Disney movie. It was July, and I was wearing shorts and a too-tight T-shirt.

Jean-Luc coughed. "More of you to love?"

I slugged his arm, not hard, but enough to make him grimace. "Not funny."

Although I knew I'd put on a few pounds, I'd been living in denial. Since I had gained so much weight—the top button of my skinny jeans had flown off and ricocheted off the wall and almost hit the cat in the eye—apparently it was time to stop cooking French meals in American-sized portions. And maybe eat cheese and baguettes in moderation, as well as the *confit de canard* or *cassoulet de Toulouse*, two regional specialties cooked in duck fat.

Oh, but it was soooo good.

Good—until I hopped onto the scale and took a good look at myself in the mirror. Sure, some women looked fantastic with a couple of extra pounds, maybe more, on them. I wasn't one of them. At five-foot-five, my frame was small, and so were my features. My eyes were tiny, my lips were thin, and I didn't have a defined jawline. I held my weight in three places—my face, which looked puffy and bloated; my stomach, which now had a *pneu* (spare tire), or muffin top; and my ass, which I could feel moving like a wave when I walked. Since I'd last seen Doctor K, I'd put on three more kilos, and I couldn't blame the extra poundage on baby weight. I knew my healthy weight, one hundred and thirty pounds, give or take, but I now weighed well over one hundred and fifty pounds. Shock set in.

Elvire had given me permission to borrow her bicycle to get some exercise—and I'd read somewhere on the Internet that one hour on the bike burned around four hundred calories. Before swimsuit season was upon us, I wanted to burn all the damn calories I could. I wanted to release any anger I'd felt over the two consecutive losses. I wanted my muscles to hurt.

"Wear a helmet," said Jean-Luc before I took off.

"I'm not five years old," I said.

My legs pumped fast as I churned them through the town, on the bike path, past the kids' school, and onwards. Which, with my luck, meant I ended up getting a little bit disoriented and lost. No longer on the bike path—to my left was a median, to the right a torn-up gravel sidewalk with a very high curb, and behind me a couple of cars.

I was totally in the way with nowhere to go.

But then an opportunity presented itself: a driveway where the curb stood lower. I pedaled faster and faster, making my move so the cars behind me could pass. And that's where I made my mistake. I'd misjudged the curb. And the gravel. I wiped out in the parking lot of a pet store, skidding on my arm and thigh with the bike on top of me, my right arm taking most of the weight. Immediately, the two cars trailing me pulled over. In shock, I just held my arm, which was completely shredded, the blood not watery but thick and tarlike.

Great. Now that I was falling in love with France, the country was trying to kill me. Old, fear-filled Sam flashed in my eyes.

A woman and her young daughter stood over me. The woman had short chestnut-colored hair and kind brown eyes. Her daughter was an adorable towhead with shoulder-length hair and big blue eyes, around four years old. She wore a pink sundress. I wanted to tell her how cute she was, but I could barely form words. Instead, I apologized over and over again in French and said that I was American, as if that explained everything.

The woman crouched down next to me and took my arm. "I used to be a nurse."

The man from the other car walked over with a blanket, placing it behind me with worry pinching his lips.

"This wound needs to be cleaned," said the woman. "I'll do what I can, but the gravel is embedded into your skin. You need to get to the hospital immediately for stitches. Lie down."

I could only nod, French words and nausea spinning around in my brain. The woman instructed her little girl to stand over me, to block the sun beating down on my head. This adorable angel giggled as a gust of wind lifted up her dress, flashing her white panties. This made me chuckle; her mom, too. I was surprised a child of her age wasn't flipping out at the sight of my arm, but she just smiled, and fetched things from the car when her mother asked for them. The man paced in the background.

"Is there anybody we can call?" asked the woman when she finished bandaging up my arm.

"*Mon mari*," I said. My husband. And I was dreading contacting him. He'd been right about the helmet, after all.

The woman pulled out her cell phone. "What's the number?"

I was trying my best to keep from throwing up in shock, and I couldn't remember the number. I was only able to get the first few digits out. I made a move to reach for the hand-me-down iPhone my sister had given me, but wasn't able to retrieve it because I was shaking and my arm hurt.

"My cell phone is in my back pocket," I said. "I can't reach it."

The woman managed to commandeer the phone. When she handed it over, it was covered in sweat. Now, I suffered with both pain and embarrassment. It took a couple of minutes until I was able to get it working, and with shaky fingers, I called Jean-Luc.

"I've been in a bicycle accident. I'm okay, but I've got to get to the hospital for stitches. Please, can you come get me?"

Both the man and the woman stayed by my side until my knight in a silver Ford arrived. Jean-Luc threw Elvire's bike in the back hatch, harrumphing about how I should have worn a helmet. I must have said *merci* about a million times to the people who came to my aid, but in a rush to get to the hospital, I didn't think to get their names. The car tore out of the gravel parking lot, and before I could blink, or cry out in pain, I was in an emergency room in Muret, the next town over, with a gas mask on my face, being cleaned up and stitched up with fishing line.

The following day I had to get a tetanus shot. And I was petrified of needles. I visited our family doctor's office during his open hours, where he explained I needed a prescription and wrote one up. I made my way to the pharmacy, picked up the shot, and headed back to the doctor. He didn't even blink at me in recognition, even though I'd just seen him an hour prior. After the doc administered the shot, I said, "Wow, that didn't hurt at all!"

The doctor wrote a prescription for bandages, so that they would be covered by our insurance and I wouldn't be charged for them, along with a mild painkiller for the pain I was still experiencing, and we set an appointment for the following week, when he'd remove the *points de suture*. I was really over hospitals. And doctors. And nurses. And stitches.

At home, I peeked under the bandage. The wound was ugly and unforgiving. It appeared as if a wild animal had attacked me, which would have made for a better story. Bruises decorated my entire right side, from ribs, to my ass, to my thighs and calves. In addition to my miscarriages, now I was scarred for life.

MAKING ENDS MEET

EVERYBODY WAS TAKING ADVANTAGE OF the beautiful French summer and the fact you could travel a mere two to four hours and find yourself in a completely new landscape. My lunches in Toulouse with Les Chicks were few and far between, but we did manage to squeeze in a dinner where our significant others would meet at Monique's gorgeous apartment in the center of Toulouse.

I called Monique, a bit scared. "What are you making?"

She laughed. "I may not like cooking, but I know how to entertain," she said. "We're going to do a *pierrade*. Everybody will cook for themselves! Hey, do you have one? We might need two, seeing that there will be nine of us, including Kissa."

"That's an awesome idea," I said. "I'll bring mine."

I did have a *pierrade*, a stone grill that is plugged in and placed in the center of a table, kind of like a hibachi. Cooking the meats—duck, chicken, and steak—is the responsibility of the guests, and the meal is accompanied by a variety of sauces and vegetables, like potatoes and zucchini.

The local bank gave us points at the end of the year, and Jean-Luc let me pick out something we needed. Thanks to the bank, I'd just received a free panini maker, which when folded down flat served as the grill—my own little *pierrade*.

"Do you want me to bring dessert too?"

"That would be awesome," said Monique.

After we hung up, I called Jean-Luc to clear the plan with him. He, of course, had no objections to having dinner with my friends. "What should I make for dessert?" I asked.

"A crumble," he said, referring to one of my specialties. "Apples, pears, and red fruits."

"I'm on it."

Cooking a crumble was easy. Peel the apples. Peel the pears. Chop them up into little squares. Put them in a baking dish. Add in red fruits—raspberries, currants, strawberries, and maybe some blueberries or blackberries (okay, not red, but considered to be part of the group). Making the mixture was sensual. Massaging flour, brown sugar, and butter together until it crumbled. A little cinnamon. A dash or two of rum. And, oh, the scent while it baked in the oven.

We ordered a pizza for the kids and made our way to *centre ville*. I was excited to finally meet my friends' other halves. We sat down for the *apéro*—snacks and drinks—the get-to-know-you session for our men.

Jean-Christophe, JC, as Monique had described, was tall, dark, and handsome. He also had the most adorable space between his two front teeth. Funny and welcoming, it was as if I'd already met him. I now knew why Monique had "claimed" him with "he's mine" many years ago. Like Jean-Luc, he was personable and funny. He made rum cocktails with freshly squeezed juice.

Philippe, Oksana's partner, had also brought champagne. A former chief of police in Paris, he was a *huissier* in Toulouse, a man who upheld the law and made sure people paid their dues. A dashing and charming man, he had dark hair, wore glasses, and spoke with exuberant hand and eyebrow gestures.

Chris, Trupty's new squeeze, was a sweet, ginger-haired Englishman who had lived in France for fourteen years running a *gîte*, a bed and breakfast, three hours north of Toulouse in the Aveyron. Although Chris was the quietest out of the bunch—which I suppose was inevitable when you put three boisterous Frenchmen and one soft-spoken Englishman together—he seemed to be enjoying himself. In fact, the men got along so well with one another that we had to play musical chairs and switch seats so the girls could get a word in edgewise—guys on one end of the table, girls on the other. It was nice to see these new connections forming right in front of us.

"Once everybody is back from summer vacations, the next dinner is at my house," said Oksana.

We all raised our glasses and toasted, making direct eye contact with each person as the glasses clinked. Five out of the eight of us may not have been French, but we'd all been here long enough to know the customs of the land.

. . . .

Jean-Luc sat me down. "Do you remember when I told you I bought an investment property outside of Paris in Orly with the children's mother?"

"Yes."

"Well, the renter hasn't paid in four months. The last check he sent bounced."

"What do we do?" I asked. "Can we kick him out?"

"No, French laws protect the renters. He has a three-year lease. And the only way to get him out is to start the eviction process."

"So, let's do it."

"I want to be fair. I talked to him earlier. He's promised to pay. But…"

"Give him one more month," I said.

A wire for two months of rent came in the next day. Still, the whole situation didn't feel right.

Although we had everything we needed—friends, a family, a roof over our heads, food on the table, and a car—living in France was expensive (our groceries were at least two hundred euros a week), and although I was writing and picking up the odd freelance design job, I wanted to pitch in more financially.

My mom would call and say, "Why don't you teach English? Why don't you do this? Why don't you do that?" And, for the thousandth time, I had to explain that not only did I need to be certified to teach, but the certification process cost over fourteen hundred euros and teaching posts were rare, snapped up by the Brits who *already* had teaching backgrounds and taught "proper" English.

So when Monique emailed me a job listing for the American Presence Post Toulouse, an arm of the consulate, I was thrilled. It was a marketing and PR position, one I thought I'd be great for, especially since the major duty was building relations between the French and Americans.

Yes! I could do that! Why not? I was already building those skills.

In addition to Claude and Paulette, who treated me like their beloved granddaughter, I'd befriended many of our neighbors, most of them over the age of seventy. Take Monsieur Gregory, for example. One day, I'd noticed M. Gregory working in his yard in his usual uniform of a blue button-down garden coat, green rubber shoes, and black cap. I walked over, smiled, and introduced myself. He invited me into his garden, the prettiest and most manicured in the neighborhood, while telling me—with wild gesturing—about how he was also an immigrant and how his parents had moved to France from Italy during the war. His kind blue eyes sparkling, he loaded up a bag with tomatoes, peppers, and a few eggplants. I made a *Tian Provençal* that night and a homemade ratatouille, the latter of which I brought over to him and his wife Jeanine.

Pétanque was *de rigueur* among the men and played in the small park across the street from our house. Not many women joined in on the fun, but Jean-Luc and I played *pétanque* with Max, and, more than a few times, one of the neighbors, like Mr. Gregory, would race over with their set of steel balls asking if they could join in. Then the games always got serious. I got pretty good at *pétanque* fast. And, soon, I knew just about everyone in the neighborhood.

I looked at the rest of the job requirements. There were two problems: the deadline to mail in my resumé was that day; and I was supposed to be able to speak and write in French at an advanced level. I decided to go for it anyway. I polished up my resumé and sent it via email, alerting human resources to the fact that I'd only just heard about the position and pleading with them to consider me for it. I also wrote that I wasn't quite a level four with my French, but I managed. This was a lie. At best, I was at level two.

The following day, a man named Laurent called to schedule an interview. He spoke fast, and I found myself wondering: why in the world, if this job was for the American post, wasn't he speaking English?

We hung up, and I flew upstairs to my computer, pulled up the job listing, and studied the list of requirements. I looked up all the newspaper companies in our region, the Midi-Pyrénées. I memorized all the local universities and Franco-American organizations. I combed through UNESCO and the American Consulate's site, printing out document after document.

Overstuffed with information, I crammed the night before my big interview at the consulate. I arrived fifteen minutes early for the *rendezvous*, expecting to see the American flag hanging somewhere— all stars and stripes and red, white, and blue. There was nothing of the sort, no clue that a post for the American consulate was located in the old building. I checked the address again. Indeed, I was at the right place. I opened the door and headed inside, found the buzzer and rang it. The voice that greeted me was, of course, French. I was told to take the elevator to the second floor.

A security guard asked for my cell phone and any electronics. I handed them over. He placed them in a plastic bag, explaining I'd get them back when the interview was over, then he ushered me through a security scanner, similar to that of an airport. I walked into a waiting room, noting how small this office was, and took a seat. A man with brown hair, brown eyes, a five-o'clock shadow, and a blue suit walked in right after me.

"Samantha," he said, holding his hand out. "It's nice to meet you."

I recognized him from the picture I'd found online. I turned my head, surprised. "I wasn't expecting to meet the consul himself."

"Only for two more weeks. My replacement starts soon. You'd work with her." I must have looked confused. After an awkward pause, he continued. "I've accepted a post in China. I'm going back to the States to learn Chinese, and then I'm headed for Beijing."

"Oh," I said. "How exciting. The wild, wild East."

"Yeah, it is. Well, I won't be interviewing you today. Laurent has that particular honor. Good luck with everything today. You've got quite an impressive resumé. We were really happy to receive so many qualified candidates this year."

The consul shot me a two-finger salute before heading into his office, and then my competition entered the room. I said a friendly "Hello," only to learn the opposition wasn't so affable, nor were they American. One of the ladies was an angry Frenchwoman, about thirty-two, with a permanent scowl, dark hair, and dark eyes. The other woman was an even angrier Englishwoman who immediately started bitching about everyone and everything. For a minute, I was confident. I did an internal happy dance, maybe the Cabbage Patch and the Lawnmower at the same time. This job would be mine!

Hope faded as Laurent, the interviewer, explained the purpose of the interview, which was a test. We had a little less than two hours to translate two articles—one from French to English and one vice versa. Then, we were to answer two pages of questions in French, one dealing with comprehension, the other with PR. I'd been studying all the wrong things. I should have been brushing up on my grammar skills, my conjugations. Sweat dripped down my back as I attempted the translation from English into French, hoping I wasn't writing complete and utter nonsense. "Is it hot in here or what?" I asked and fanned my neck with my hand.

The Frenchwoman sniggered. The Englishwoman said, "It would have been bloody nice if they told us this post wasn't for Bordeaux, but Toulouse. I want them to reimburse me for my train ticket."

"The job sheet did say the post was for Toulouse," said the Frenchwoman.

The Englishwoman glared at her. The ladies dropped their heads and went back to their translations. I didn't understand why the Englishwoman was even bothering. I didn't know why I was. My pages were a mess of crossed-out phrases, misspellings. My mind was completely blank. I couldn't wait to get out of there.

On the train, I just sat there muttering, cursing myself. The woman seated next to me shifted her body to the side. One bus ride later, and I was home.

Jean-Luc looked up from his paper when I walked in. "How'd it go?"

"Well, I don't think I'll be getting that job," I said, explaining what had gone down.

"At least you tried," he said.

"Yep," I said. "At least I tried."

I had known that this job was out of my realm. But I'd been thinking about other options. And in my spare time I'd been working on it. I ran my idea by Jean-Luc.

"I'm almost finished with that story about us," I said. "The story about how we got together—"

"Nobody cares about us. Write about your mutant kid," he said, referring to the middle grade manuscript titled *King of the Mutants* I'd started writing a few years prior.

"But I think our story is one that needs to be told," I said. "It's romantic. There's something special. I know it."

"Fine. But you need to kill me off at the end."

Forget about hope, the French believed all great love stories must come to a tragic ending, or at least be plagued by misery and loss.

"Jean-Luc, I'm writing a memoir, our story. I can't kill you off. It wouldn't be the truth."

"Romance by itself is boring," he scoffed. "You have to kill me."

I'd love to say this was an argument, but it wasn't. It was a debate. And the French love a good debate, regardless of the topic. Politics? Religion? Art? Literature? It's all game. Come prepared, because they'll come at you with very compelling ways to win their point. I had to stand strong and not back down.

"Women need hope. I'm not killing you off."

"You have to." He crossed his arms over his chest. "Kill me."

"Fine. How do you want to die?"

"A heroic death, one that will make women cry. Maybe you're pregnant, in the hospital, waiting for me. I'm on my way to see the birth of our daughter or son. And I die, on the road, after trying to save another pregnant woman from a burning car and there's a big explosion—"

"No. That's horrible."

"I suppose you have a better suggestion?"

I choked back my laughter, almost moved to tears. Boy oh boy, did I have a few scenarios for him. "Well, you love scuba and you want to dive with the giant squid off the coast of Oregon, right?"

"Yes."

"Good. So you're diving in really deep waters with the giant squid—"

"Uh-huh." By his excited tone, the glint in his eye, I could tell he liked the idea. So far.

"Okay. One of the squids is going to fall in love with you. I don't know if it's male or female, but whatever, does it matter? Anyway, the giant squid is going to wrap you in his or her tentacles and drag you down to the bottom of the Pacific Ocean."

Silence.

"That's how you'll die."

More silence.

"The squid is going to love you to death." Jean-Luc's lips pinched together. I wondered if my humor translated. "Get it?"

"Sam, that isn't a heroic death. It's ridiculous."

Exactly.

"Honey," I said. "I haven't been sitting in the house staring at walls and picking up lizard tails. I kind of finished the book. And I'm ready to query agents." I paused. "So, let's make a deal. If I don't get anywhere with my writing career in a few months, I'll look for a job in advertising. And, in the meantime, I'll keep freelancing."

He looked skeptical, but he agreed to my plan.

"Uh, do you mind if I use your letters and emails?" I asked, even though I'd already included them.

"Why would I mind? Those letters are yours."

I'd titled the book *Seven Letters from Paris*, and to keep with the theme, I sent out seven query letters each week for three weeks, hoping to get seven full or partial requests. *Jackpot*. I received a few rejections. Some agents never responded. But I had my number. Seven.

Three months later, I landed a stellar agent at one of New York's best boutique agencies. I'd never been so excited to receive "a call." Stephanie was passionate about the story, but told me that I had to go through one or two rounds of revisions with her. But we had time. In fact, the *New York Times* had just come out with an article bashing memoirs. She wanted to wait until things cooled off. I was fine with that. I had a real live agent, one who loved my story. I jumped into my dreams, no longer just a fantasy in my head. Of course, I shared my news with Jean-Luc.

His response was, "Don't get too excited. You don't have a deal until it's done."

Leave it to my rocket scientist to ground my pie-in-the-sky fantasies on Earth.

DIVING RIGHT IN

S OON, SUMMER WAS IN FULL swing and our family was taking a
longer road trip for Jean-Luc's biannual scuba diving excursion.
We were heading six hours away by car to L'île de Porquerolles—an
island off the coast of the Mediterranean Sea near Toulon—home
of enormous fish called *morue*, cod with lips so puffed out they
made Angelina Jolie's look small, but (thankfully) no giant squids
that would fall in love with Jean-Luc and drag him down to a
watery grave.

Prior to leaving, when our family doctor removed my stitches
from my cycling accident, he informed me that I couldn't go into
the water, which left me feeling supremely disappointed. But at my
checkup with Doctor K, a simple appointment to make sure all the
"material" from my last miscarriage had cleared, I asked for a second
opinion. He gave the go-ahead to swim, but also encouraged us to try
getting pregnant again.

"You poor thing," he said. "Please don't let all this stop you and
Jean-Luc from trying again." He patted my arm. "It wasn't anything
you did, Samantha. It was just your body's way of rejecting a baby
that wasn't meant to be. If you want to become pregnant again, you
will and you can." He winked. "I have a good feeling about this."

"Is one month long enough to stay on the Pill?"

"Usually I recommend two, but you're free and clear. Everything
looks healthy. Just give your body some time to heal. And I don't see

any reason you can't swim on your trip; salt water will be good for you, but make sure you keep the wound clean and dry afterward."

Doctor K's positivity rubbed off on me. I left his office with a smile on my face, but it turned into a frown the following day. My arm itched so badly it felt like ants were swarming underneath my skin. I squeezed the bandage tighter onto the wound, swearing the family doctor had forgotten a few stitches. Once again, I walked the three blocks to his office during the open hours. I showed him the wound, pointed out a little piece of what looked, to me, like fishing line. He told me it was just my skin healing, asked for his twenty-three euros, and sent me on my way.

On an early morning in Hyères, we caught the dive boat with the rest of Jean-Luc's scuba club, skimming the turquoise waters our way to the Mediterranean paradise that is L'île de Porquerolles, passing sailboats and motorboats, great and small, and the occasional yacht. Warm summer breezes whipped in our hair, and fifteen minutes later, the rugged natural landscape of an island with cliffs dotted with hundreds of umbrella-shaped Aleppo pine trees and sandy beaches came into view.

I cozied up to the group, not worrying if I was conjugating verbs right or, more likely, wrong, and when they asked if I'd dive, I told everybody about my war wound. "No, I can't. I fear the wet suit will rip my skin. But no worries, the kids only get to dive once, so I'll hang out with them for most of the trip."

At least that's what I thought I'd said.

"The island is big," said Carole, one of the wives. "Cars are prohibited. The only way to get around it and to the beaches is by renting bicycles."

My eyes darted to my bandaged arm. Max and Elvire glanced at me, disappointment darkening their eyes. My stomach lurched.

"It's okay," said Max. "We don't have to rent bikes if you don't want to."

I wasn't going to be a downer. Wasn't I the type of woman who, when she fell off a horse (or bike), brushed the dirt off and got back on, yelling giddy-up? "Max," I said, "If the only way to get around the island is to rent bikes, that's what we'll do."

"Are you sure?" asked Elvire.

"Yeah, I'm sure," I said forcefully, my voice exuding the confidence my twisted guts did not feel. The boat pulled into the dock and, to hide the fear in my eyes, I put my sunglasses on.

Because Jean-Luc's company worked on defense projects for the French government, we were able to stay at the Hôtel Igesa, which was usually reserved for the Department of Defense. To my delight, instead of sharing accommodations with the kids, we were only sharing a bathroom. Elvire jumped with joy; she wouldn't have to sleep in the shower due to my snoring. Since the hotel was a former military base, our rooms were basic and barracks-like. But who cared? Who wanted to stay in their room when they had a beautiful island to explore? Plus, the compound was charming, with its pink sand–colored buildings. The paths to the beaches and the town were filled with flowers and towering trees, with the sweet symphony of cicadas buzzing in tune with my happy heart.

After dropping off our bags, Jean-Luc took off with the kids for the morning dive, and I walked through the village amongst the flowers, meeting cat, after cat, after friendly cat. The town itself was laden with oleander and bougainvillea, which climbed up the whitewashed houses, giving them bursts of vibrant colors—oranges, hot pinks, deep purples, and reds. In the distance, the sparkling sea beckoned. I decided instead of listening to our general doctor, I'd follow Doctor K's expert advice. I was ready to swim, let my cares float away, not letting a little flesh wound stand in my way. Plus, my small backpack was loaded up with extra bandages, tape, painkillers, and antiseptic. I walked to the nearest beach, and I swam and I read and I napped.

It was when I was cleaning the gash I noticed the little filament sticking out. Skin didn't knot, nor did it look like fishing line. I raced to my room to grab a pair of tweezers, poured antiseptic on them, and pulled, teeth clenched. There was no pain, but a sense of release as the fishing line unraveled out of my skin. Jean-Luc walked into our room.

"That crackpot of a doctor didn't miss one, but two stitches." I waved the tweezers victoriously in my hand. "I think I got all of them. But you check." I held out my arm, twisting it so Jean-Luc had a better view, and handed him the tweezers. He pulled another stitch out. This one was at least two inches long. I flopped back on the bed, breathing out a sigh of relief, the feeling of ants dancing under my skin now gone. "We need to find a new GP stat. No wonder he never has a wait at his office."

Jean-Luc's laughter started out soft and then it exploded. "Honey, I think I just played doctor."

I wiggled my brows. "Can I play nurse?"

Jean-Luc was about to lock the door to our room when the knock came.

"I'm hungry," said Max.

Jean-Luc sighed. "Let's head to lunch."

Jean-Luc took off with the diving club early in the morning, and the kids and I rented bikes so we could discover everything this Mediterranean island paradise had to offer.

"*T'as mis de la crème solaire, Elvire?*" I asked. Did you put on sunscreen?

"*Non, pas encore,*" she said. Not yet.

Unlike Max, who was a deep shade of brown, Elvire's porcelain complexion was white and creamy like milk, and she was already turning pink. I handed her the bottle. With my backpack loaded up with my arsenal of medical supplies, sunscreen, a camera, and three bottles of water, we sped down one of the trails. Well, the kids did. I was like a grandmother at first, pedaling so slowly I might as well have been going backwards. The kids raced on before me, stopping and waiting when they realized that I wasn't behind them. As dirt and rocks swished under the tires, my stomach twisted into knots, and I prayed silently, finally suggesting that we lock up the bikes and discover a hidden trail by foot. Because wouldn't *that* be exciting?

Max and Elvire screeched like banshees as the vegetation became thick. We were climbing over thorny bushes and two-foot high croppings, when I finally put a stop to my very bad idea. The plants were cutting into my legs. I had burrs in my hair. "Let's go find those hidden coves," I said. "By bike."

On the way, we stopped at one of the larger beaches to cool off—because we could. The day was ours. We stumbled down a long dirt path, kicked off our flip-flops, and made our way to the sand. In the distance, sailboats bobbed in the water. Elvire yelped when she dipped her toes into the sea.

"Is it cold?" I asked.

"*Non, mais il y a beaucoup de méduses.*"

I was about to ask her what in the world a *méduse* was, when Max grabbed a stick and hoisted a large, jiggly jellyfish out of the water. He ran toward Elvire with it. Then, chased her down the beach. I plopped down onto the sand and pulled out my camera, snapping picture after picture. Five minutes later, the kids splayed out next to me, breathless.

"Some water? And then we'll find the other cove?"

The kids shot me the thumbs-up.

I pulled out a map and we backtracked to the path that would take us to the other side of the island. We traversed a vineyard, taking in the sweeping landscape, perfectly spaced vines on each side. Besides the occasional cat, there wasn't another soul in sight, and it was as if we had the whole island—nature—to ourselves. When we finally reached the small rocky cove, our bodies glistened with perspiration, and limestone cliffs soared high above our heads. The water was so clear we could see the sand on the bottom. Even better, we didn't see a single jellyfish. We stripped down to our bathing suits and dove right in. Refreshed, I climbed up onto the rocks to watch the kids splash around. They pointed at me and giggled.

"What?"

They didn't stop giggling.

"What?"

"From the back we thought you were Natasha for a second," said Elvire.

Max laughed harder. "She had a big butt."

"*Enorme*," said Elvire.

Out of the mouth of babes. I was a pork roll on the island of Porquerolles. I cringed, thinking about the twenty or so pounds I still needed to lose. Speaking of loss, they'd never brought her up before. "Do you ever miss her? Natasha?"

Their mouths twisted into an expression I could only describe as sheer and utter disgust. "*Non*," said Elvire. She launched into a breathless five-minute speech about how living with Natasha was like living with a big baby, how immature she was, and how she cried all the time and barely spoke to them. When she did, it was only to tell them what to do. Max's eyes went wide, and he bobbled his head in agreement. Wildly animated, he told me about how one time he had thrown a stuffed animal at her and how she'd burst into tears, darted up the stairs, and locked herself in the master bedroom. When she finally came out, she wouldn't look at him.

I was stunned. "I hope you think things are different with me."

"*Non*," said Elvire, a wicked light sparking her eyes. "It's the same."

I jumped into the water and splashed her. "Take that back."

Max jumped onto Elvire's shoulders and dunked her under the water, swimming away before she could take her revenge. Elvire popped her head out of the water and treaded in the sea. "*Tu m'aimes?*"

Do you love me?

I bit down on my bottom lip, keeping my emotions at bay. "Of course," I said, and then I dove into the water and pulled her under. The three of us swam and splashed for a good half hour until another couple entered the cove. The kids and I exchanged quick glances. I nodded. It was time to leave. We were the family Vérant, on our own private adventure. No strangers allowed.

Once again, we were on the bikes, stopping to take pictures of the cliffs, a random horse, or the occasional tiger-striped cat—like the one Elvire had found at the old windmill. On the way to a beach on the south side of the island, the bike path became rockier and rugged. The kids zoomed ahead. I yelled for them to slow down, but they didn't hear. There were too many rocks, the incline was too steep, and I was petrified to pedal faster. With my heart racing, I yelled, "*Lentement!*"

Slowly!

I was two hundred yards behind them when it happened. It took about three seconds, but seemed like slow motion. My heart stopped. I screamed as Max and his bike did a one-hundred-and-eighty-degree flip. Max's feet were in the air and he smashed to the ground, his bike landing on top of him. One of his flip-flops flew into the bushes. I hopped off my bike, throwing it to the side of the path, and ran as fast as my own flip-flopped feet would allow. "Max, I'm coming. *J'arrive. Je viens.* Oh my God."

Elvire just stood over Max, her jaw dropped, looking absolutely dumbfounded. "Elvire, don't just stand there! Move the bike off Maxence."

She didn't budge. I pushed my legs to move faster and approached Max. His eyes were squeezed tight as he held back his tears. I lifted the bike off his little body. "Max, just stay quiet. Don't move." I grabbed a towel, lifting his head ever so slightly. "Does your neck hurt?"

"*Non,*" he said. I placed the towel under his head and assessed the damage. He had a huge scrape on his right arm, just above his elbow, in the exact same place as mine. Remaining calm, I pulled out the arsenal of supplies from my backpack and cleaned the wound. He clenched his teeth as I poured the antiseptic. I exhaled a sigh of relief. It wasn't a deep cut. We wouldn't need to get stitches. I bandaged his arm. "Can you sit up?"

"*Oui.*"

"Does your head hurt?"

"*Un peu.*"

A little.

I handed him an aspirin and helped him to a sitting position.

Elvire fetched the water bottle. He chugged it. Since we were three kilometers from the village, I told Max we were just going to sit for a while until he felt better. Then, we'd walk the bikes. His bottom lip quivered, but he didn't cry. A big hug was in order. "I'm proud of you, Max."

"*Pourquoi?*"

"You've been very brave."

Ten minutes later, we began the uphill climb and, once the trail became manageable, Max decided he didn't want to walk; he wanted to ride. And so we did. We returned the bikes in the village and I bought the kids ice cream cones, not caring that we were supposed to eat lunch in ten minutes. Today, it was dessert first.

19

LA GUERRE DES BOUTONS (THE WAR OF THE BUTTONS)

In the middle of July, the kids were taking off for their grand-mother's house in Provence. Before they left, I wanted to spend as much time with them as I could, which meant dancing in the kitchen with Elvire when I cooked or playing baseball or pétanque with Max. After a quick game of catch in the park, Max and I were walking home when we passed by some bushes with orange and red berries. I grabbed a hearty handful of them and yelled, "*La Guerre des Boutons,*" a French movie for which I'd recently seen the preview, and I threw them at Max, starting our own little war.

From behind the bushes, an old woman screamed, "*Qu'est-ce que vous faites?*"

We stopped mid-throw, berries flying into the air and splattering on the ground. Max looked at me. I looked at him. We clasped our hands over our mouths. What were we doing? What was I doing was more like it. I may have been *une femme d'un certain âge,* but I'd always had the heart of a child, and it had just been unleashed.

An older woman, around seventy, with gray-blond hair, peered at Max and me over the hedge, her cold blue eyes narrowed into a glare.

Instead of running away giggling, I apologized profusely, explain-ing that we were just having some fun. She harrumphed and shook her finger. "Leave my bushes alone," she said.

Max and I tucked our chins into our necks, trying to keep straight faces, while nodding and saying *désolé.* Once we were out of earshot, though, we couldn't stop the laughter. Max had his afternoon snack and went up to his room. I sat on the couch, checking email and Facebook.

A knock came at the door. By the shape of the shadow, I assumed it was my neighbor, Claude. But instead of Claude, a short, boxy man stood in front of me, a packet of cigarettes in the front pocket of a dirty T-shirt. His nose reminded me of a half head of garlic, the nostrils flattened on the sides. In one hand, he held an apple. In the other, he held a pocketknife, which he waved toward a white truck while explaining that he was selling vegetables and fruits. They were organic, direct from the producer. If I didn't have cash, I could use my debit card.

"*Venez voir!*" he exclaimed. Come see!

If he'd come to slit my throat, I figured I'd already be dead. And, thankfully, this guy wasn't a cop. Like I'd be arrested for throwing a handful of bush berries? I walked over to the truck, noting the prices were very reasonable and by the kilo. The man stabbed the apple with his pocketknife, slicing off a piece.

"*Alors, goûtez-le,*" he said. Taste it.

I eyed the apple, which looked nice and juicy. Then, I eyed the man's dirty fingernails and his rusty knife. I wasn't going to have a Snow White sleep, waiting for my prince to come and kiss me. "*Non, merci,*" I said. "*J'aime pas les pommes, mais les enfants les aiment.*"

I don't like apples, but the kids do. Was that polite?

The man shrugged and ate the slice, juice dripping down his chin.

They did look delectable. I decided to purchase some apples, shallots, and two varieties of potatoes, around twelve euros' worth. I finished my order and he handed me the bill. It was over one hundred euros?

"*Pardon?*" I questioned.

He told me I had to buy twenty kilos of each item—not one kilo.

"*Non, non, non,*" I said. "*J'ai mal compris.*" I misunderstood. Seriously? What was I going to do with over one hundred kilos of produce? Where would I put it?

The man tried to convince me to buy, buy, buy! The more I said *non*, *non*, *non*, the angrier he became, steam practically rising from his bald potato head. He stormed away, screaming and swearing and shaking his fist. Immediately, I called Jean-Luc, my hand trembling as I punched in his work number.

"What?" he said. "That's illegal. Vendors aren't allowed to sell to you at your house. It's a trick to get the old people to open up their pocketbooks. *Une arnaque.* A scam. Did you get the license plate number of the truck? We need to call *les gendarmes.*"

"I wasn't exactly thinking of that."

Nope. Unless I was absolutely, positively sure who was on the other side of it, I vowed never to open the front door again. And, just in case, the next day I brought the woman with the bushes some roses from my garden. And that's how I made a new friend in Marie—a woman who complained way more than I did about anything and everything. Like Marie, I believed I was just stating the facts, like it was hot inside without air-conditioning or I was tired, thanks to Beepy the Frog keeping me up all night. Much as I loved his melodies, it was difficult to sleep with his incessant noise. Jean-Luc, on the other hand, never uttered a word of complaint. He could lose a limb and smile. He was even-keeled like that. Les Chicks wondered if he was really French.

Unlike most French women, who are usually more reserved in the beginning of a friendship, Marie confided in me right away. She invited me into her garden, introduced to me to her cats and rosebushes. An older woman in her seventies, Marie had lost her husband years ago. To what? I didn't ask. I just let her talk.

"My children live close by," she said. "But I don't see them very often. They're busy with their own lives, their kids, and don't have much time for me."

"Are you lonely?" I asked, my heart breaking for this woman.

She sighed and said with a shrug, "It's just life. And I'm proud of my children." She laughed and took my hands. "I'm just an old lady. Thank you for listening to me."

Well, she had every right to complain. About the garbage men who didn't do their jobs right. About the loud kids in the park who littered. About how it seemed everybody she knew was passing over to the other side. About life in general. Thankfully, she didn't mention weird Americans who ripped a couple of berries off of her bushes. Before I left, she retrieved a pair of garden clippers from her jacket, cutting the most beautiful roses I'd ever seen and handing them over. To me.

That day, I cooked way too much food for a dinner party with Christian and Ghislaine, the main course a barbecued *gigôt d'agneau* (leg of lamb) pierced with garlic and pine nuts and wrapped in rosemary. For the *apéro*, I'd made a chickpea, olive, and roasted pepper and garlic tapenade. I turned to Jean-Luc and said, "I'll be right back. I'm going to bring some of this over to Marie."

"Sam," he said, "you don't really know her. And, in France, we don't do that."

I put my hands on my hips and said, "Well, I'm not French. I'm American. And I *do* do that."

Marie was shocked when I rang her bell and offered her a Tupperware filled with the dip. Her hand went right to her heart. "Thank you for thinking of me," she said.

Amazing what a friendly "*bonjour*" and a smile could do.

. . . .

It wasn't all fun and games or avoiding killer vegetable salesmen in the south of France; we had a lot of hard work ahead of us. Jean-Luc had a plan.

"We're going to convert the garage into a fourth bedroom," he said.

"Why?"

He pointed to my stomach. "We may need it."

I wasn't so sure about trying again. It had only been a few months since I'd last miscarried. "Or maybe we won't."

"Don't be a pessimist," said Jean-Luc.

"I'm being a realist."

"How's this for real? When your parents and sister come to visit, where will they sleep? We need a fourth bedroom."

He was right. And he said the right thing, one that didn't set my hopes too high. A little part of me wanted to try again. Plus, it was the end of June, and my parents and sister were staying with us in the end of August. "Fine. You win. But who is going to do all the work?"

I knew his answer before he uttered his response. It would be us. Hiring workers in France was tough, because the government taxed the wages paid to the contractor, up-charging sixty percent, sometimes more, to cover social security, insurance, and health care. Basically, we would become an employer. So if we hired a worker who wanted to charge us one hundred euro an hour, we'd actually be paying one hundred sixty euro an hour. Jean-Luc worked with the government on defense projects and, alas, he was against "black market" workers. I had nearly snapped putting together IKEA furniture. I couldn't imagine the stress of building a room.

Jean-Luc, like most Frenchmen, received more than his share of vacation days. Sadly, we were using most of them to fix up the town house prior to my American family's arrival, and we'd do it while the kids were at their maternal grandmother's house in Provence for six weeks. After dropping the kids off at the airport, we pulled up to Leroy Merlin, a hardware store similar to Home Depot.

"So, where is all the stuff in the garage going to go?" I asked with a sigh.

"That's why we're here. First, we need to pick out an *abri de jardin*."

"An *abri*?"

"A garden cabin."

Three hours later, we finally decided on a pine frame, reminiscent of a little home one might find in the woods of Canada, complete with a little window and windowbox. Jean-Luc filed the necessary paperwork with the *mairie* (you need approvals for everything in France), cleared out a space in the back of our yard, and, since the cabin didn't come with a floor, he set a cement foundation and built one himself.

When the cabin arrived two weeks later, I was happy to learn that the kit we had ordered was as simple as putting a Lincoln Log cabin together—just a whole lot bigger. With the main structure completed, Jean-Luc worked on the roof while I applied a coat of weatherproofing varnish to both the outside and the inside. Jean-Luc could be a little bossy, and I almost quit.

"Don't forget to varnish in between every crack," he'd say.

Or "Don't let the paint drip like that."

Or "Don't forget to paint around the window."

I was tempted to hand him the brush and say, "Don't tell me what to do," and once or twice I threatened to walk off the job. But Jean-Luc would just laugh. And his laugh was infectious. We both had our tasks, and we got them done. Then it was time to plan the bedroom. Since we only had one and a half bathrooms, I wanted to include a shower and sink in our plans—an open Italian design of sorts. We spent the next weekend at Leroy Merlin, choosing tiles for our bathroom, fixtures, wood flooring, and paint.

When I moved to France, I never thought I'd learn how to cut and lay tile, put up drywall, lay down a wood floor, or install a ceiling. But, on and off for a month, that's what we did. My back hurt five million ways. My legs ached. My head felt like it was going to split open. During the work, I had to keep telling myself that the end result would be worth the frustration.

My biggest freak-out moment came when we were working on the open bathroom. I'd picked out a large square tile with a faux mosaic pattern, which was supposed to be centered on the floor. Neither of us had taken the shower basin into account, and Jean-Luc was about to install the signature tile in a spot where the sink would completely cover it. And, considering there was only room for four large tiles, it wouldn't be centered, the position going against all design sensibility.

"Stop!" I said. "You can't do that."

Jean-Luc shook his head and reached for the tile.

"If you put that tile down, I'm lifting it right off."

"We bought it. We're using it," he said.

I had to think quickly. Thankfully, we'd also had to buy a box of the plain tiles, so we had enough to finish the job. "Wait," I said. "I have an idea. We can use it on the interior shower wall. Like a signature piece."

He scratched his chin. "It's heavy, but, yes, that might work."

"We can make it work," I said, whispering, "but it has to be centered."

Day after day, we quipped, and we sighed, but always came up with a solution in the end—not one fight threatening to shake the foundation we were building. Sometimes, just like in a marriage, when dealing with home renovation projects, it was necessary to compromise. And, once everything for the bathroom was installed, it looked beautiful—especially the mosaic tile.

"Next summer we'll redo the kitchen," said Jean-Luc. "I don't like it. It's old and needs to change."

I cringed. We were just finishing up the first renovation project, and he was already planning the next. While we did get severely irritated and frustrated with one another at times, we didn't argue, yell, or fight. I'd like to think it was because of how our relationship had begun—with letters and email—and that we communicated well. Jean-Luc had another theory: we were like bonobo chimpanzees. Apparently, the bonobo strategy was to have sex to keep conflict and violence out of their lives. Make love, not war!

And that's all I have to say on the subject.

JEAN-LUC'S CRÊPES

Prep time: 10 minutes
Cook time: 30 minutes (plus 45 minutes resting time)
Makes: 10 to 12 crêpes
Great for: a family meal, dessert, or a snack
Wine suggestion: Bordeaux

- 2 cups all-purpose flour
- 3½ cups whole milk*
- ¼ teaspoon salt
- 3 large eggs
- 4 tablespoons butter, melted
- Vegetable oil, for coating pan

Combine the flour, milk, and salt in a medium mixing bowl. In a separate bowl, whisk the eggs until foamy. Little by little, fold the eggs into the flour mixture. Add the butter, and mix well. The batter shouldn't be thick, but fluid. Place the bowl in the refrigerator, letting the mixture set for about 45 minutes. When ready, coat the bottom of 12-inch nonstick pan lightly with vegetable oil, and heat the pan on a medium-high burner. Once the pan is hot, ladle the batter into the pan. Quickly swirl the pan so the batter spreads evenly. Once the edges are slightly browned, flip the crêpe. Cook for about 1 minute more. Place the crêpe on a plate, cover with a warm kitchen towel, and continue stacking the crêpes, one on top of the other, under the towel until all the batter is gone. Fill the crêpes with your favorite sweet ingredients like fruit, jellies, jams, or Nutella, or use one of the recipes below for savory crêpe options.

* *Jean-Luc's recipe is more fluid than others. "Crêpes should never be thick like a pancake," he says. Hence, more milk.*

My Mom's Chicken and Mushrooms in a Cream Sauce

Prep time: 15 minutes
Cook time: 10 minutes

- 8 premade crêpes
- 2 tablespoons unsalted butter
- 1½ cups mushrooms (Portobello, porcini, *cèpes,* or white), sliced
- 3 chicken breasts, precooked and sliced
- ¼ teaspoon nutmeg
- 1½ cups *crème fraîche* or sour cream
- ¼ cup dry white wine
- ¼ cup tarragon, plus extra for garnish
- ¼ cup chives, chopped, for garnish
- Salt and freshly ground black pepper, to taste

Heat the butter in a large pan over medium heat. Add the mushrooms, sprinkle with salt, and cook for 5 to 7 minutes. Add the chicken, and sprinkle in the nutmeg. Once warm, add the *crème fraîche*, wine, and tarragon. Season with salt and pepper. Fill each crêpe, folding like a burrito. Garnish with chives and more tarragon. Serve with a crisp green salad with balsamic vinaigrette.

Maxence's Ham and Cheese Crêpes

Prep time: 5 minutes
Cook time: 10 minutes

- 8 premade crêpes
- 4 slices deli ham, cut into ½-inch wide strips
- 2 cups gruyère (or similar), grated
- Freshly ground black pepper, to taste

Place a crêpe in a pan over medium heat. Sprinkle ¼ cup of the cheese in the center of the crêpe. Once the cheese begins to melt, add the ham, and season with pepper. When all the cheese is melted, fold the crêpe like a burrito with a spatula. Repeat.

CHICKEN TAGINE WITH APRICOTS, PRUNES, AND ALMONDS

In France, our North African neighbors influence more than a few dishes. A tagine is a beautiful clay pot with a cone-shaped cover, making meals easy to serve. Although my cooking style is not typically Algerian or Moroccan, I've experimented with quite a few recipes using traditional ingredients. And, you bet, I'll be experimenting with more.

Prep time: 20 minutes

Cook time: 60 minutes

Serves: 6

Great for: simple dinner party

Wine suggestion: Beaujolais or Moroccan rosé

FOR THE CHICKEN:

- 6 tablespoons unsalted butter
- 6 chicken breasts or thighs
- 2 tablespoons paprika
- 1 tablespoon *herbes de Provence*, plus extra for seasoning
- 4 cloves garlic, peeled, de-germed, and finely minced
- 1 large yellow onion, peeled and roughly diced
- 1 teaspoon ground cumin
- 1 tablespoon ground cinnamon
- 1 tablespoon fresh peeled ginger root, finely minced
- 1 teaspoon saffron
- 1 tablespoon tumeric
- 2 cups chicken stock
- 1 cup green or black olives
- 1 (12- to 15-ounce) can chickpeas, drained
- 1 red or yellow pepper, roughly diced

- 12 dried apricots, roughly chopped
- 12 dried prunes, roughly chopped
- 3 tablespoons honey
- 2 lemons, juiced
- ½ cup slivered almonds, for garnish
- ½ cup flat parsley, finely chopped, for garnish
- ¼ cup Lemon Confit à la Marocaine (p. 194), diced (optional)
- Salt and freshly ground black pepper, to taste

FOR THE COUSCOUS:

- Couscous, about ½ cup per person*
- 1 tablespoon paprika
- 1 lemon, juiced
- Vegetable stock, about ½ cup per person
- Salt and freshly ground black pepper, to taste

Heat a dash of olive oil in a large pot or Dutch oven over medium-high heat. Season chicken with the salt, pepper, 1 tablespoon of the paprika, and *herbes de Provence*. Cook for about 5 minutes on each side, until lightly browned. Transfer to a plate, and set aside. In the same pot, heat another dash of olive oil. Add the garlic and onions, cooking about 5 minutes, or until translucent. Stir in the cumin, the remaining paprika, cinnamon, ginger, saffron, and tumeric, and cook until fragrant. Return chicken to the pot. Add chicken stock, olives, chickpeas, peppers, apricots, prunes, and honey, and bring the mixture to a boil.

Reduce heat, cover, and simmer for 30 minutes. In a small heated pan, toast the almonds. 10 minutes before serving the chicken, stir in the lemon juice.

To prepare the couscous, place the uncooked grains in the

tagine or serving dish. Sprinkle with the paprika. Add the lemon juice to the vegetable stock, and bring to a boil. Pour the stock over the couscous, and cover. After 5 minutes, fluff the grains with a fork.

Place the chicken stew over the couscous in the tagine or serving dish. Garnish with parsley, toasted almonds, and lemon *confit* (optional). Pour any remaining stock into a gravy boat. Along with the stock, serve the tagine with a jar of puréed pimento peppers on the side.

* *One part couscous to one part vegetable stock.*

LEMON *CONFIT* À LA MAROCAINE (PRESERVES)

Prep time: 15 minutes
Cook time: 4 weeks rest time
Makes: 1 jar
Great for: tagines, salad dressings, risottos, vegetables, and seafood

- 1 Mason jar
- Kosher or rock salt
- 4 to 5 small organic lemons (like Meyer lemons), washed well
- ¼ cup water

Fill the bottom of 1 mason jar with the salt, just enough to coat the bottom. Trim the ends of each lemon, and then slice the lemons in half. Cut an X in the top of each half, almost quartering them, but making sure to not slice through to the bottom. Stuff each lemon half with salt and push into the bottom of the mason jar, sour face down, to release the juices. Fill the jar completely. Boil the water, and add to the jar, pouring over the lemons. Close the jar and store in a cool, dark place for 4 weeks—preserving the lemons. Then, store in a refrigerator until ready to use. When ready, discard the pulp—it's the peel that is used. Rinse the lemon rinds in cold water to remove excess salt. Dice the rinds and add to your meal.

SAM'S TOULOUSIAN FRENCH CREOLE GUMBO

Prep time: 40 minutes

Cook time: 2 hours

Serves: 8 to 10

Great for: dinner party or family meal with leftovers

Wine suggestion: Cahors or Fronton

- 3 boneless, skinless chicken breasts
- 3 tablespoons extra virgin olive oil
- 1 pound andouille (or other pork sausage), sliced in rounds
- ½ cup vegetable oil
- ¼ cup all-purpose flour
- 5 to 6 tablespoons butter
- 1 large onion, peeled and diced
- 4 cloves garlic, peeled, de-germed, and finely minced
- 4 celery stalks, diced
- 1 green pepper, seeded and diced
- 1 red pepper, seeded and diced
- 3 to 4 tablespoons Cajun seasoning, premade or DIY*
- ½ cup flat parsley, coarsely chopped, plus extra for garnish
- 4 cups beef stock, homemade or from bouillon cubes
- 1 (14-ounce) can tomatoes, with juice
- 2 tablespoons tomato paste
- 2 to 3 bay leaves
- 3½ cups okra, fresh or frozen, sliced in ½-inch-thick rounds

- 32 to 40 pieces uncooked shrimp, peeled and deveined
- Salt and freshly ground black pepper, to taste

Poach the chicken for 8 to 10 minutes in a pot of lightly salted boiling water. Remove with a slotted spoon, and set aside.

Heat the oil in a Dutch oven (or a large heavy pot with lid) over medium heat. Add the sausage, cooking until browned on all sides, and remove, also setting it to the side. To make the roux, add the vegetable oil to the same pot, using the grease of the sausage for flavor. Sprinkle the flour over the oil, add 2 tablespoons of the butter, stirring constantly with a wooden spoon, about 15 minutes, until the mixture turns a dark, golden color.

Add 2 more tablespoons of the butter, the onion, garlic, celery, and peppers to the pot. Stir, and reduce the heat to low. Season with the Cajun seasoning, salt, pepper, and ¼ cup of the parsley. Cook for another 10 minutes, until fragrant. While this cooks, shred the poached chicken with your fingers.

Add beef stock into the pot, along with the canned tomatoes, tomato paste, bay leaves, and cooked chicken and sausage. Bring to a boil, then reduce heat and cover. Simmer for 35 to 45 minutes. Add in 2 cups of the okra. Cover again, and simmer for another 45 minutes.

Add the shrimp and remaining okra 15 minutes before serving. Cover and cook for 15 minutes until ready to serve. Remove the bay leaves, serve over rice (along with a few bottles of hot sauce!), and garnish with parsley.

* *This seasoning is something I make myself, and you can too! Just mix equal parts (about 1 tablespoon of each) garlic powder, paprika, onion powder, oregano, thyme, and cocoa powder. Then add about ½ tablespoon red pepper flakes and a dash of cayenne pepper. You can store this in a plastic container.*

ISABELLE'S *GÂTEAU FONDANT À L'ORANGE*

Prep time: 15 minutes

Cook time: 35 to 40 minutes

Serves: 8 to 10

Great for: This cake is fresh, moist, and delightful—it's great any time!

Wine suggestion: Champagne!

FOR THE CAKE:

- ¾ cup unsalted butter, softened
- ⅔ cup granulated sugar
- 1 cup all-purpose flour
- 1½ teaspoons baking powder
- 3 eggs
- Zest from 2 oranges, finely chopped
- 6 oranges, juiced (separate into juice from 2 oranges, and juice from 4 oranges)
- ⅛ cup confectioners' sugar

FOR THE PINEAPPLES:

- 1 tablespoon unsalted butter
- 6 to 8 pineapple slices, canned or fresh
- 2 to 3 tablespoons brown sugar

Preheat oven to 325°F. In a large mixing bowl, combine the butter with the granulated sugar using a handheld blender. Add the flour, baking powder, and eggs, and mix well. Add the orange zest and juice from 2 oranges, and mix well. Pour into a lightly buttered springform baking pan, and bake for 35 to 40 minutes.

In a separate bowl, pour in the remaining orange juice. Add in the confectioners' sugar, whisking lightly. Take the cake out of the oven. Pour the juice mixture over it, and let the cake cool.

In a separate pan, melt the butter until it foams. Sprinkle both sides of the pineapple slices with the brown sugar. Place the pineapple slices in the pan and cook, about 2 to 3 minutes on each side, until golden brown. When the cake is cool, place the pineapple slices on top. Cover the cake in plastic wrap, and refrigerate for at least an hour before serving.

Ingredient Four

PASSION

20

THE AMERICAN INVASION

AMILY IS THE CRAZIEST KIND of love. And now that I was finally settled and happy in France, I couldn't wait to share my new life with my parents and sister. But, before my family would see Cugnaux and Toulouse, they were going to experience the sea and the sun of the Mediterranean. Isabelle had invited everybody to stay with her and Richard in Provence for a few days, so my family was flying into Marseille and out of Toulouse. Jean-Luc and I drove the four hours to pick them up at Marignane airport. My mother bounced up and down with excitement, like a hyperactive kid that had eaten way too much candy.

"Aren't you tired?" I asked.

"How could I be? This is the best trip ever," said my mom. She put her arms around my sister and me, the three of us crammed into the back seat of our Ford. "I've got my two beautiful girls, my husband, and my amazing son-in-law. I'm so excited! I'm going to see France through the eyes of a Frenchman."

Jess and I jabbed her in the ribs. Jean-Luc eyed us in the rearview mirror, his eyes crinkled with laughter. He shook his head, but didn't say a word.

"What?" asked my mom.

"Come up with your own material. You just quoted one of Jean-Luc's old letters," I said.

"I did?"

"Sam, did you let your parents' dogs read my letters, too?" asked Jean-Luc.

Then, he burst out into a wide grin, his laugh warm and soft and infectious.

"Welcome to France. Your tour guide for the next ten days is the incredible Jean-Luc," I said. "I really hope you guys got a little sleep on the plane, because he has a nonstop itinerary planned. There's a party at Isabelle's tonight. Maxime, her son, is heading off to Canada in a few weeks for university. It's a welcome party for you, a good-bye party for him."

My dad turned to face us, his jaw dropped. He looked exhausted from the long flight and probably wanted to relax. But Isabelle had already planned this get-together months in advance. I gave him my Cabbage Patch Kid closed-mouth smile. Forty minutes later, we pulled up to Isabelle and Richard's, a beautiful Provençal home painted pale yellow with dark green shutters and a terra-cotta roof. I loved the warmth of this home at Christmas, and it was even better in the summer. The garden was in full bloom, bright, big, beautiful roses in every color. The pool sparkled in the sunlight, reflecting the sky, the Garlaban Mountains in the distance peeking through the tall pine trees surrounding the property. The cicadas chirped out their melodies. It was a Provençal paradise. I especially loved the thatch-roofed outdoor kitchen with the long table overlooking all of this beauty, now set up for a family gathering.

"I am 'appy to meet you," said Richard. Unfortunately, Richard hadn't been able to attend the California wedding. A doctor, he'd just opened up a new radiology center and couldn't get away. He and Isabelle embraced my parents and sister in an enthusiastic round of *la bise*. "Welcome!"

"Your home reminds me a little bit of ours in California," said my mom. Her assessment was true, and probably another one of the million reasons I loved visiting Provence. It was home. It was family. And everyone was together. "You'll have to visit us sometime," said my mom.

"What did she say?" asked Richard, and I translated.

"Tell her when we come to visit, we're not staying for four days, but for four months."

"What did he say?" asked my mom, I told her, and we all burst out laughing.

While my parents and sister unpacked and settled in, Jean-Luc and I headed off to Meme's to kidnap the kids for one night. They would spend more time with my family back in Toulouse. Soon, the kids were swimming in the pool, playing with their cousins—Maxime and Steeve, and his fiancée, Laura. Isabelle was preparing for the night's festivities, so I offered to help. Unlike me whenever I hosted parties and dinners, she was completely unstressed. This was—and is—the French way. Tonight was a cocktail *apéro-dinatoire*—not a formal dinner, but rather a selection of hot and cold finger foods served buffet style. Although she had hired a caterer to provide most of the dishes, Isabelle had also made a few quiches, *les tartes salées* (savory tarts), and a huge bowl of pasta salad. I helped her set up the chairs, dishes, and wine glasses. My French was improving every day, and conversations with Isabelle were easier to manage. We spoke about life in general, my miscarriages, and her first marriage to the father of her two sons, Steeve and Maxime. As long as Isabelle's ear was mine, and there were no intruders, I'd been dying to find out one thing. "Do you and Richard ever plan on getting married?"

She broke out into a wide grin. "*Et, alors*, I should be Madame Richard next summer, the wedding right here in the garden, just like you and Jean-Luc!"

I gave her a hug—the big American kind. "An early *félicitations!*"

By nine p.m., the house was packed, the party in full swing. Jean-Luc's mother was still in poor health, so she wouldn't be in attendance, nor Michel, his hermit crab of a brother, but his dapper dad, André, was coming over with his sister Muriel, Alain, her husband, and their kids, Anaïs and Arnaud. Spicy rum punch was poured and the revelry began. There were four Americans and thirty French, which also meant *la bise* didn't end. Richard was seated at the head of the long table in the outdoor kitchen. "Jessica, do you have a boyfriend?" he asked and I translated.

"No, not right now."

"*Eh ben*, I have the perfect guy for you." He paused, dramatically, until everybody had his full attention. "He's very handsome. A doctor, like me, he's in a good position. He's in excellent shape. He's funny, charming, and he has a lot of friends…" His smile turned sinister. "But there's just one little problem…" Another dramatic pause. He held up his hand, leveling it two or three feet from the ground. "He's a very little man." Richard waited for the laughter to die down, and continued. "Nobody's perfect, Jessica."

Jessica turned to me, mouth dropped, eyes streaming with tears of laughter. "Tell him I like my men tall."

"Tall, you say?" He held up a finger. "*Eh, ben*, I know another man for you. He's very handsome. He's in a good position. He's in excellent shape. He's funny, charming, and he has a lot of friends…but there's just one little problem…" Another dramatic pause. "Do you own a razor?"

Jess nodded, understanding the French.

"Good," said Richard. "Because he's completely covered in hair and needs to be shaved every two or three days."

I clasped my hands over my stomach, which hurt from laughing so hard. For once, I wasn't the target of the *familial* hazing. Richard, now in clown mode, launched into a few more potential prospects, changing Jessica's ideal mate right after "But there's just one little problem," offering to set her up with a mute quadriplegic, a toothless drunk missing most of his fingers, and a guy who might be half-monkey. Richard was in rare form tonight. And he wasn't even drinking.

"Tony," said Richard when the laughter died down. "Do you like Elvis?"

"*J'adore* Elvis," said my dad. Having studied the language of love in high school and college, my dad used to be fluent in French. He'd even traveled by motorcycle throughout France and Europe in his

twenties. Now that he had shaken the jet lag off, the basic skills
were coming back to him.

"Me, too." Richard pulled out his cell phone and played a YouTube
video of Elvis singing "Hallelujah." He sang along at the top of his
lungs, standing up and belting out the chorus.

"Oh no," I said with a giggle. "*Pas encore*, Richard." Not again.

Jean-Luc's father's eyebrows lifted. He shook his head. "I have a
very bizarre family."

A very bizarre family that I loved.

My mom pulled me aside. "How on earth do you deal with the
language? My head is spinning." She lowered her voice to a whisper.
"I don't understand anything they are saying. I just nod and smile."

I thought about my first Christmas in France, when I had felt out
of place and could barely speak, let alone understand, the language.
"Believe me, Mom, it took some getting used to. And I still do a lot
of smiling and nodding—especially when they talk fast."

The Americans didn't retreat to bed until well after midnight.

Save for Jean-Luc and me, nobody woke up until eleven the next
morning. I stayed at Isabelle's when Jean-Luc dropped the kids back
off at their grandmother's, just in case my parents needed a translator, coffee, or breakfast. Then Jean-Luc's job as French cruise director began. We piled into the car, taking off for Aix-en-Provence for a
late lunch. My mom and sister were antsy—there were shops, shops
and more shops, and they were ready to go nuts. At the open-air
market, my mom bought a panama hat and Jessica bought *herbes
de Provence* grown in Provence. In the late afternoon, we found
ourselves back at Isabelle's, relaxing and floating in the pool listening to the cicadas—a good thing, too, because from here on out the
action would be nonstop.

The next morning's agenda included a quick coffee and a couple
of croissants, followed by a drive to the small medieval village of Le
Castellet, inland from Jean-Luc's hometown of La Ciotat. We hadn't
even been there a second when my mom and sister beelined into one
of the shops selling French linens and soaps. My dad rolled his eyes.

"Your wife," said Jean-Luc, "does she not like history?"

"Oh, she does, but only the history of Coco Chanel." My dad nodded his head toward me. "You're lucky the shopping gene skipped a generation with this one."

Jean-Luc put his arm around me. "*Oui*, Tony, I am. She is a very special girl."

"Sam, go get your mom," said my dad.

Per her usual habits, my mom just liked to look; most of the time she couldn't make up her mind, so she rarely actually purchased anything. After I dragged my mom away from some lavender-scented soaps, which, thanks to me, she already had at home, Jean-Luc's posture straightened, and he announced in a low voice, "Next stop on the frog tour. A quick glimpse of La Ciotat and then the beach of Cassis."

As we set off on another adventure, Jean-Luc pointed out the local sites on the way—the old shipping yard, the Eden theater, where the first movie in the world was shown, and the beach where and he and his friends had picked up girls from all over Europe. He pulled the car over on the cliffs separating La Ciotat from Cassis, offering my parents and sister the awe-inspiring view he'd already shared with me.

"I'd love to see this from the water," said my mom.

"That's tomorrow. My friend, Gilles, is taking us out on his boat."

"Wonderful!" My mom clapped her hands together like a small child. "What was his wife's name again? I really liked her. It was so nice of them to come to your wedding."

"Her name *was* Nathalie."

"Did something happen to her?" asked Jess.

"In a way. She and Gilles are now divorced."

Time to change the subject. "Who wants mussels?" I asked.

From the highway, the breathtakingly beautiful colors of the magnificent landscape were especially vivid in the summer—yellow, salmon, and orange buildings settled among a backdrop of green. Cassis itself was nestled in a bay, surrounded by lush vineyards and, on the shore, sheltered inlets known as *calanques*. Because we'd arrived late, we had to park rather far from the village. But that was okay. There were free *navettes* (buses) to take us into town. After a lunch of salads with *chèvre chaud* (warm goat cheese) and mussels, which were technically not in season, but still tasty, we found an open spot on the beach and settled into the rocky plateau—watching adorable French children play, some of the little girls topless.

Regarding that stereotype: most women in France don't sunbathe topless, unless they are under the age of ten, over sixty, or at a nude beach in Cap d'Agde. When we were in the Porquerolles, I'd asked the kids what they thought about the older ladies splashing in the water, breasts out.

"*Bof. C'est naturel,*" was Max's response. It was natural.

And that was very true. It was natural, not exhibitionism or even sexual—just a human body. Not that I'd ever sunbathe topless in public. I tried it once when I was nineteen, when traveling Europe with Tracey, only to learn that I'm not wired that way. I came back to Syracuse University, and one of the bartenders yelled, "Hey, I know you! I saw you topless in Greece! Your nipples are the size of dimes!"

So, yes, the ladies were staying in the confines of my bikini top.

My dad and Jean-Luc were in the water for over an hour, smiling and laughing and talking. This, for me, was a rare occurrence. My dad and Chris, my ex, had never truly bonded. Not like this. My mom noticed the connection as well. She propped herself up on her elbows. "He's so nice."

"He is."

A spark of hope lit up her eyes. "Are you going to try for a baby again?"

Oh God, not that question. Instead of putting myself on the defense, I was honest.

"Well, I'd like to become pregnant before my birthday, which gives us two months, and then I don't know. It's hard with you and dad being so far away. And Jean-Luc's sisters don't exactly live around the corner. There's a lot to think about. *On verra.*"

We'll see.

Jean-Luc padded his way over to the shore, my dad close behind. "We've got to get going," he said. "Tonight, we've been invited over to my co-worker's, Simone, for an *apéritif.* She and her husband have a house in La Ciotat, right on the water." He looked at his watch. "We have just enough time to head back to Isabelle's, shower, and change, and then we'll make our way back here." Jean-Luc cleared his throat. "Oh, before Simone's, we're stopping by my parents'."

On the ride over into La Ciotat, Jean-Luc overexplained his family's situation, saying things like, "They don't live in a place like Isabelle's. It's simple. It's where I grew up," and, "My mother is in really bad health. She might be killing my father. I'd like for them to move, but she refuses."

My dad put a stop to his insecurities. "Jean-Luc, they raised you. And obviously they did a great job."

Jean-Luc's eyes met mine in the rearview mirror. "You and Anne did a pretty good job, too."

The visit with Jean-Luc's parents was short, but sweet. Unfortunately, Madame Vérant's health had declined even more since the last time we'd seen her. As we made our way back to the car, I grabbed Jean-Luc's hand, squeezing it. "I wish my father would put her in a home. He really can't take care of her anymore. It's too hard on him," he said and turned to my family. "I'm sorry about that."

"What's to be sorry about, Jean-Luc?" asked my dad. "Your parents are wonderful."

"*Alors*, they're mine." Jean-Luc blew out the air in between his lips. "On to the next stop."

After another round of champagne toasts and light-hearted conversation at Simone's home, we found ourselves seated on the inside terrace of Chez Tania. Situated in the *calanque* de Figuerolles, the restaurant offered a view of the sea and the famed *Bec de l'Aigle*, a rock cropping reminiscent of an eagle's beak. We'd be eating under the full moon, enjoying the music of the symbol of Provence—the cicadas. The view of the sea and the rising cliffs bathed in the orange and pink sunset was breathtaking.

. . . .

The next day, before setting off into the wild blue yonder on a boat with the even wilder Gilles, Claude, another childhood friend of Jean-Luc's, invited our family over to his house for an *apéritif* at ten-thirty in the morning. My parents were thrilled. Claude and his wife, Danielle, had also made the trip for the California wedding, and my parents loved both of them, as did I. How could we not? They were, as the French say, *chaleureux*—warm, open, and friendly. Claude greeted us with his huge, toothy smile and a bottle of champagne, explaining that Danielle was at work and sent her hellos.

"Isn't it a little early for that?" asked Jean-Luc, eyeing the champagne bottle, and my dad agreed.

My sister said, "It's never too early for champagne."

"When in France," said my mom.

I loved visiting Claude, not only to see him, but also his unbalanced cat, Mario, who randomly tipped over for no reason at all. Soon, Mario had my whole family in stitches, running around in the yard and falling down like an old drunk. My mom gushed about how much she loved Mario and Claude's beautiful Provençal home—the ironwork, the tiles, and the well-equipped country kitchen. Claude raised his glass. "I have an idea. We can do a house exchange one year! I'd love to go to California again."

They toasted, and I wondered if Claude knew exactly what he'd just gotten himself into, because on the ride to Saint-Cyr-sur-Mer, the village in which Gilles docked his thirty-foot speedboat, the house exchange was all my mother could talk about. We picked up some *jambon* and *fromage* baguettes at the local *boulangerie*, and, in less than ten minutes, we were zipping off into the Med with our crazed captain, Gilles, the wind whipping through our hair, the water glistening ahead of us. Gille's nineteen-year-old daughter Julie and her friend were joining us as well, and we stopped to pick them up at a little port in La Ciotat.

A beautiful girl, Julie was tall with shoulder-length dark brown hair. She was wearing oversized black sunglasses, which in typical French fashion, she placed on top of her head when the required round of *la bise* was swapped. In a dash of sophistication, her pearl earrings matched her tiny bikini. Her friend, whose name I didn't catch, had a sexy look about her—long sun-kissed hair that reached the middle of her tiny back. She didn't have love handles or a double chin. I cringed and put my T-shirt on to hide the rolls on my stomach, the baguettes. The two taut, tanned beauties left to make themselves comfortable on the bow of the boat.

At least the other view inspired awe instead of making me feel like a manatee.

Dotted with umbrella pines, the majestic clay-colored cliffs rose high into the cloudless sky. Gilles pulled out of the little harbor. We toured the many *calanques* of Cassis and La Ciotat, drinking a rosé from Bandol, the wine bearing the name of the region a mere twenty kilometers away, and stopping to swim in clear and surprisingly warm waters.

The next day, we met up with Christian and Ghislaine, who had an apartment in St. Tropez, at the famed coffeehouse with the red awning of Sénéquier. For their last night, Muriel hosted a family barbecue, another evening filled with love, laughter, and wine. We were living *la belle vie*—a great ending to our last twenty-four hours in Provence.

"I can't wait to see your home," said Jess.

"You will. But we're making two stops first."

My parents and sister had experienced life on the Mediterranean Sea; now it was time for some history. On the way back to Toulouse, we visited Arles, known for its bullfights and two-tiered Roman amphitheater, which dates back to 90 AD, a magnificent structure where chariot races were in fashion and gladiators fought. Then, it was onto the medieval and fortified village of Carcassonne (a standard stop for any guest), and where my mother was less than impressed with the shops selling swords and "knight-wear." We didn't get home until seven in the evening.

Jean-Luc gave my family the tour, showing off the room we'd just built and all his handiwork. I shut myself in the kitchen cooking, wanting to introduce my family to one of the specialties of the region: *saucisse de Toulouse,* which I'd serve with a trio of peppers and onions, along with a salad. My mom and Jess rested as Jean-Luc and my dad left the house to pick up Max, Elvire, and a rental car at the airport, since we wouldn't all fit in one car the next few days.

Over dinner, my dad's eyes bugged out when Jean-Luc told him that we would leave early in the morning, before nine, for the next day's full-day tour. My dad wasn't used to running around nonstop— only working nonstop. This was good for him. We were taking them to some of our favorite places, incredible villages. After all, the town built into the cliffs, Rocamadour, was a must-see. And we'd be nuts if we didn't take them to Saint-Cirq-Lapopie and Cordes-sur-Ciel.

Jean-Luc smiled at Jessica, poured her glass of wine. "Is there anything in particular you'd like to do?"

Jess nodded. "I'd love to visit a vineyard."

"Me, too," said my mom.

"Which is why we're going to Saint Émilion. Again, we have to leave early as it's two and half hours away and we have to be back in Toulouse by eight." Jean-Luc paused. "Christian and Ghislaine are hosting a dinner for your final night."

"Will we see Toulouse?" asked my mom.

"If there's time," I said.

With the itinerary Jean-Luc had planned, there wouldn't be. But my life was in France now; my family could always come back.

21

DIGGING UP ROOTS

U NTIL I QUALIFIED FOR A ten-year card (requiring three years of marriage to a French national and four years of living in France) or, better yet, dual citizenship (five years of living in France, still married), I would be stuck in the blue, white, and red tape of having to renew my "green card" every year. But an immigrant had to do what immigrant had to do. No exceptions.

Four months prior, I'd submitted my *dossier*—a folder filled with exact same papers from the previous year—at the *préfecture*. I kept my *récépissé*—a temporary receipt that proved my legal status in France was on the up and up—tucked safely in my wallet. Exactly two and a half months after my first card had expired, the notification came in the mail, a postcard alerting me that the card was finally ready to be picked up. Before they closed, I headed to the local treasury to pick up the *les timbres fiscaux*—eighty-seven euros of tax stamps. No stamps, no card.

The weather was unusually hot for mid-October, eighty-four degrees in the shade, and the kids were out of school for the La Toussaint holiday, home with us for a week before they flew to Provence to visit Meme. Honestly, it was hard keeping up with the time the kids had off from school. Along with all of the holidays, *les grèves* (strikes) seemed to hit France on a monthly basis. Teachers, like the people working at the *préfecture*, were under the umbrella of *les fonctionnaires* (civil servants), and if given a reason to strike, that's exactly what most of them did. In France, substitute teachers didn't exist, which blew my mind, and left me scrambling to prepare more than a few impromptu lunches for the kids on days when they were unexpectedly home from school.

Max was playing video games on the Wii in the living room, whistling. Elvire was in her room, no doubt, watching a dubbed version of *Gossip Girl* or *Pretty Little Liars* on her computer. Either that, or she was spaz-dancing with a hairbrush in her hand, pretending she was a pop star. I went back to chopping up rosemary for my potatoes as Jean-Luc fanned the barbecue.

From upstairs, Elvire screamed, "Max, *arrête de siffler!*"

Elvire was mostly angel with a little devil thrown into the mix—basically a one hundred percent, occasionally hormonal, almost fifteen-year-old girl. Growing up right before our eyes, her figure and facial features had transformed from a child's into a woman's practically overnight. With her beautiful, thick auburn hair and blue, feline eyes, she was beautiful, but didn't know it yet. I was dreading the day she started to date. So was Jean-Luc—even though Elvire was a strong-headed girl who wasn't afraid of speaking her mind, especially when it came to her younger brother.

"Max!" Elvire yelled again. "*Arrête de siffler. C'est énervant.*"

"*Tais-toi,*" he yelled back. "*C'est toi. T'es énervante.*"

Elvire's bedroom door slammed. Max whistled, louder.

"Max!!!"

This war of "shut-ups," whistles, screeches, and door slams went on for another five minutes. They were both being *très énervant*—very annoying—and I was getting a headache. Before a migraine set in or Elvire came downstairs and the argument escalated into a tear-filled, red-faced wrestling match, I stepped in to mediate.

"Max," I said, poking my head into the living room. "Stop whistling, please."

He shifted his eyes from side to side. "It wasn't me. It was my doppelgänger."

I had to laugh. Along with "freak," "weirdo," and a whole slew of other words I probably shouldn't have taught him, his English was improving. He continued whistling, the tone a little softer.

"Max," I said, using my patented step-parental growl, and the house went quiet.

When it came to the opposite sex, I wasn't worried about Max. No, it was the girls I feared for. I knew his father's history, every last sordid detail of it, and the reason as to why Jean-Luc had concerns for Elvire. The French had an idiom: "*les chiens ne font pas des chats*" (dogs don't make cats), which didn't make sense until Jean-Luc later explained that it was like the American expression "an apple doesn't fall far from the tree." Given either scenario— dogs and cats or apples and trees—one day, just like his dad, Max would be a real heartbreaker.

Max looked up from his video game, raised a quizzical brow. "*Quoi?*" I was staring at him. Like a weirdo.

"*Rien,*" I said. Nothing. "Can you set the table?"

"*Deux secondes,*" he said.

Unlike Elvire, whose "two seconds" lasted twenty hours, I didn't have to ask him twice…and then ten more times. Although it had taken some time, through trial and error, I had this whole foreign stepmom thing down, locked and loaded. Kids would be kids, no matter what country they were from. Which made me question if having a baby with Jean-Luc was still a possibility. I threw some fresh rosemary into the potatoes and stirred, lost in my thoughts. If having a biological child wasn't in the cards for me, at least I had a good man, who vacuumed, mopped, and worked the grill, and two kids, who were, for the most part, well behaved. I opened up a bottle of Cahors wine, known as Malbec in the U.S. Other than having to go to the *préfecture* in the morning, I was lucky in life, and I had no complaints. Kelly Clarkson belted out her latest song, the off-key lyrics of which Elvire now sang in her room.

"Elvire," I said, loud enough for her to hear. "Your windows are open and the neighbors can hear you."

"*Tu chantes comme une casserole,*" said Jean-Luc from the garden, teasing his daughter about singing like a pot—another one of those odd French expressions.

Silence.

We were eating barbecued *merguez* (spicy sausages) that Jean-Luc had grilled, along with my famed "I could eat-the-whole-pan-but-I'll-restrain-myself" sautéed potatoes, which were crunchy and golden on the outside, soft on the inside, and an endive salad with lemon-mustard vinaigrette, when I announced that I'd be heading into Toulouse the following morning to finish up my paperwork.

"Can I come with you?" asked Elvire.

Was she crazy? I wrinkled my nose. "But I'm going to the *préfecture*. It's, well, *un vrai cauchemar.*"

A *real* nightmare. I was pretty sure the *préfecture* liked torturing us immigrants, watching us squirm in our chairs as we waited in never-ending purgatory.

"But I want to go shopping at Place St. Georges. I need some things for school."

My upper lip curled. Which one was more painful? The *préfecture*? Or shopping with Elvire? Her eyes pleaded with mine. Jean-Luc raised his eyebrows. Guilt set in. Just like an immigrant, a step-by-stepmom had to do what a step-by-stepmom had to do. "Fine," I said. "But we have to pick up my card first, *d'accord*?" I turned to Max. "Do you want to come, too?"

Max held up both of his hands in the stop motion, his teeth clenched in mock fear. Like me, he knew that shopping with Elvire was like having an annoying song stuck on repeat.

"By the way, Elvire," I said. "We have to leave early. No later than eight. If we're not there right when the *préfecture* opens, we could be there for days."

The next morning, Elvire was in her slow-motion teenaged-*Matrix* mode and we didn't leave the house until a quarter until nine. When we got to the *préfecture*, I raced to the ticket kiosk and grabbed my number. There were fifty people ahead of me—at least.

I shot Elvire a look, but didn't say a word. Thankfully, we were able to find some seats in the hallway. I pulled out my iPad from my bag, opened up an iBook, and said, "Looks like we'll be here for a while."

Before she snapped in her earbuds, she said, "I don't like it here. The people are *bizarre*."

It was true. On this day, it was as if someone had unlocked the door to an insane asylum and ushered all the crazies to the *préfecture*. An hour later, Elvire jabbed me in the ribs. "*Regarde*," she whispered. "That woman? With the man?"

It was hard not to notice them. An elderly, platinum-haired Frenchwoman wearing tight, leopard-print spandex and mile-high heels was canoodling with what appeared to be her very much younger Nubian lover. And by canoodling, I mean her tongue was in his ear. But who was I to question love? The brash public display of affection was a bit too much for Elvire.

"*C'est dégueulasse*. Really disgusting."

"What about the kids at school?"

"That's normal. They're not *old*."

"Have you kissed a boy?" I asked, seeing an opportunity for open communication sans her dad.

"*Pas encore*," she said. Not yet. "But I want to. Not like that, though." Her brows furrowed. "I don't have a boyfriend."

"Well, one day you will, and when you do, you can talk to me about anything." To be clear, I had to add in, "Anything at all."

"*Je sais*," she said. "I will. Just don't tell papa."

I did an internal happy dance.

Two hours later, we finally left the *préfecture*, my new card in hand, for our next adventure: shopping. I survived the day, Elvire was happy with her purchases, and we didn't go over budget on her selections (which included one cute T-shirt with a graphic print of a mustache on it but, unfortunately for my favorite boots, no shoes). More importantly, we'd opened up to one another even more, building up a mutual trust. Plus, Elvire now understood my frustrations of being an immigrant in France a bit better—and maybe the importance of being on time. Then again, life never moved fast at the *préfecture*.

At home, Max eyed me curiously. "Why do you have a dark stripe on the top of your head?" he asked.

He was referring to my roots. I explained that I color my hair, have it highlighted. He pointed to my head. "*Mais*, your hair is black. But only the top."

"It's not black. It just looks that way because of the contrast of light and dark. My natural hair color is just like yours—*châtain*," which was medium brown that turns blond in the summer (sometimes with the help of Sun-In or lemon juice or highlights and hair dye).

Elvire sauntered into the kitchen. "You look like *une moufette*." She picked at my scalp like a monkey grooming its young. "This is not natural. And you have a gray hair. You're old."

"I'm not old. And I do *not* look like a skunk. I was born blond, and I don't look good with dark hair. It doesn't match my complexion." I brushed Elvire's hand away and bolted upstairs to my box of photos, and raced downstairs with baby pictures in hand. "See? See? I was blond. And I don't have gray hair. I don't. It's just a strand of glittery blond."

The more I explained, the more the kids laughed.

They had me. And they knew what they were doing.

I looked in the mirror. For the past year, in order to save money, I'd been doing my color myself, picking up boxed kits at the grocery store. Put it this way: Tweety-Bird yellow with dark roots wasn't a good look. And those "glitter" strands had to go. Clearly, it was time for me to get to the hairdresser, so I called and made an appointment for the following day. I also made one for Max, whose hair was so long and out of control he was beginning to look like an orphan or the long-lost twin of Justin Bieber. We couldn't send him to his grandmother's like that. Surely, she'd scream!

Max walked into Hairmes (yes, *Hairmes*) at eleven-thirty. I'd been at the *coiffure* since nine, my hair now plaited into layers of foils. Max grimaced and choked back on his laughter as he took a seat. I was sure he wanted to pretend he didn't know me. But I didn't let that happen. He sunk into his chair. It didn't help matters when I caught Max's eyes in the mirror and did robot moves while mouthing, "I come from planet Freak."

Michel, the owner of Hairmes, laughed his butt off, as did Laure, my hairdresser.

On the way home, Max, his haircut short and spiked with gel, and me, my now-blond hair no longer skunk-like with no signs of "glitter" strands, grabbed a baguette for lunch at the local *boulangerie*. The scent of fresh buttery bread warmed my soul as we opened the door. The bell jingled and the woman I'd become friendly with as my confidence with the French language turned from mouse voice to full and strong greeted us, clapping her hands in delight. "Oh, is this your son?"

Max's mouth twisted. I couldn't tell if he was offended or not. He did the sort-of motion with his hand. "No," I said, reading the signs. "My stepson."

"Oh," she said with surprise. "You look alike. Look at his eyes. They're just like yours."

I caught Max hiding a little smile before his gaze darted to the tartes. For a moment, it was almost as if he seemed proud, not embarrassed of me like he'd been at the hairdresser.

"What can I get you?"

"I'd like to try something new." I read the names of the varying baguettes. "I'll take the Avey-blah-blah-blah."

Max smirked. "Blah, blah, blah?"

And he was embarrassed again.

The woman said, "Repeat after me. *A-vey-ro-naise.*"

She rolled her r heavily, the way of the South. I repeated her, light on the r.

"*Non, non, non.*" Her kind blue eyes met mine. "*Rrroh. Rrroh. Rrroh! Aveyr-r-rrrro-naise.*"

I gave it the good old college try. "*Avey-r-rrr-ro-naise,*" I said, sounding more like a cat coughing up a dozen hairballs.

"Better," she said, handing me a paper-wrapped baguette. "Your French! It is improving!"

Fresh-baked bread under my arm, Max and I left the shop and walked the two blocks home. He tapped me on the arm. "Don't ever speak like that woman," he said. "It was bizarre."

"Does it bother you she thought you were my son?"

"No, it was funny."

I bumped him with my hip. "Want to race? Last one home is *un oeuf pourri*."

By the way Max knitted his brows, "rotten egg" didn't translate. But it didn't matter. He got the gist of it. Max took off before I could explain, leaving me smiling in his dust.

22

DREAMS CHANGE

ONE MONTH BEFORE MY FORTY-SECOND birthday, I knew. My period was two weeks late. My breasts stung to the touch as if live wires electrocuted them. I was super sensitive. This time, instead of crying during a Disney cartoon, I sobbed through a dubbed version of *Glee*. It wasn't even sad. And when I sprayed my wrists with Opium, I found myself dry heaving over the porcelain bowl. Not to mention the scent of the salmon baking in the oven, which, before I'd made it, had sounded good. Now, the smell coming from the oven made me sick. Suffice it to say, instead of going to the pharmacy to grab a test, I called Doctor K to make an appointment for the following day.

"You're six weeks along," he said. "And, listen, we've got a fetal heartbeat."

He waved his magic wand over my belly and turned up the volume on the machine. A frantic heartbeat thumped, the sound like an echo of a train rumbling down the tracks. My own heart beat faster. Jean-Luc stepped over from his seat, grabbed my hand, and we listened to the life growing inside me. "Everything looks great. Perfect." Doctor K broke out into a wide, happy grin. "Would you like a printout of the ultrasound?"

I nodded my head yes, trying to think positively, but I couldn't. I'd already been down the road called "getting my hopes up" two times before. What if? What if? I regarded the grainy image with trepidation. Nope. No horns.

Jack (or Jill) the Bean, this time, you better stick.

"If you feel anything is wrong," said Doctor K, "don't hesitate to come see me as many times as you want to, every week if you want to."

I sat up and pulled my shirt over my belly. The first time I'd miscarried had happened at eight weeks, but I didn't know until week twelve. The second time, I'd been a little over five weeks. I was now six weeks along. "I'd like to come back in two weeks, just to check in."

"Not a problem."

We set the appointment.

Once again, I made the calls—first, Tracey, then my sister. I saved my mom for last. This time, she knew better than to express her excitement. We were all keeping our cool, trying to remain level-headed in case of another disaster.

Right before a lunch with the girls, I checked my email. My New York literary agent, Stephanie, had sent a message letting me know that she had sent out the pitch for *Seven Letters from Paris* in the agency newsletter. Ten editors, five from the same house (which was unheard of), and two from another house and the same imprint, along with three others, had requested the manuscript. I was a nervous wreck, hoping for good news on all fronts.

When I met up with Monique, Oksana, and Trupty for lunch in Toulouse, they ordered wine. I opted for plain old water—clearly a giveaway. Monique picked up on it first. "You're pregnant."

"Looks like the cat is out of the bag," I said.

"Stay away from cats!" said Monique.

Oksana stood up from her chair to give me a hug. "Do you think France puts folic acid in its water? Because I need some."

My nerves settled down the next time I saw Doctor K. Not only was I eight weeks along, but the fetal heartbeat was strong at one hundred sixty-seven beats per minute, the fetus itself measuring sixteen millimeters. I let out the breath I'd been holding, seemingly for the past two weeks, and then I scheduled another appointment for the following week. Just to be sure.

I was cautiously optimistic. And I had reason to be.

Two days later, it was as if all my pregnancy symptoms had disappeared overnight. My breasts were still full, yes, but they didn't hurt at all. I checked the Internet. Maybe, just maybe, my body was adjusting to the hormones. But I should have been tired. And I wasn't. I should have been mildly nauseated, a sign, apparently, of a healthy pregnancy. But I wasn't. I felt normal. And normal wasn't good. I called Doctor K, explaining my fears. He had me come to the clinic the next day. Jean-Luc and I sat in the waiting room, rigid.

I went absolutely numb when Doctor K delivered the news. My gut instinct had been right; there was no fetal heartbeat and, according to the measurements, I'd lost the pregnancy only the day before. Doctor K's hand shook when he ran the wand over my belly again. "I don't understand what happened. Everything was fine three days ago."

All cried out, I could only stare at the ceiling, shaking my head. "Will I have to do another D&C?"

"I'm afraid so." He sucked in his breath. "I'll call down to surgery and see if we can schedule you in for tomorrow."

It was as if someone had lobbed five thousand baseballs into a glass house. And I was that glass house, my dreams of having a biological child of my own blown to smithereens.

I was shattered.

The next day, before I left the hospital after the procedure, Doctor K sat Jean-Luc and me down, presenting us with a few options: I could have a series of tests done to see if we could pinpoint a problem; perhaps my blood wasn't delivering enough oxygen to the fetus. If I got pregnant again and if I had this issue, I'd have to give myself a shot every day during the entire term of the pregnancy; I could see a fertility specialist, although, he said, I obviously don't have a problem becoming pregnant; or, I could curb this baby-making activity by going on the Pill.

He urged me to keep trying.

I bit down on my bottom lip. "I don't know."

"We'll figure it out," said Doctor K.

On the car ride home, Jean-Luc and I weighed all the pros and cons. My parents and his family were far away, too far to lend a hand. We'd be the oldest parents in preschool. With his fiftieth birthday approaching the following year and me still reeling from my forty-second, after three consecutive miscarriages, the answer for me was clear.

"We have to really want this," I said. "Really, really want this. Like more than anything we've ever wanted in our entire lives."

"'Oney, I only want what you want."

"I'm tired of getting my hopes up. I'm tired of the crushing disappointments." My shoulders shook and I slumped in my seat. "I'm just tired. I'm tired of feeling like this."

Back when we had first started trying, Jean-Luc and I had agreed; if I were to get pregnant naturally, it would happen—no planning, no fertility treatments, and no pressure. But now all I was feeling was pressure. I didn't know if my body, my mind, could deal with another loss. Plus, because of my age, the chance of having a baby with health issues had risen exponentially and, along with that, there was always the possibility of having twins, which would be a whole different challenge.

"I think having a baby would really mess up our family dynamic. You already have two kids. I think of them like my own—"

"But, 'oney, I thought this was your dream."

Was it? I thought of the car ride from Chicago to California with my mother right after my divorce. My mom had had big aspirations when she was younger. She was going to be a famous ballerina, dancing in *Swan Lake*, fluttering around in tutus and pink satin toe shoes with the New York City Ballet. But then she met Chuck, my biological father, married him, and moved to Los Angeles at the age of nineteen. When she became pregnant with me, her toe shoes were hung up on a hook of unfulfilled dreams. Chuck abandoned my mom and me when I was six months old, leaving us for another woman. My mom was forced to move back home to her parents, too young and broke to care for an infant on her own.

At the time, I was about to find myself in the same position she'd found herself in so long ago—broke, heavy-hearted from a breakup, and about to move back home to my parents. The only difference was that I wasn't twenty-one with a small infant; I was almost forty and childless. I'd asked my mom if she ever regretted putting her dreams aside for me. She looked at me like I was nuts and said, "Dreams change."

They did. I was so thankful for my dad, the one who raised me.

"Love doesn't only come from DNA," I said.

Jean-Luc squeezed my hand. We were in agreement. But this decision, I felt, was not ours alone. I was close with the kids, more than close, so I sat Max and Elvire down when we got back to the house. Elvire's eyes glistened with tears when, with a shaky voice, I shared the devastating news. Having just turned twelve, Max was too young to understand terms like *fausse couche* (miscarriage) and why they were an emotional roller-coaster ride of epic proportions, but he was sweet.

"*Ça va?*" he asked, his bottom lip puffed out with concern.

"I'm fine. I just have a few questions for the two of you." I paused, swallowing back the lump in my throat. "Would you be upset if I can't give you a brother or sister? Or do you like the way things are now? Just me, the two of you, and your dad?"

Max grimaced. "It's up to you."

Elvire nodded her head in agreement. "You're kind of old. The baby has a chance of being born with major problems, come out—"

Either she'd been talking to her grandmother or she'd been studying fertility in school.

"So, you're against the idea, I take it?" I asked.

It didn't take a translator to read the *real* message veiled in both of their eyes. Right then, I knew that my decision *not* to have a biological child of my own was the most selfless thing I'd ever done. I wrestled Max into my arms. "So, since I'm not going to have one, do you mind if I pretend you're a baby for two seconds?"

Naturally, a massive pillow fight ensued.

With the threat of a cloud of goose feathers exploding over our

heads, those pillows and our laughter knocked me right into acceptance. Sure, I was sad about the loss, but I no longer felt shattered. In
less than a few minutes, my *family* had glued the pieces of my heart
back together. I knew the kids would never call me "mom." And I
was okay with that. For me, having their love was more than enough.
Max and Elvire would benefit from the way my parents had raised
me—supported and cared for no matter what.

"Can we have American breakfast tonight?" asked Max.

Homemade hash browns and cheesy scrambled eggs—food was
the way to this little man's heart, especially when it was prepared
with love. Hold the veggies. And the tuna noodle casserole. Shame
I wasn't able to find American bacon in Toulouse. Believe me, I'd
looked everywhere.

. . . .

Shortly after this third consecutive loss, my agent, Stephanie, emailed
to schedule a call. I was hoping for good news. I needed it.

"Well, I have some bad news," she said, and my heart dropped
into my stomach. "I'm leaving agenting and going to work for a
publisher." She paused. "The good news is you'll be placed in the
hands of one my co-workers, Susan. She loves your story. And I'll
transfer you over to her once we're done."

I blew out a sigh of relief. She wasn't dumping me. "I'm so sorry
you're leaving. I hope it's for greener pastures."

"It is. And just so you know, I loved working with you."

"Me, too. Thanks for everything," I said.

"No problem."

I bit down on a fingernail. "While I have you, any news on the
submissions?"

She sucked her in breath. "Well, I'm afraid I have more bad news.
Please remember that this was only the first round, and all of the
rejections were positive. They all loved the story and your voice, but
they didn't like the epistolary format. Too many letters and emails

driving the plot forward was the general consensus. I'll send them on to you in a few…"

My throat constricted. My book was rejected. My body rejected the baby. I wanted to throw up. I was sick of rejection.

"Don't worry. You'll find a publisher. I believe in your book. And I believe in you. There are lots of other imprints and houses out there."

My response came out as a gurgle.

"Are you ready to talk to Susan?"

"Yes." There. I got one word out.

"You'll be in good hands. Keep in touch."

Stephanie transferred me to Susan. And, from the moment she opened her mouth, I knew we didn't have a connection. I wanted to rewrite the story based on the comments—to eliminate all the emails and just keep Jean-Luc's letters. She told me not to rewrite anything, that the only way I stood a chance of publication was if I got an article published in the "Modern Love" column in the *New York Times*. I figured I'd listen to her. She knew what she was doing, right? And, at the time, I figured having an agent was better than not having one at all.

A few days later, I received an email from the agent who had filled Stephanie's position. His email said something like, "I'm sorry, but we've reached the end of the line with *Seven Letters*." He urged me look for representation elsewhere. I googled him to learn that he represented manga. I was livid, shaking in my shoes, steam-coming-out-of-my-ears mad (also very hormonal). So, I forwarded Susan the email, copying the owner of the agency and this random dude.

Forgive me if I'm wrong, but I thought I was working with Susan.

I received a reply a few hours later, explaining that it was an internal communication mishap, that, yes, I'd been assigned to Susan. No apology.

Needless to say, my relationship with my new agent wasn't off to a great start. I cried for about an hour, and then I got over it. Although sad, I was feeling good about the decision Jean-Luc and I had made regarding our family. I didn't need another outside influence I couldn't control bringing me down. I needed to get back to and embrace my life. So while I worked on writing the "Modern Love" article, a little voice inside of me said, "Sam, you should also follow your gut instincts and rewrite the book."

And that's exactly what I did.

. . . .

Along with the parties and lunches, I was most looking forward to two things this holiday season: my parents and sister were spending Christmas with us at Isabelle's; and my core group of friends (Monique, Trupty, and Oksana, plus our significant others) were spending a weekend away at Trupty's boyfriend's *gîte* in Valon, a tiny village in Aveyron.

The kids were invited but, wanting to avoid the boredom of adult conversations, opted to stay home. (I also told my neighbors to keep an eye on our house *just in case* Elvire, soon to be fifteen years old, took advantage of our departure to sneak back into the house to throw a party).

To say that Jean-Luc was nervous about leaving the kids alone was an understatement. Although French parents were generally less obsessive than Americans when it came to their kids' activities, that didn't mean they didn't worry. In France, young adults often lived at home while attending university and, according to statistics, more than half of children between the ages of eighteen to thirty still lived at home to save money.

Oftentimes, Jean-Luc and I discussed our childhoods. Like me, Jean-Luc had his first job at the age of sixteen. He worked at the shipping yard in La Ciotat. I worked at The Limited (where I spent my paychecks on clothes) followed by a pharmacy, and then taking orders at Talbots (where I didn't spend my paychecks on clothes, but saved up for my first car—a burgundy 1978 Oldsmobile Cutlass Supreme with white pleather interior). But times changed. Today, the majority of teens in France don't work. They call it the "dependent generation."

Still, it was important to me for the kids to be independent. I never relied on my parents to wake me up in the morning for school; I had an invention called an alarm clock. Somehow I convinced Jean-Luc that they would be just fine on their own for one measly night. Fine, Elvire's first cooking attempts were a bit of a disaster—specifically the time I was out of town when she attempted to make spaghetti, not realizing that you had to push the noodles into the water with a wooden spoon so they were completely covered, and she'd called me up, wondering why the pasta was only half cooked. But, by this point, Elvire had spent enough time in the kitchen cooking and singing with me. She knew how to cook basic dishes as well as a few desserts, such as *gâteau au yaourt*, a simple cake made from yogurt, a staple in any French home.

Regardless, before we left, Jean-Luc instructed the kids.

"Don't forget to turn off the gas. You don't want to burn the house down."

"Don't leave the water on."

"Don't forget to feed the cat twice a day."

"Don't stay up too late."

"Don't forget to do your homework."

"*Oui, je sais, Papa*," said Elvire with an eye roll, and a sigh. Yes, I know, Dad. She practically pushed us out the door.

Jean-Luc posted the neighbors' number on the refrigerator. "If there are any big emergencies, call Claude and Paulette. And don't forget to lock the door."

He called them every two hours. "Everything okay?"

I could hear Elvire's sigh. "*Oui, Papa.*"

. . . .

On the three-hour drive from Toulouse to Valon on Saturday morning, Jean-Luc informed me we were headed to *la France profonde*—deep France, the winding route taking us by forests, rivers, and towns dressed up for Christmas.

Valon was a very tiny village of around twenty old, beautiful homes, centered around its *pièce-de-résistance*, the Château de Valon, a twelfth-century fortress with a panoramic view of the Gorges de la Truyère, lush mountains, and forests. A layer of fog made it appear as if it were floating in the clouds.

A charming stone home, Chris's *gîte* was absolutely amazing, and even more impressive was the fact that he'd restored the property from ruin, including the roof. In addition to the main house, which had four bedrooms, there were two bedrooms in a downstairs apartment, a barn that Chris was in the process of converting into a one-bedroom apartment, and an art gallery.

After dropping off our bags in our room, Jean-Luc and I joined our friends for lunch, the vichyssoise soup I'd prepared in advance and served, with a crisp salad, crusty baguettes, sausages, cheeses, and *foie gras* filling our bellies. Trupty and Chris had constructed homemade ornaments from branches they'd found in the forest, tying them with raffia into the shape of stars, and embellishing them with dried oranges.

Since the weather was more than agreeable, we took our coffee outside at a picnic table, the view overlooking the valley, and then we headed off to Conques (a beautiful medieval village on the pilgrimage route of Saint-Jacques-de-Compostelle), before exploring the Christmas market in Mur de Barrez, where we came face-to-face with *Le Père Fouettard*, the whipping father who, according to French legend, accompanied Saint Nick on December 6 to dispense lumps of coal or to flog the naughty children.

At night, together we cooked up a feast—Oksana's famed *chapon* (a capon, or castrated rooster) in a kiwi sauce, my roasted potatoes, and Trupty's eggplant and zucchini blinis. Our resident non-cook, Monique, played sous-chef.

"See, I can do this," she said.

Side by side, everybody chopped and laughed, the men working just as hard as us ladies, preparing the *verrines* for the *apéro*. It was a real group effort. After dinner, we exchanged Secret Santa gifts by the fire. And we girls hadn't forgotten that it was Oksana's birthday the week before. When she saw the extra gift we'd all pitched in for, a spa day, she burst into tears. In the morning, we hiked through the forest, discovering rivers, old barns, and wonderful beehives, the weekend deepening our friendships even more.

This was the magic of the holidays. This was the magic of friendship.

Let the *Festi Noël* begin.

23

THROW PAPA
FROM THE PLANE

T HE "MODERN LOVE" ARTICLE I'D written for my new agent, Susan, was rejected. She barely replied to my emails after that. So I made the hard decision to leave the agency. Having an agent who wasn't passionate about my work, in fact, was far worse than not having an agent at all. I called her up and said thanks, nice knowing you, but I think it's time we part ways. She didn't argue.

Of course, I had a backup plan. Jean-Luc had always joked that women were like monkeys (bonobo chimps?), and that they wouldn't leave quietly unless they had a firm grip on another branch. Well, I had a new branch. For three months, from the cold months of December to February, I rewrote that damned manuscript. When I was finished, I contacted an editor who was now freelancing, Jay Schaefer. He'd worked with Frances Mayes of *Under the Tuscan Sun* fame when he was with Chronicle Books. How did I find him? Google. Along with my book proposal and sample chapters, I'd sent a few initial questions when I first made contact: "Does my book stand a chance at publication? Or am I smoking a crack pipe?"

Jay got back to me immediately. He didn't make false promises of any kind. But he said what mattered: he believed in my story, and he could help me structure it better. Plus, he'd help me revise the book proposal, make it shine. There was just one problem: he didn't work for free…and I didn't have any money.

I thought about just giving up. But that wasn't like me. I believed in my story, too, felt it needed to be told, thought it was something women could relate to. A second chance at life and love? What if I had given up on my life in France when the going got tough? Nope, I was a fighter. And I had other people who believed in my writing, namely my mom. And boy oh boy, was she spurring me on. She offered to give me the small loan I needed. Actually, *offered* isn't the right word. She insisted, wouldn't take no for an answer.

Before I signed on the dotted line with Jay, I enlisted an army of beta readers to read my new draft—friends, family members, and other writers. The consensus was the same.

"Sam! Get your story out there! You can do it!"

I hired Jay, and a new round of edits began.

I'd jumped feet first into this French life. I'd jumped into following my dream of becoming a writer. I'd jumped into motherhood. The seasons were changing. I was changing. And, by the time April rolled around, I wanted Jean-Luc to know exactly how it felt when you took a big leap of faith.

. . . .

Max and Elvire were the masterminds behind the whole operation. For weeks, the kids and I plotted and planned: Daddy was going down on his fiftieth birthday.

Instead of the *moelleux au chocolat* with the *cœur fondant* (chocolate lava cake) he'd anticipated, Elvire placed an envelope on her father's dessert plate. Jean-Luc's brows furrowed when he pulled out our handmade card. Max and I exchanged nervous glances. I placed one hundred sixty euro on the table. "I paid half—for the deposit. This is the kids' portion."

I didn't know what surprised him more, the fact we'd bought him a parachute jump for his fiftieth birthday, or that Max and Elvire had actually pitched in for the gift, using their savings on him instead of buying video games or clothes. Once he'd processed what we'd done, Jean-Luc's eyes lit up. "I've always wanted to do this."

Jean-Luc's excitement reminded me why I'd agreed to book the skydive in the first place. I wanted him to experience the thrill and exhilaration, the adventure, of leaping into the blue skies of the French countryside, right into the unknown—the equivalent of how I'd felt when I'd landed in France to meet him years ago. Indeed, it was the perfect gift for his fiftieth birthday.

"Okay," I said. "You have to call them to book it."

He set the date for the end of May.

If Jean-Luc was going to jump out of a plane, certainly I could get over my fear of flambé for our second wedding anniversary dinner. Jean-Luc had cooked this particular recipe—shrimp with Pastis— many times before, me always playing sous-chef, slicing and dicing the shallots, parsley, and garlic. This time, I was going to light the match. To my delight, I didn't burn the house down or singe my eyebrows off. One shrimp may have escaped the pan, but the cat was happy. And so was I.

We'd promised one another no presents, but over dinner—the flambéed shrimp with Pastis served with steamed rice and a mango, avocado, and tomato salsa—Jean-Luc surprised me with a bracelet. The chain was thin, the jewel in the middle an amethyst heart, which rested right on my pulse.

Dinner wasn't the only thing on fire that night; my heart was, too. He whipped out a pair of opera tickets and placed them on the table. I didn't think it was possible, but I loved this man more every day.

"They're for next weekend," he said. "I picked them up at work."

"How'd you know this was my favorite opera?" I said, trying to find my breath. "Thank you."

"You never have to thank me, Sam."

Oh, but I did.

Three years ago, when I had left a loveless marriage, filed for bankruptcy, become a dog walker, and moved back in with my parents in Southern California, I thought things couldn't get any worse. But after tracking down Jean-Luc, my life, even with all of the problems and stress, just got better and better. This wonderful man had managed to open up my heart—fully and completely—to love.

. . . .

It was five minutes after six. Jean-Luc raced into the house and kissed me. "Are you ready, my love? We have to go." His gaze darted to my three-inch heels and moved up my legs. My black fitted dress came below the knee, but, by the way his jaw dropped, I was pretty sure Jean-Luc knew I was most likely wearing sheer black thigh-highs. "*Oauh*, you look incredibly sexy. Maybe we should stay home?"

"No way, José. *Madame Butterfly* is my favorite opera." I placed a twenty-euro bill on the kitchen counter, and yelled up to the kids. "We're leaving now. Order a pizza."

"*D'accord*," said Elvire.

"We'll be back around eleven," said Jean-Luc. "And you better be in bed."

"*D'accord*," the kids answered in unison, followed by giggles.

We locked the front door and headed to the car, knowing full well that when we got home, those sneaky adolescents would have been watching for the lights of our Ford and would race to their rooms, pretending to be asleep. All par for the course. Jean-Luc floored it to the Halle aux Grains Theater in Toulouse, one hand on the wheel, the other inching its way up my thigh. He snapped the top of my nylons. "I like these."

"I know you do."

We drove by the Canal du Midi, passing dozens of bicycle riders, some of them with flowers in their baskets, some with bread under their arms; past the street of the school where I'd taken my French lessons; past a sign for the *préfecture*, where I'd picked up both my driver's license and *carte de séjour*. And a funny thought occurred: I really didn't feel like an immigrant anymore. I'd settled into this life.

Jean-Luc parked the car and, hand in hand, we strolled to a café to grab a quick bite to eat before the show, taking a table by the window. Jean-Luc's hands and eyes didn't leave mine until the waiter brought us the menus.

"*Vin rouge?*" asked Jean-Luc. I nodded and he ordered a demi-carafe.

Two *chèvre chaud* salads and a basket of crusty bread later, and we were seated in the first row of the theater, the stage so close I could almost touch it. Jean-Luc's hand rested on my thigh. He eyed me mischievously. The musicians in the orchestral pit warmed up their instruments, violins and cellos humming. Finally, the lights dimmed and the maestro took his place on the podium. The moment the first soprano's note reached my ears, a lump formed in the back of my throat and shivers ran down my spine, the harmonious melodies pulling on my psyche. I was left breathless, barely able to move during intermission.

Yet, it was the second act I was most looking forward to. Right when Cio-Cio San sang "*Un Bel Dì, Vidremo,*" the opera's most illustrious and haunting aria, the tears I'd been fighting welled up. Never giving up on love, Cio-Cio waited for Pinkerton, her American husband and a United States Naval Officer, to come back to her, faithfully watching for his ship to enter the port every day since he'd left her three years prior. Suzuki, Cio-Cio's maid, gathered flowers to prepare for Pinkerton's arrival.

In the darkness of the theater, tears of happiness glistened on my cheeks, the lyrics taking on new meaning. *Un Bel Dì, Vidremo:* One good day, we shall see. Unlike Cio-Cio, who soon found out her devotion was all for naught, that day had come for me and, thankfully, there would be many more. My arm slid under Jean-Luc's, and our fingers intertwined like vines. I placed my head on his shoulder. "I left you at a train station twenty-three years ago."

"And I'm so very happy when you came back to me you didn't leave."

So was I. I suggested that one day we take a trip to Paris, to retrace the steps we first took together.

"One day," said Jean-Luc. "One day."

Un Bel Dì, Vidremo: One good day, we shall see.

. . . .

Jean-Luc and I had many good—no, great—days together. The romance between us thrived, regardless of the hurdles we had to jump over along the way.

The night before his big leap, I joined Jean-Luc at the table on our deck. "Did you check the company out, to be sure it's safe?" I asked for the thousandth time. Just the thought of Jean-Luc catapulting from the side of a plane from four thousand meters and free-falling at over two hundred kilometers per hour sent shivers of dread down my spine. "I'm not sure I trust what I found out about the company on Google, and not just because it's written in French."

"They're fine, Sam." Jean-Luc placed his elbows on the table and leaned forward. "Didn't you find me on Google? Were you sure I was safe?"

A dash of déjà vu: we'd had this conversation many times before. I spouted off my canned response. "That's different. We already knew one another. We reconnected. You were the one who got away—"

"And, now that you caught me, you're throwing me out of a plane?"

"Yes," I said. "Yes, I am."

In the morning, wispy clouds filled the cornflower blue sky, the temperature a perfect seventy degrees. Jean-Luc woke up at sunrise, raring to go. Max had a big rugby tournament, so he wouldn't be accompanying us.

On the hour's drive to the Gers region, Elvire sat in the backseat listening to her iPod, Jean-Luc guided the car with one hand casually draped over the steering wheel, and I tried not to flip out in the passenger seat. Instead, I focused on the French countryside, no longer reminiscent of a flat suburb of Toulouse, but undulating with cow- and sheep-dotted hills. And I wondered if livestock could cushion his landing.

It was two in the afternoon when our silver Ford rumbled down a dirt road to the jump site. We parked the car, and I took in my surroundings. Ten brightly colored parachutes danced in the sky, a whimsical mobile of reds, blues, bright greens, and yellows. Directly in front of us stood an open barn-like structure, its floors covered in glossy, oversized French movie posters where people suited up—one guy dressed in a cow costume, udder and all. Fifty or so Belgian soldiers wearing army fatigues, and all sporting the same buzz cuts, made their way to a military plane. The place looked well equipped and, more importantly, legit—if I didn't factor in the human cow.

I was feeling better about the whole situation until a parachutist landed in the distant cornfield. Good God almighty, what if an unforgiving corn stalk impaled my husband? Mouth agape, I turned toward Jean-Luc. "You don't have to do this. You can always change your mind."

"Sam, why are you nervous?" he asked. "You're not the one jumping, I am."

Per my usual Lucille Ball–like methods, I masked my paranoia. "There's something I didn't tell you. The kids and I bought the bargain jump and you won't have a parachute." I paused. "You're insured, right?"

A white truck emblazoned with the company's logo screeched onto the lot, a thankful distraction from my off-color joke and Jean-Luc's impending response. A parachutist hopped out of the passenger door and swaggered into the barn as confident as Val Kilmer in *Top Gun*, shooting everybody the thumbs-up with one hand, and picking cornhusks out of his pants with the other.

Jean-Luc nudged me in the ribs. "*Tu vois?* Everything is cool."

Much to my chagrin, we paid the remaining balance for the jump with the money the kids had given.

Elvire and I listened in while Jean-Luc received his debrief, in which a stocky instructor manhandled my husband's body into the three positions one assumes during a tandem jump, a strange *kama sutra* of sorts. Five minutes later, Jean-Luc's back and thighs were encased in a harness. I broke out my camera with a quivering smile when Jean-Luc strutted toward the red and gray prop plane.

After a rumble and a roar, the plane disappeared into the horizon. Fifteen stress-filled minutes later, I caught a glimpse of the first jumper, a tiny dot no larger than an ant, followed by another minuscule blip, then another. Elvire pointed. "There he is. There's Papa. I see the parachute. It's the red one."

Every worry I'd had washed away.

The first of the parachutists, a woman, landed gracefully with her tandem partner, as did the second, also a woman. Jean-Luc's red parachute made its approach. Instead of landing on his feet, he and his partner skidded across the ground like a human train—Jean-Luc the engine, his instructor the caboose. Jean-Luc's face wore an odd expression. He stood up and walked toward Elvire and me, holding his rear.

"Are you okay?" I called out.

"I'm fine."

"What happened?" asked Elvire, her eyes round with concern.

Jean-Luc burst into laughter, turned, and wiggled his behind. "My pants split open!"

I was thankful he'd worn boxers and hadn't flown commando.

Once he stopped dancing around for his amused audience, Elvire and I barraged him with one question after another: "Did you like it? Was it worth it? Were you scared?"

"*Alors*, we were up in the air and they announced we would jump in two minutes. They opened the door and I could barely breathe. My instructor stood behind me, holding onto the sides of the plane. My feet dangled over the edge, the wind whipping my feet. I was like a puppet hanging there. And then we were in the free fall. Adrenaline took over…"

Yep. He liked it. And this gift was worth every last darn *centime*. Jean-Luc's love, his warm laughter, had tipped into balance the anxieties I'd had about jumping into a new life, and the nagging voice in my head had begun to change its tune from "I can't do this. I'm going to die!" to "I'll really regret this if I don't give it a try." When push came to shove, I realized a big part of me was fearless. If there was anything I'd learned on this trajectory we call life—it's that sometimes you just have to take a leap. Well, that, and when parachuting, it might be a good idea to pack a second pair of pants.

Jean-Luc's hand clasped mine.

I mumbled, "And now you know exactly how I felt when I landed in France."

JEAN-LUC'S FLAMBÉED PASTIS SHRIMP

Prep time: 15 minutes

Cook time: 10 minutes

Serves: 4 to 6

Great for: a dinner party or a healthy summer meal

Wine suggestion: fruity rosé like Bandol or Vin des Sables de Camargue

- 3 to 4 cloves garlic, minced
- 5 small shallots, peeled and finely chopped
- 2-inch piece fresh ginger root, peeled and finely chopped
- 24 to 48 uncooked shrimp, skin on (6 to 8 per person)
- ¼ cup Pastis*
- ¼ cup flat parsley, chopped, for garnish
- 1 lime, sliced in 4 wedges, for garnish
- Salt and freshly ground black pepper, to taste

In a large skillet, warm a dash of olive oil over medium-high heat. Add the garlic, shallots, and ginger, cooking until softened and fragrant. Stir in the shrimp, cooking until they begin to turn pink. Add the Pastis and light it with a match. Carefully, shake the pan gently, tossing the shrimp. Once the flame has settled down (if it doesn't, snuff it out with the cover of large pot), return the pan to low heat.**

Season with salt and pepper, garnish with parsley, and serve warm with steamed rice, mango-avocado salsa (p. 244), and wedges of lime.

*   *Can't get your hands on Pastis, the anise-flavored liqueur? You can always use tequila, rum, absinthe, ouzo, or Cognac as a tasty substitution.*

** *Flambé at your own risk—please be careful!*

MANGO-AVOCADO SALSA

Prep time: 20 minutes

Cook time: 30 minutes (to chill in refrigerator)

Serves: 4 to 6

Great for: summer picnic or on the side of seafood dishes like shrimp

- 2 avocados, peeled and diced
- 2 tomatoes, diced
- ¼ red onion, finely minced
- 1 mango, diced
- 1 handful flat parsley or cilantro, finely chopped
- ½ jalapeño pepper, seeded and minced
- 1 lime, juiced
- Freshly ground black pepper, to taste

Mix all the ingredients in a bowl. Chill in the refrigerator for about half an hour, or until ready to serve. Serve with tortilla chips or as an accompaniment to a seafood dish like Jean-Luc's Flambéed Pastis Shrimp (p. 243).

MOELLEUX AU CHOCOLAT
WITH A CŒUR FONDANT

Prep time: 15 minutes

Cook time: 10 to 12 minutes

Serves: 6 to 8

Great for: an easy and delicious dessert

Wine suggestion: sparkling Chenin Blanc

- 1 (200-gram) bar dark chocolate (70 percent cocoa)
- 1 stick unsalted butter, plus extra for greasing ramekins
- 4 eggs
- 1 pinch ground cinnamon
- 1 pinch salt
- ⅔ cup brown sugar
- ½ cup all-purpose flour, plus extra for coating ramekins

Preheat oven to 350°F. Butter and flour 8 four-inch ramekins. Break the chocolate into small pieces, and melt in the microwave at 20 or 30 percent power for 30 seconds. Stir, and repeat, continuing until the chocolate is smooth. Melt the butter in the microwave the same way.

In a large mixing bowl, beat the eggs, cinnamon, salt, and sugar with a whisk. Add the melted butter, and whisk again. Little by little, add the flour, whisking into the mixture. Finally, add the melted chocolate, mixing well. The color of the batter should be chocolate brown. Pour the mixture into the ramekins. Bake for 10 to 12 minutes, or until the cakes are puffed up; they may still look a little uncooked, but they won't be flat. Cool for at least 2 minutes before loosening the cakes out of the ramekin. Serve with vanilla ice cream and cherry compote (p. 298), fresh raspberries and a dollop of whipped cream, or crème anglaise.

SAUTÉED ROSEMARY POTATOES

Prep time: 15 minutes

Cook time: 25 minutes

Serves: 4

Great for: side dish for meat, chicken, or fish

- 4 tablespoons extra virgin olive oil
- 8 medium-sized red or gold potatoes, diced into ½-inch cubes (1 cup per person)
- 3 sprigs fresh rosemary, needles removed and stem discarded*
- 3 to 4 pinches *fleur de sel*, kosher, or sea salt
- Freshly ground black pepper, to taste

Heat the oil in a Dutch oven or deep, large pan on high heat. Add the potatoes and stir. Cook for 10 minutes, then turn the heat down to medium-low. Add the rosemary and salt, tossing all ingredients together. Cook for 20 to 30 minutes until the potatoes are golden brown on the outside, tossing occasionally. Season with salt and pepper.

* *If you can't find fresh rosemary or don't have it on hand, use dried rosemary or a few pinches of herbes de Provence or thyme.*

ELVIRE'S *GÂTEAU AU YAOURT* (YOGURT CAKE)

Prep time: 15 minutes
Cook time: 30 to 35 minutes
Serves: 6 to 8
Great for: breakfast or a snack

- ¾ cup plain or Greek yogurt
- ¾ cup sugar
- 1¼ cups all-purpose flour, sifted
- ¼ cup canola oil
- 1 teaspoon baking power
- ½ teaspoon salt
- 1 teaspoon vanilla extract
- 2 large eggs
- 1 lemon, juiced
- 1 lemon zest, finely chopped
- 1 cup strawberries, sliced

Preheat oven to 375°F. Using an electric mixer, combine all ingredients in a large mixing bowl, mixing until smooth. Bake in a lightly oiled loaf pan for 30 to 35 minutes. Let cool. Serve with fresh, sliced strawberries.

Ingredient Five

LOVE

STEPMOTHER'S DAY

I'D DECIDED THAT STEPMOTHERS GET the shaft. So, I came up with a new holiday: Stepmother's Day, which takes place on the Sunday in between the French and American motherly-love events. I picked the day because I didn't want to upset the kids by making them feel as if I were competing with the memory of their mother. But I was doing all the things mothers do. Surely I deserved one tiny moment of appreciation. Flowers? Bring them on! A day off from cleaning? Yes, please.

With three miscarriages behind me, I needed this. And I was pretty sure Jean-Luc and the kids didn't realize that I wasn't quite over the pain of three consecutive losses. Because how could I be? The sadness just crept up unexpectedly. I should have received an Academy Award, one that I'd accept with a fake smile plastered across my face. I was happy, yes, but I always found myself questioning what could have been. Don't get me wrong; I wasn't needy. But my inner strength, that woman who said everything was going to be fine, could only take me so far. And grief was something that took time to come to grips with. I had three scars on my heart. But they could be healed. *Give me one day. Just one day,* I prayed.

So I wasn't opaque, and I didn't hide all of my feelings as I'd done when I first moved to France. I told my family exactly what I wanted, needed, dropping not-so-subtle hints here and there. Because when I looked at Max, Elvire, and Jean-Luc, sometimes these losses ripped me to the core. Max and Elvire were such beautiful kids—smart, too. What would the three babies I'd lost have looked like? Me? Him? Her?

"Don't forget. Tomorrow is Stepmother's Day," I said.

I've never understood why women get so angry when their significant other forgets a big event like a birthday or an anniversary—why not just remind them? Jean-Luc might have been a rocket scientist, but he was also a bit absentminded, forgetting where he put his keys and phone. With me around, he'd *always* remember a significant event.

"How could we forget when you've been reminding us for the past month?" said Jean-Luc. He rolled his eyes. "It isn't even a real holiday."

"Yes, it is," I said. "It's 100 percent real. And it's extremely important to me."

In the morning, I was in the kitchen having my coffee. There were no flowers, there was nothing. And I was seething. But, before my mind could spiral into deep depression, I heard Jean-Luc and the kids giggling in the dining/living room. "What's going on in there?" I asked.

"Happy Stepmother's Day!" they yelled, racing up to me with a gift—an orchid in a cute wooden box with a "*Bonne Fête Belle Maman*" sign in the shape of a daisy. *Belle Maman* was stepmom in French. This made me all kinds of happy. I knew I'd forced the fake holiday on them, but it was nice of them to pull through. I didn't cry until they handed me a small puzzle. Once I finally managed to piece it together, I flipped it over, and in Elvire's creative marker writing, the card read: "*Nous t'aimons, nous t'aimerons toujours car tu seras gravée dans nos cœurs et aussi car tu es la meilleure. Gros bisous, Max, Elvire, et Bella.*"

We love you, we will always love you because you will be engraved in our hearts and also because you are the best. Big kisses, Max, Elvire, and Bella.

"Thank you. This is the sweetest holiday *ever*," I said. "Tonight, I'm making a strawberry apple crumble for dessert."

This statement was followed by hugs—real, hard loving hugs.

Jean-Luc kissed me on the forehead. "Go relax," he said.

"Thank you," I said. "It…it…it means the world to me," I said with a stutter, so touched.

"I know."

As a family, we normally cleaned on Sundays. The kids did the upstairs and their bathroom. Jean-Luc vacuumed and mopped (he didn't like the way I did it, so I wasn't going to change my wily ways). And I tackled all the surfaces in the kitchen, our room, and the living room, as well as the never-ending piles of laundry.

I was so emotional by this point, I could only think of one thing to say. "Really? I don't have to clean today?"

"No," he said. "Elvire will be doing your portion."

"*Mais,* Papaaaaaaaaa," said Elvire.

I ignored her. "Honey," I said, turning to Jean-Luc, "Sometimes I act like I'm stronger than I really am."

"Sam, I know. And it's because you have a heart."

. . . .

Part of living a passionate life together means sharing one another's passions. In my case, this meant scuba diving in the summer and skiing in the winter, two sports that made my heart race with fear, two sports the kids and Jean-Luc enjoyed immensely, two sports I was completely miserable at. But a family that plays together stays together, and I set a goal to try to kick my nerves to the curb and to learn how to breathe—extremely important when it came to diving.

In late May, we headed to the Costa Brava region of Spain for the biannual scuba trip with Jean-Luc's work group. I'd say we went to Spain—but the Catalans are very proud to be Catalan (they even have their own flag), and so our destination was Catalonia.

On the three-hour drive, I had to smile. I loved this aspect of French life. When I lived in Chicago, I could visit Lake Geneva, the Indiana dunes, the Michigan beaches, or go apple picking in the fall. But in southwestern France, I could visit another country.

We were staying at a "camping" site, consisting of plots of land for camping cars and tents, as well as bungalows, which was what Jean-Luc had booked for us. "Camping" sites in France and Spain came complete with restaurants, swimming pools, and entertainment. This location also had a dive center and an aviary filled with tropical birds.

Set beside a pond, dotted with grass umbrellas, our accommodations were adorable. The bungalow had a front porch, a small kitchen/living room, and three bedrooms. The kids were thrilled to have their own rooms.

Many familiar faces from the Porquerolles trip, as well as a couple of new ones, surrounded us. But I was too nervous to talk to anybody—mostly because it was time for me to fling myself backwards off the side of the Zodiac into the Mediterranean. Admittedly, this experience was quite fun, much like doing a somersault underwater. The moment I emerged, I shot Jean-Luc the okay sign. So far, so good. We swam about sixty feet to the area the boat captain had pointed out, where the depth of the water was around six meters, perfect for a discovery dive. Once there, Jean-Luc stopped and removed the regulator from his mouth. "Ready to descend?" he asked.

Swimming at the surface with a twenty-pound bottle of air strapped to his back was child's play for Jean-Luc, but I wasn't used to this kind of effort, especially in a rough sea. Instead of catching my breath, I held it in, the water churning like my fear. Finally, I sucked in a mouthful of air and took the regulator out of my mouth. "Aren't you going to give me any instruction?" I asked, panting.

"You've done this once before."

"Two years ago," I said, remembering my first *baptême de plongée* (introductory dive) when Jean-Luc took the kids and me to Spain for a long weekend. My instructor was a fiery, redheaded Catalan woman whose wet suit was equipped with red horns on the hood and a pitchfork tail on her rear. I didn't hate the experience. But I didn't really love it. "She didn't speak one word of English," I continued. "What if I missed something important? I mean, I could run out of air and die or get compression sickness."

"Don't be ridiculous. Put the regulator back in your mouth," said Jean-Luc. "Just breathe. You'll be fine."

"I can't do this."

"You can," he said.

But I couldn't. Not when I was close to hyperventilating. Fins between my legs, I swam back to the Zodiac, Jean-Luc in tow. After removing my weights and dive vest, the captain and another diver hoisted me up. The kids raised their eyebrows. I knew what they were thinking: *loser*. Disappointment set in. I had dreams of diving in tropical waters, sea turtles and manta rays surrounding us, my family by my side. Which was the reason I wasn't going to give up.

Before the second outing, a simple beach dive at a natural park called Anse de Paulilles, located in the beautiful department of Languedoc-Roussillon-Midi-Pyrénées in the Pyrénées-Oriental region, almost eased my frazzled scuba-diving nerves.

The drive along the sea was spectacular. Lush vineyards, which produced the wonderful white and rosé wines named after the town of the same name, Collioure AOC (*Apellation d'Origine Contrôlée*), and *châteaus* on one side, and the glistening sea, rocky cliffs, and sandy and pebbled beaches beckoned to us on the other side. To the south was Banyuls sur Mer, known for its fortified AOC dessert wines and also its sweet and mellow vinegar. A mere twenty miles from the Spanish border, we were in Catalan country, the weather as sunny and warm as the people.

The park of Anse de Paulilles was beautiful, the fern-bordered path taking us through beautiful Mediterranean gardens and exotic vegetation, through forests of pine, olive trees, and a pasture with two adorable bushy-eared donkeys. Apparently, the land used to be owned by a former dynamite factory, but it had been sold to the *Conservatoire du Littoral* so that the natural terrain of seventeen hectares would be protected against real estate developers. The buildings of the former dynamite factory now housed a museum on the heritage of traditional Catalan boat repair. All of this—the museum, the nature trails, and beach—was free to the public.

One of the dive masters had set up the day for the families of the club's divers, and he'd coordinated a truck to take our equipment down to the small, rocky beach. Which was a relief, seeing how heavy the equipment was, especially the air bottle, and we had to walk about a mile. Today, there were mostly little kids doing their *baptême de plongée*, and a giant baby: me. Jean-Luc and I suited up and made our way down to the shoreline.

"Ready?" he asked.

"As I'll ever be."

We swam for a few minutes, and I was able to acclimate myself before the descent. Jean-Luc guided me under water, and after a few moments, my nerves settled, and I was no longer sucking in air like a Dyson vacuum cleaner set on high. My breath became more stable, and I was feeling at ease. Everything was going swimmingly until Jean-Luc pointed out the small octopus, and pushed me toward it, face-forward—as if I'd miss this creature with bulbous yellow eyes and suction-cup-encrusted tentacles scurrying around in the sand. My body flailed. Jean-Luc led me to the surface.

"Did you see the octopus?" he asked.

"How could I have missed it?" I replied. "When you're pushing my face into it?"

Jean-Luc laughed.

To me, this wasn't funny. "I think I want to take the diving course in the pool."

Baby steps. Baby steps. Baby steps.

"Good idea," said Jean-Luc.

"Wait. Who is the instructor?" I asked.

"I am."

Uh-oh.

After all the home renovation projects we'd done together, I wasn't looking forward to Jean-Luc bossing me around. Oh, the things we do for love.

25

GET ME TO
THE CHURCH ON TIME

I SABELLE AND RICHARD WERE GETTING married this summer at their home in Provence. Max and Elvire would stay with us at their house for a few days, so they could spend some time with the Vérant side of the family, playing with their cousins and swimming in the pool, not to mention participating in the very competitive ping-pong tournaments, before heading to Meme's.

André and the rest of the Vérant siblings, along with Jean-Luc, had finally convinced Jean-Luc's mother to move into the *maison de retraite*, the retirement home, in La Ciotat. André simply couldn't take care of Marcelle anymore.

I understood Marcelle's initial fear. One day, one of my neighbors, a woman about the same age as Marcelle, knocked on my door. It was raining out, and she stood on my front stoop shivering. So was her little dog, a Yorkie.

"*Je peux entrer?*" she asked. Can I come in?

I was a bit worried about what Bella would do to her Yorkie, but of course I said, "*Oui, oui, oui, entrez.*"

The old woman was breathless. I heard words like "my son" and "my daughter," and "I don't want to go." Meanwhile, I'd thought she'd locked herself out of her house. So, I invited her inside, sat her down at the dining room table, and offered her a cup of coffee and some biscuits. I asked her if we could call somebody. The woman shook her head no. Elvire came downstairs. I was supposed to take her shopping. I shrugged, my posture letting her know that I didn't know what to do. An hour later, the woman hadn't moved. Elvire was getting impatient. I asked the woman if I could walk her home. Hesitantly, she agreed.

The front door of her town house was wide open. She hadn't been locked out after all. I escorted her in and went back home. Elvire was happy when I returned and said, "*On y va.*" While Elvire and I were pulling out of our parking spot, I saw the woman knocking on my neighbor's door. Sylvie let her in. Later that day, I found out from Sylvie that the woman was hiding from her children; she didn't want to be sent to a retirement home. She didn't want to leave the home she knew, her dog, or her cat.

I thought of my grandmother, Nanny. She lived in Virginia with my Aunt Laura. Although her health wasn't the greatest, due to emphysema, she got around just fine. She still played bridge with her friends and, when she wasn't winded, the occasional golf game. More like Nanny, this woman obviously wasn't having any major health issues that I knew of, like Jean-Luc's mother. Bedridden or in a wheelchair, Marcelle couldn't move; she definitely needed professional care to shower, to go to the bathroom, and more. But surely this woman's family could care for her? Perhaps they just didn't want to. I tried checking on her a few days later, but nobody answered the door.

The kids, Jean-Luc, and I didn't know what to expect at the *maison de retraite* when we visited Marcelle. At first, it was a strange experience. More like a hospital, the place wasn't exactly homey. We sauntered into the main room, followed by the eyes of every inhabitant, their curious faces marked with wonder, some with jealousy: *Who are they here for? Are they here for me?*

Marcelle was sitting at a table with André. She saw us first. "*My* family!" she said with a cackle.

Seems there was some competition at the nursing home.

As we exchanged *la bise*, Marcelle eyed me. "What's your name again? MMA?"

MMA was the acronym for a health insurance agency.

"*Non, maman,* this is Samantha, my wife," said Jean-Luc.

"Oh, yes! I remember her now!" She grabbed my hand, squeezing it tightly.

Jean-Luc's father shook his head. "She's doing better here, but sometimes she still forgets things."

"I forget nothing," said Marcelle.

The kids shifted in their seats.

Marcelle commandeered a packet of Gauloise cigarettes from her wheelchair and started to count them. A woman scurried up behind her. "You can't smoke in here," she said, her voice a high-pitched whine. It was like she was the nursing home tattletale.

"I'm not smoking in here," said Marcelle with a perfunctory nod. "We're going outside."

André wheeled Marcelle toward the doors, leading to the outside terrace, and we followed. Marcelle muttered under her breath, "I don't like that woman. I know she stole one of my cigarettes. I only have three left. And I had four."

Once we were seated at an outside table, André reached into the front pocket of his plaid shirt, whipped out a pack of cigarettes, and handed her one. "You're only allowed five a day, remember that."

Both of Jean-Luc's parents had quit smoking for many years, but had recently picked up the habit again. Isabelle, Muriel, and Michel also smoked. Jean-Luc had never taken one puff in his life.

"I know," said Marcelle.

"Maman," said Jean-Luc. "Do you like it here?"

"I do," she said. "Papa comes to visit with me every day. The food is wonderful. And they give me snacks just like when I was a little girl." She paused. "The only thing I don't like here is that old fart, the one who stole one of my cigarettes." She pointed. "Oh, look, there's the cat. He lives here. Samantha, can you fetch him?"

And so I did, placing the fuzzy creature in her lap. Marcelle smiled. "I love it here. There's less stress on my husband, too. I was hard to take care of."

André's posture straightened and his eyes brightened. Save for the fact it was hard seeing a wife, parent, or grandparent in this situation, this home was the best thing for Marcelle. Jean-Luc blew out a sigh of relief.

. . . .

Like Jean-Luc and me, Isabelle and Richard had a garden wedding at their home catered by *un traiteur*, the party preceded by a formal civil ceremony at the *Mairie* in La Ciotat. Isabelle wore a silver and black dress and was glowing with happiness. Richard looked dapper, dressed to the nines in a designer suit. Probably French, right? André was a fiercely proud Papa. Jean-Luc and the kids were happy, too.

I understood the customs now. Yes, we waited, sometimes awkwardly, until all the guests arrived before making a beeline to the *apéro* bar. Yes, we swapped *la bise* with everybody, no matter if there were over one hundred people in attendance at a party. Yes, we danced until five in the morning. This was the way of the French. And, yes, I was even making all those ridiculous mouth sounds I used to make fun off—the raspberry farts, the breathless *oui*s, the *pffftp*s, and the *paf, paf, paf*s!

I still may have pronounced *un pull* (sweater) like *une poule* (chicken), which confused the woman at the local clothing boutique, but, even with the curveballs life had thrown at us, I was glowing in the independent phase of this Frenchified life. Which made the marriage of Isabelle and Richard all the more fun.

At one point, I was expecting Richard to belt out one of his Elvis songs. He didn't, but that didn't put a damper on the evening. Especially when I considered Jean-Luc's dancing. The man didn't leave the floor until well after three a.m., the kids and me by his side. Elvire shot me a glance at one point. "*Regarde Papa. Je suis morte de rire.*"

Look at Papa. I'm dying of laughter.

"Oh, he's just getting into it," I said. "But he'll never compete with our kitchen dancing."

"Um," said Elvire, "he's rolling his shoulders. And look at his face! It's so intense."

"He was young once, too."

"I don't even want to imagine it. Look at him now!"

Jean-Luc was undulating like a snake, legs spread, knees dipping. He was surrounded by three of Isabelle's friends, busting the moves of all moves. As much as I loved his enthusiasm, I couldn't contain my laughter. "I love your dad," I said.

Elvire and I lost it, almost falling down to the ground.

It was a beautiful night in the garden under the stars. I had to give props to Isabelle. She'd been completely creative. Over dinner, she'd hidden a paper chef's hat under one of the place mats at every table. Whoever had the hat had to carve the main course, a *gigôt d'agneau* (leg of lamb), tableside. Every detail was perfect—from the table decorations she'd made herself, to the floral arrangements. Everything. Richard, my full-fledged and wonderful brother-in-law, was in charge of the wine. Let's just say that it was beyond fantastic.

The following day, we were in the pool waiting for the *méchoui* (a full grilled lamb stuffed with couscous), a traditional meal in Provence after a marriage, when I noticed it skimming the waters: a blue *libellule* the size of my fist. I raised my arms into a touchdown position. The dragonfly darted over my head, and then performed a gravity-defying act over the pool. They may not have had humming-birds in France, but that didn't stop me from appreciating the tiny, beautiful things in life. I raised my arms again. Repeat.

"What are you doing, *Americaine*?" asked Richard.

I pointed to the dragonfly. "Look! It's so beautiful. A *libellule*."

His eyes crinkled with mischievous delight. "Your French has gotten worse."

Jean-Luc's sister, Muriel, poked him in the ribs. "No! It's much better! She's almost fluent. Do you remember the first time she came to the house? She didn't understand a thing. It was impossible to communicate with her."

"She still doesn't understand anything," said Richard, bumping my hip with his.

The dragonfly buzzed Richard's head.

"*Tu vois*," I said, shaking my finger. You see? "Even the dragonfly doesn't agree with you."

While my French may have gotten better, sometimes my accent still got in the way. I offered to help the man tending the *méchoui*. He was short and tan, his skin scorched by the sun, and he wore white chef's pants, a black T-shirt, and a checked chef's apron. I'd never seen a barbecue like this before. He turned the lamb on the iron spit by hand, roasting the meat until perfectly golden, the juices dripping into a tray.

"Do you mind if I take a few pictures?" I asked, trying to make up my mind if this tradition, which came from North Africa, was beautiful or barbaric. "I like sharing my French life with my family."

His jaw dropped in shock. "You've never seen a *méchoui*?"

"Nope."

"Go get your camera. Share, share, share! This is one of the best meals in the south of France. Soon, I'll be stuffing the lamb with couscous." He brought his fingers to his lips, blowing a kiss. "Delicious."

After I took a few shots, Gustave handed me a platter with small brown blobs on it. Instead of offering my family members the kidneys (*les reins*), I offered them queens (*les reines*) and reindeer (*les rennes*) and received many confused looks. Yes, all these words had slight pronunciation differences that mattered, but thankfully, my French *faux pas* didn't have a sexual innuendo attached.

Jean-Luc called everybody to the table. As I sat, he kissed my shoulder. "Love you," he said.

"*Je t'aime, aussi*, honey," I replied.

Richard eyed me wickedly as he poured me a glass of rosé. "*Alors, Americaine*, what do you call Jean-Luc? Besides 'oney?" (The whole family made fun of me when I called Jean-Luc honey. They repeated it over and over again. 'Oney! 'Oney! Seriously, I was the one who should be making fun of them, considering the French don't pronounce their Hs.)

With all the home renovations we'd been doing, only one word had come to mind: hammer. "*Quelque fois, je l'appelle le marteau-piqueur.*" Whoops.

I didn't say "hammer," like I'd meant to, which was *marteau*. I'd said "jackhammer," which had just as strong a sexual connotation as in English. There was only one thing to do before the familial hazing continued: tease myself and laugh right along with them. I wrapped my arm around Jean-Luc and said, "*Mon bonobo.*"

As the laughter died down, I thought back on all the moments I'd experienced in France, especially when the going got tough, and I just had to giggle. My French life wasn't so different than my former life after all. The food may have been different, the landscape may have been different, and some of the customs may have been different, but the love I had for this home and my family wasn't so different at all.

"What's so funny, *Americaine?*" asked Richard.

"Some days are so perfect, I just have to laugh."

Richard raised his glass. "*Tchin-tchin.*"

26

FRIENDSHIP IS ALWAYS IN SEASON

STRAWBERRIES—SPECIFICALLY THE SWEET, LITTLE plump delights known as *gariguettes*, a small, tasty, and expensive hybrid cultivated in the south of France—were in season. We'd come back home from the market with two full *barquettes* of the sweet and scarlet beauties. I cut off the stems, helping Jean-Luc make his delectable strawberry soup—a blended concoction made with *crème fraîche*, strawberries, sugar, and maybe a little vanilla extract and/or rum.

"You know," said Jean-Luc as he pulled the food processor out of the cabinet. "You're not supposed to *faire la bise* with our vegetable vendor."

"Well, we hadn't seen him a while," I said. "He didn't seem to mind. Plus, he gave us two free avocados, parsley, and a couple cloves of garlic."

"Guess he likes you," said Jean-Luc.

"He likes us, *mon petit chou*. You two were chatting up a storm. I kept hearing the word pigeon."

"He used to raise pigeons. Then, he got divorced. His wife hated the birds. Now, he's remarried."

"Are you sure he's French?"

"Why?"

"Well, that's a lot of information to share."

Jean-Luc laughed. "Do you remember that English couple I

told you about? Nicola and Martin? They just moved here from Singapore? Their son, Aidan, plays on Max's rugby team?"

I nodded.

"I was thinking to invite them over for dinner. They live in Cugnaux and I don't think they know too many people. They have another son Elvire's age."

"*Pourquoi pas?*" I said. Why not?

We'd recently finished our kitchen renovation, which also included putting a new tiled floor in the foyer and installing new pine floors in the living room. I ran my hand over the countertops and cabinets that Jean-Luc and I had installed last month, proud of our accomplishment. We'd demolished the old kitchen, built sometime in the 1970s, only to find a ten-by-three cement base we'd had to jackhammer down to lay the new pale gray ceramic tiles. We'd constructed every single cabinet by hand, and then hung them on the freshly painted gray walls.

Although frustrating at times, the backbreaking effort was definitely worth it in the end; the kitchen is my favorite room in the house. It's where I sing and dance while cooking with Elvire, where I happily prepare Max his new favorite meal, an American breakfast of homemade hash browns and cheesy scrambled eggs, and where Jean-Luc and I discuss future plans and dreams over a glass of wine, the places we'd like to see, the adventures we'd like to experience.

I was proud of our endeavor—and the fact Jean-Luc and I didn't kill one another during the process. *Bricolage* meant construction or creation. Just call me Bricowoman—although we did have a few issues. When we cut the work surface for the sink and stove, it got chipped. Rather than let that get us down, we got creative and bought small tiles to cover up the damage. And I may have put together the cabinet for the sink wrong—the interior bar askew. And Jean-Luc may have accidently drilled two holes straight through to the living room. But in the end, everything worked out. We definitely had a one-of-a-kind kitchen. Oh, and joy to the world, I had an ample amount of cabinet space for my expanding collection of kitchen tools.

"Should I make something French? Or something English?"
I asked.

Jean-Luc grimaced. Like most Frenchmen, when he thought
of British food, Jean-Luc thought of boiled meats, jellies, greasy
fish and chips, and sausages came to mind. In 2005, French presi-
dent Jacques Chirac had delivered his infamous put-down: "You
can't trust people whose cuisine is so bad."

Even I'd been subjected to the food snobbery of the French, like
when every person I'd ever met asked me if I cooked American. And
I was like, American? What's that? Hamburgers and hot dogs? Yes,
I cooked these meals, but give me some credit. So did the French!
While I avoided bringing up tuna noodle casserole or cooking it
again, I politely explained that America—land of the free, home
of the brave—was a melting pot, infused with Spanish, Mexican,
Cuban, Indian, Italian, Polish, Greek, Chinese, Korean, French—the
cuisine of basically every country on this beautiful planet of ours. I'd
end my monologue with, "Unless I'm hosting a dinner party, I cook
simple meals: quiches, lamb, chicken, spaghetti, fajitas…"

Once this information was processed, the typical response was:
"*Alors, tu prépares les repas familiaux, comme nous.*"

Yes, I prepare family meals, just like you.

Jean-Luc texted Martin and invited his family over, also asking
if there were any dietary restrictions. Nicola offered to bring dessert.

"I hope she doesn't bring a dry pudding," said Jean-Luc.

"Honey, when my family lived in London, the food was amazing."

My parents had moved to Hampstead in 1989 while I was attending Syracuse University. That was the summer Tracey and I decided
to travel Europe while we had the opportunity. This was the summer
I'd met Jean-Luc.

"I don't believe you," said Jean-Luc.

"You're being impossibly French."

And he was. Because Nicola brought over the most delicious
strawberry torte we'd ever tasted. From the *apéro*—chips for the kids
and an artichoke-parmesan dip for all, served with bread, and small

bites of olives and tomatoes, to dinner, a *pot-au-feu*, to that wonderful, flaky strawberry dessert—everything flowed, even the conversation. At one point, I swore Elvire was flirting with Prentice, Nicola
and Martin's older son. She flipped her beautiful, auburn hair over
her shoulder and then she giggled. Also, she was trying her best to
speak English. Tall, with dark hair, big blue eyes, and a cute accent,
Prentice was a teenage girl's dreamboat.

I smiled to myself, remembering what it was like to be her age.
Then, I turned to Nicola. "Your boys go to the International School
in Toulouse, right?" She nodded. "Do they like it here?"

"It's been a big change for them. They really miss their friends
in Singapore."

"What about you? Are you having a difficult time? It's a bit of a
struggle at first, yes?"

"It's been quite the challenge." Nicola seemed nervous and out
of sorts. Just like I had been in the beginning. I told her about
my difficulties integrating, especially those first few months. She
nodded, hanging on to my every word. We were one. She knew I
"got" her. "I was worried that nobody in Cugnaux spoke English
because we don't speak French," she said. "Thank you so much for
inviting us over."

I nodded with understanding. When your world is thrown off
kilter, family and friendships meant more.

I raised my glass. "Here's to our families and to new friends. And
I have tons of people to introduce you to! There's Kathy, another
American the next town over. She makes an amazing *tian Provençal*!
I met her through my first French friend, Caro, who also lives in
Cugnaux. She used to be married to an American and speaks
English. Plus, there's the Toulouse Les Chicks. We just started a
book club. You should come to the next meeting."

In fact, so many people had come into my friendship mix, I had
more friends than I knew what to do with. There was Melissa, an
American who had moved here from Star City in Russia with her
aerospace husband; Zoe, a yoga teacher from Australia; Lindsey, a

veterinarian from Canada; Kristin, a teacher from South Dakota; Charley from England; and two other French girlfriends—Céline, a teacher in Toulouse, and Elodie, an attorney. I'd joked that we should start a gang and come up with some kind of initiation. Instead, we started a book club—really more of an excuse to get together and drink wine.

"I'd love to go," said Nicola.

"Great! Our next get-together is in two weeks. We meet on Sundays, so we can head into Toulouse together. Plus, I'm having lunch with Kathy and Caro next week. I'm hosting it. So, you'll definitely have to come to that, too."

The worry vanished from Nicola's kind face, her eyes brightened, and she blew out a sigh of relief.

. . . .

By the time August rolled around, my manuscript was ready for the world. It had been polished, fine-tuned, and polished again. I'd been a writing workhorse. Jay connected me to an agent, telling me to offer her an exclusive. I wasn't so sure about that. I'd always been told to query widely. But he knew the business. And I did not. So, I just hoped. And I prayed. And I opened up a bottle of wine. The agent emailed me back the day I queried her. She was looking forward to the read.

This is the one! This is the one! She's going to join team Seabiscuit!

I liked to call myself Seabiscuit, after the little horse that proved all the naysayers wrong when he finally found people who believed in him and became a champion. Like Seabiscuit, I had my team. Max noticed my excitement. "Did you sell your book?"

"No, not yet. But there is a chance."

"Am I in it?"

"Of course. It's a memoir."

"You used my name?" he asked, and I nodded. "I think I should get paid. Or you can't mention me."

I took a sip of wine. "Fine, how much?"

"Two hundred euros."

I raised a brow, took another sip of wine. I was being strong-armed by a twelve-year-old. Admittedly, I found it hilarious. I laughed. "Fine."

"I'll be right back with the contract."

Max ran upstairs. A few minutes later, he thrust a paper in my hands. There was one line written on it, reading that I, Samantha Vérant, would pay Maxence Vérant two hundred euros if my book was published, followed by a bunch of squiggly marks, filling the page, and a place for both of us to sign. He handed me a pen. "Here."

From then on, I had nothing to do but wait. So, while I was waiting, I decided to revise my middle-grade novel, *King of the Mutants*, the story about a sideshow attraction on the search for his roots and his identity. I believed in this work too. Like my memoir, it held a piece of my heart. And, in a funny way, I related to the main character, Maverick. All those alienating experiences I'd had when I first moved to France helped me to shape the story.

. . . .

After a year of lessons in the pool with a drill sergeant (Jean-Luc) as my instructor, I was ready for my level one scuba certification. Over the winter, I'd tackled my fear of skiing and was now doing blue runs with the family. If I could conquer a mountain, certainly, a little water wouldn't hurt me. But when we loaded up the car for Cap d'Agde on the Mediterranean coast, I was expecting calm waters, warm weather, and an underwater adventure, not a Navy Seal exercise.

The first dive was brutal. Swimming fifteen feet to the buoy took great effort and, thanks to the twenty-pound lead baby, other-wise known as the air bottle, strapped to my back, I was completely winded. The water was freezing, and I wore a surf shorty under my seven-millimeter wet suit. And I was still cold. A spark of panic set in as the waves tossed me around like a shark torturing a baby seal before he ate it. I tried to swim and grip a rope hanging off the side of the boat, thinking, *I can't breathe. I'm going to die. What am I doing? This is supposed to be fun; it isn't. It's torture! Kill me now!*

But I wasn't going to let fear hold me back. Not this time.

Families that play together…stay together. Think positive thoughts. Such as a dream trip to the Seychelles or the Maldives.

This time I knew what to do. I took slow, purposeful breaths to calm my nerves before the descent. We performed all level-one tasks—removing our masks, motioning for a loss of air and supplying another diver with the "octopus" (spare regulator), checking air levels, and stability exercises, the most important being the ascent. The first dive lasted about twenty-five minutes. I wasn't wearing gloves; my hands were blocks of ice. Apparently, I was a masochist. But, after three more dives, one of which had zero visibility and required us to use a string to guide us, I was a masochist who was now level one certified.

I faced my fears, and through diving I finally learned how to breathe.

27

LIFE IS A BOWL OF CHERRIES, EVEN WHEN THERE ARE PITS

WONDERFUL THINGS WERE HAPPENING AT every turn, but bad news hits you when you least expect it. Jean-Luc's mother passed on to the other side, dying peacefully in her sleep. This time our trip to La Ciotat was somber, filled with tears, not laughter and revelry. Then, the renter in the Paris apartment completely vanished, never returning one of Jean-Luc's calls.

"You have to evict him. We can't take this. We can't support him. Honey, you should call Philippe," I suggested to Jean-Luc. "He's a *huissier*."

"Can you get me his number?"

Done.

What we found out from Philippe wasn't good. Unfortunately, in accordance with French law, you couldn't boot someone out during the winter months (October to April). If the deadbeat renter didn't leave willingly come April or before then, it could take up to three years to get rid of him. All Jean-Luc wanted to do was sell the place, but his hands were tied. We couldn't change the locks and put the renter's belongings in storage. If we had done that, Jean-Luc would get a thirty-thousand-euro fine and face time in prison. When it came to real estate in France, the laws in France protected the renters, not the owners. There have been horror stories about professional squatters—people who take over your house when you were on vacation. If you didn't have an alarm system, or if there was no sign of a break-in, all these squatters had to do was send mail to themselves at your address or change the utilities to their name—and *voilà*—you'd have to start the eviction process, which, again, could take years. It was nuts.

Jean-Luc had never wanted to purchase the apartment in the first place; he'd been pressured into it when he was with Frédérique. It was supposed to be a nest egg. But it wasn't. It was a constant nightmare.

Jean-Luc started the process to evict the renter. And we lost more money, hiring a *huissier* in Orly. The trial was set for November. Which meant the renter didn't have to leave until April, if he left at all. We held our breath, hoping everything would work out. For now, there was nothing more we could do, save for losing nine hundred euro a month.

The pressure was on, simmering like a *pot-au-feu*.

On April 22, I decided that the rules of publishing weren't working for me. A few months prior, the agent who had the exclusive look at the manuscript declined representation. Through referrals from Jay, I'd tried three or four more agents. They all came back with rejections, hesitant to take on a book—even though rewritten from the ground up—that had already been shopped, although very lightly.

But I was a fighter. I wouldn't give up, not when I'd worked so hard and had come this far.

So I decided to break the rules. Did I really need an agent? Of course, self-publishing was an option, but I wanted the guidance from a traditional publisher. That's when I found Sourcebooks. They accepted unsolicited manuscripts from unagented authors. And, the more research I did on them, namely the Paris-based memoirs they'd put out, the more I believed I'd found the perfect home for my memoir. I popped open a bottle of wine. And, nervous as hell, I sent off my book proposal and a query letter. Then, I crossed my fingers. According to their site, I wouldn't hear back from them for six to eight weeks. Until then, my book would rest in what was called the slush pile.

While I was in fighting-for-my-writing mode, I also sent a query off for *King of the Mutants*, my middle grade, to an up-and-coming independent publisher. One week later, I had an offer of publication. I realized I could write. I had a voice. And it was time for people to hear it.

In the beginning of June, it had been more than six weeks and I hadn't heard back from Sourcebooks. I figured they weren't interested. So I decided to break more publishing rules, contacting three editors at the big houses who had seen the first draft of *Seven Letters* and had given very positive feedback along with their rejections. It was a risk. But I was a risk-taker now. And, as they say, no risk, no reward. I figured, I wasn't actually sending out an "unsolicited query." These editors had all seen the manuscript before. My letter was sweet and polite. I reintroduced them to the book, explaining I'd left my agent and had hired an editor to help me structure it better. Two of them got back to me immediately. They remembered my story and they were anxious to see it again.

And then Murphy's law threw me for a loop. I woke up to an email from Anna, an editor for Sourcebooks, alerting me to the fact that she loved my book proposal and sample chapters. Could I send her the full manuscript? Three days later, she sent me another email to schedule "the call." We talked about the book and the changes she wanted to make to it. Did I agree with her suggestions? You bet I did. Plus, she was so sweet and kind and passionate about the story. She also told me that in three years she had never made an offer for a book she'd found in the slush pile. When she made the offer for publication, I was quick to say yes. I'd found another member of "Team Seabiscuit."

My *squees* could be heard to my former home in California.

It did put me in a slightly awkward situation, as I had to contact the two editors who had requested the manuscript, plus the third who hadn't responded yet, letting them know *Seven Letters from Paris* had received an offer…and that, after much thought, I'd decided to take it, because it truly was the right home for the book. All three responded with hearty congratulations. And, thankfully, the two editors who had the manuscript in their hands hadn't started reading yet.

I was doing a happy dance in the kitchen when Max came downstairs. "You sold your book?"

I nodded, smiled, and took a sip of wine.

"Don't forget. I get two hundred euro."

I grimaced. I'd forgotten about the contract he had me sign. Smart kid. And note to self: never sign contracts when you've been drinking wine.

A few days later, Anna sent me the final contract. I looked at the proposed publication date of October 2014. That was the same month my middle-grade novel was going to be released. So, yes, I had a romantic memoir and a book about a boy who was part alligator on the search for his identity coming out at the same time.

. . . .

All of a sudden, spring turned into summer, and our garden was in full bloom, the cherry tree dotted with plump red fruits. It was *clafoutis* time.

The kids and I gathered the cherries so that Jean-Luc could make his famed dessert. As he poured the batter into the baking pan, Jean-Luc insisted that you couldn't seed the cherries or it ruined the taste. I wasn't going to argue with my Frenchman. We spit the seeds out. Classy. Adding to the spirit of revelry, when I was dropping off my dossier to renew my *carte de séjour*, I found out that after three years of marriage I now qualified for a ten-year card. If approved, I didn't have to go to the *préfecture* every year, submitting my dossier filled with all the same paperwork months in advance. I came home, filled with excitement—happy-dance crazy. I wanted to share my good news.

Jean-Luc was hacking away at my favorite rosebush, the one climbing up the back of our town house. Apparently, one thick branch had wedged its way under the small, tiled roof hanging over the kitchen. "Stop! It's like you're cutting off my arm," I said, my demeanor shifting.

"Would you rather the roof falls down, crushing somebody?" he asked.

I had to think on this. For me, this rosebush symbolized my growth in France, rooting itself to this place as I'd done—no matter what the weather brought. "Well…"

"Sam, enough with your clown-school drama," said Jean-Luc.

I narrowed my eyes into a glare. "Fine. But only the wayward branch. And if you kill this rose bush, I'm not going to be happy. I might chop something else off. Keep that in mind."

"I'm scared," said Jean-Luc.

"You should be," I said and he laughed.

"Not funny," I said, making a motion to cut my throat with my finger. "I'm serious."

The phone rang, saving Jean-Luc from my rosebush wrath. I went into the house to answer the call, cringing at the sound of Jean-Luc's saw. Caller ID displayed Tracey's number. "I have big news," she said.

"Can't wait to hear it." We had unlimited calling to the U.S. and sixty or so other countries for an extra seven euro a month. Tracey was calling from her cell. "I'll call you right back." And so I did.

"I'm pregnant," she said.

I sucked in my breath.

After one round of IVF, Tracey was now twelve weeks pregnant with a healthy baby girl. Naturally, she asked her decades-long best friend to be the godmother. Naturally, I accepted. Although I was thrilled to bits for her, twinges of jealousy sparked my nerves like live wires and I found myself questioning if I wanted to try again. As I sat on the couch, I kept coming back to the same answer, which was a resounding no. I was happy with my life and all of the decisions Jean-Luc and I made together—aside from the massacre of my rosebush. I was a mother—just not in the way I'd expected.

Sometimes you just had to approach life a bit differently.

Take sushi, for example. Although they had sushi restaurants in

Toulouse, I couldn't find the rolls I was jonesing for, like dragon rolls or shrimp tempura rolls with mango and avocado. So I made my way to the Asian grocer, the one oddly named Paris Store, bought the required materials like a rice maker and a sushi mat, and learned how to make them myself. Oksana and Trupty joined me one day, and we had a sushi-making party, coming up with creative vegetarian options using roasted vegetables for Trupty. On a roll, I decided to invent a French-inspired dish. I was cooking up slices of *magret de canard* (duck breast), steamed sticky rice, and making a cherry compote when Jean-Luc walked into the kitchen.

"What are you making?" asked Jean-Luc. "I thought we were having sushi."

"Well, it's sort of like sushi," I said. "But this is *frushi.*"

"Frushi? What's that? There's no such thing."

"Yes, there is. French-inspired sushi. *Tu vois?* I'm going to roll cooked ingredients in seaweed and slice them up."

"So you just made this up? Like Stepmother's Day?"

"That holiday is 100 percent real," I said, giving him the stink eye, followed by a smile. "And so is frushi. Taste."

Focusing on the things I missed from my American life had proven to be futile. I didn't miss anything anymore. Not when I had everything I needed—like a loving husband and two adorable kids. When dreams change you just had to roll right along with them. Kind of like sushi. Or Frushi. Whatever.

SWEET SIXTEEN

EVEN WITH ITS TWISTS AND turns, nature eventually takes its course, and everything just flowed, the time sped up by happiness. That summer, our family dove in Mediterranean waters. In the fall, we celebrated Thanksgiving, introducing my French family and friends to the American tradition, followed by another Christmas in Provence, one New Year's celebration, a couple of ski trips, and a few lunches and dinners with our friends. If life *were* like *Groundhog Day*, I'd have no problem repeating every day, every meal, or every event.

In May, that month of new beginnings, Jean-Luc and I finally made it to Paris, under both good and bad circumstances. The good: the wicked non-paying renter had finally left the apartment in Orly. The bad: it was up to us to paint it so we could sell the beast, and hopefully quick, because for the past year Jean-Luc had lost close to nine hundred euro a month and, although I'd sold *Seven Letters from Paris* and received a decent advance, my career as a writer had yet to kick off, as my book wouldn't hit the shelves for another year. We might have been struggling financially for a while, but we were rich in love. And I'm a glass-is-half-full, not half-empty kind of girl, so the trip wouldn't be all backbreaking work and no play. Before we drove the seven long hours—our car loaded up with paint, an air mattress, and cleaning supplies—I made dinner plans with Patrick, the friend of Jean-Luc's I'd met at that infamous café in Paris the summer of 1989. Although Jean-Luc hadn't kept in touch with Patrick, I'd connected with him on Facebook after Jean-Luc and I had tied the proverbial knot.

After working from sunup to sundown, Jean-Luc and I cleaned ourselves up and drove to the seventh arrondisement to meet Patrick at his beautiful apartment, a stone's throw away from Hôtel des Invalides. Patrick opened the door and embraced us, twirling Jean-Luc around. We sat down on the leather couch for the *apéro*, and we were introduced to Alexandra, Patrick's wife. Patrick popped open a bottle of champagne.

"Here's to old friends," he said.

"*Tchin-tchin*," said Jean-Luc.

Patrick served us a salmon that he'd caught and smoked himself at their home in the country. Then he told us how and he and Alexandra had gotten married on water-skis. Soon, he and Jean-Luc picked up right where they left off more than twenty long years ago, updating one another on all of life's past events—marriages and divorces, the birth of children (Patrick and Alexandra had two), and how crazy it was that Jean-Luc and I had reconnected after all those years.

"Does your friend Tracey wonder about Patrick?" asked Alexandra with a coy smile.

"She's with a man from her past, too," I said. "And very happy."

She laughed. "I wasn't worried."

From the *apéro*, it was off to a local café, where we ate a light dinner and talked about the future, and laughed about the past. We spent the evening strolling along the Seine. Instead of retracing the steps Jean-Luc and I first took in Paris together like I'd always envisioned, we created a new memory. And it was time to create a few more.

One month later, I was to chaperone Elvire and two of her friends, Manon and Emma, on a trip to California for her sixteenth birthday. Her girlfriends would stay with my family for two weeks, Elvire and I would have one week alone with my family, and then, Jean-Luc and Max would join us for three weeks. Before we left, the parents of Manon and Emma loaded me up with gifts to take to my family—tablecloths, French lotions, and chocolates. We also set a budget. Save for Elvire, I was covering the girls' meals, but not all the extras. And we'd planned on quite a few extras. The girls' mothers made me promise that they would only speak English.

My mom had been a fitness instructor for more than thirty years. She was currently teaching yoga to former soldiers suffering from pain or post-traumatic stress at the Veterans Affairs in Los Angeles. She was taking two weeks off work to spend time with me and get to know Elvire better. We took the girls to Disneyland for Elvire's birthday, and then out on my parents' boat, dolphins jumping in the wake. We had tea at the Beverly Wilshire after window-shopping on Rodeo drive. We rented bikes, one a tandem, and cruised down the path from Santa Monica to Venice Beach. We strolled down Hollywood Boulevard, laughing at fat Batman and all of the other weirdos, the girls hitting every souvenir shop along the way. We went to the Universal theme park, where we discovered the way to skip lines: head to the single riders section. I even took the girls to Palm Desert, wanting to catch up with a friend of mine of over thirty years, Debra, while I had the chance.

Jean-Luc had met Debra in October of 2009, at her 17,000-square-foot Moroccan palace.

"Is this a hotel?" Jean-Luc had asked when we arrived.

Like Jean-Luc, the girls' jaws dropped when they saw her home. Debra had hired workers from Morocco to build her masterpiece. The floors were intricately tiled. The brass lights were all hand hammered. The moldings were finely detailed, white and perfect, like the prettiest of wedding cakes. Toward the back of the home, right off the gourmet kitchen, there was a hookah room, where at the press of a button, a twenty-foot-wide movie screen would rise in front of its stunned audience. Outside, there were two pools— one was an infinity-edged lap pool, the water flowing and giving the impression it was one with the surrounding landscape; the other large and circular with built-in sun beds. It was paradise, a desert oasis of luxurious dreams.

Elvire's jaw dropped. "Where am I?"

"Paradise," I said. "With me, my mom, and my friend. And your friends."

While the girls swam in the pool feeling like princesses of the desert, Mom, Debra, and I popped open a bottle of champagne. Debra placed her hand on my back. "I've never seen you so happy. You've really hit the jackpot with Jean-Luc. He's really a great guy. I love him. And I'm in love with these girls. I'm so, so happy for you."

"You know what, Debra," I said, "I've never been happier in my life."

"Let's celebrate," said my mom, holding up her glass.

"Things work out for a reason," said Debra. "And, Sam, you deserve happiness. We all do."

We settled back on lounge chairs with smiles on our faces.

After our day at the desert, I'd signed the girls up for two days of surf lessons. It was so cute seeing them in black and pink Roxy wet suits. I sat on the beach, taking pictures and cheering each of them on as they caught a wave, gliding gracefully across the water. Elvire skipped onto the beach, breathless.

"A seal was swimming next to me," she screeched.

"That's so cool," I said. "Were you scared?"

She shook her head no. "*Mais*, cool? Our instructor, Joe, is like a character," said Elvire. "He has blond dreadlocks and he speaks so funny. What's 'rad'?"

"Rad is when your mom tries to surf," said Joe.

Elvire didn't even blink at the word "mom." My heart skipped a beat.

He dragged a long-board over, handing it over to me, along with a wet suit. "Your turn."

I gave it the good old college try. It took me three times, with Joe swimming and pushing the board behind me, until I caught my first wave. From the beach, the girls screamed, "Soooooooo rad!"

Every evening we ate with my parents, me cooking, mostly barbecues, and on more than one occasion, we went out under the stars for a midnight swim. My mom was making the girls pancakes with strawberries and whipped cream for breakfast when Rayna walked into the kitchen.

I ran up and gave her hug. "Rayna! I've missed you."

Rayna had worked for my mom for well over ten years, cleaning, but she wasn't just a hire, she was part of the family. She was an immigrant from Guatemala, and my parents sponsored her when she was on the road to becoming an American. She was also there every step of the way when I was going through my divorce and rekindling my relationship with Jean-Luc. I'd return home from walking dogs and Rayna would exclaim, "You have a package! Flowers from France!" After Jean-Luc and I reconnected, and while I was still living at home with the parental units, Jean-Luc sent me orange and hot pink roses—my favorite color combo—every three months, from a French company that delivered to the U.S.

Rayna stepped back. "You have lost weight," she said. "I liked you better when you were more *gordito*."

"*Gordito?*"

"Fatter!" she said. "Woman are always better with more meat on their bones. Promise me you won't get too skinny."

"I promise," I said. "But maybe I could stand to lose three more pounds?"

"No," said Rayna. "Be *gordito*." We talked about life as an immigrant. All the trials and tribulations. She asked me who cleaned. I said I did. And Jean-Luc too. Who cooks? Me, I said. I told her about the tuna noodle casserole fiasco. She gave me another huge, heartfelt hug and then grabbed the vacuum cleaner, about to head upstairs to the girls' room.

I blocked her path. "Don't go up there. For you, it's off limits. I'll clean it later."

But there was no stopping Rayna. Her jaw dropped. Then, she threatened to grab garbage bags to throw away all of the clothes littering the floor. "Ay-yai-yai," she said. "Never, never, never, never…"

"Teenage girls," I said, embarrassment flushing my cheeks.

The phone rang just in time. It was Jean-Luc. "The police were just here for you."

My heart nearly jumped out of my ribcage. "What? What are you talking about?"

He laughed. "Don't worry about it. They just wanted to interview you for your ten-year *carte de séjour*. Oh, and they wanted to make sure that you live here with me, to make sure we don't have a *mariage blanc*. I explained to the gendarme that you were in Los Angeles with Elvire. They want me to call when you are back in town."

"Why?"

"So they can interview you," he said.

Les fonctionnaires at the *préfecture* never mentioned an interview. Surprise! I was already nervous. Police scared the bejesus out of me. Out of all the dumb luck, the *gendarme* showed up at our home when I wasn't in town, and our marriage probably looked sketchy. But I was where I was and there was nothing I could do about it, except pray.

The girls' last night in town was July 4, and they were excited to experience an American tradition—the barbecues, the fireworks, the parties. A friend of my mother's invited us over to his house for a get-together. A woman approached as I was making my way from the outside deck to the living room. The conversation started off amicably enough. The usual—"Oh, you're so lucky to live in France! I love Paris," to "How did you meet your husband?" to "Do you have kids?" I pointed to Elvire.

"I have two. That's Elvire, my, er, uh, stepdaughter. Her brother, Max, and their dad are joining us in a few weeks…"

The woman's eyes widened as she processed my answers, and severe awkwardness ensued. Her questions now carried a judgment. After living in France, I'd become accustomed to the French way of life, especially with strangers. "On *s'occupe de ses oignons*," or minds one's own business. This woman, however, wouldn't back off. And all of a sudden she had me confessing that I'd had three consecutive miscarriages.

The woman eyed me, and then Elvire, and said, "Well, it's never too late. A friend of mine just had a baby at fifty. How old are you?" She continued to blabber on about how there is nothing like having a child of your own. I tuned her out when she brought up the latest developments on in vitro fertilization.

Once my jaw recovered from being completely unhinged, my lips clenched together into a trembling smile. "Thanks," I said, "I'll keep that in my mind," and, slowly, I backed away from the table, heading straight to the margarita bar. Screw the margarita. Give me a few shots of tequila.

Elvire noticed that I was upset and, after asking for a daiquiri for her and her friends to share, she asked why. So I told her what the woman had said. Her upper lip curled into a sneer.

"Do you mind if I just tell people that you and Max are my kids? My real kids?" I asked.

She hugged me and said, "That's fine. We are your kids. Well, almost." I hugged her back. Hard.

An hour later, my parents, the girls, and I escaped the party. We headed home for a barbecue and then over to the Malibu Pier to watch the fireworks. The night was capped off with a midnight dip in the pool.

A few days later, Manon and Emma were replaced with Tracey and her baby girl, Vivienne. I finally met my beautiful goddaughter. Happier than I'd ever been, I wasn't jealous, because I was an almost mom. And I was *almost* French.

. . . .

Back in France, my appointment with the *gendarme* was surreal. My interviewer was muscular and tan, his bulging biceps struggling against the confines of his tight uniform. His teeth sparkled, whiter than white. His hair was perfectly coiffed, gelled to perfection. He was a beefcake. Did my life in France hinge upon the opinion of a twenty-four-year-old French Chippendale dancer disguised as a government official? I waited for him to whip out a boom box, to watch him strip while I clapped along to a familiar boy-band song. But this wasn't a bachelorette party; it was serious. Victor asked a few questions, his long, dark eyelashes fluttering, like how long had Jean-Luc and I been married and where had we met. Then, he and Jean-Luc talked about scuba diving for half an hour. Before Victor left, he told me that my card would be ready in a few months. Apparently, I passed the immigrant test!

Sometimes I liked to walk in the park a few blocks from our house, to watch the children riding their bikes and scooters and the mallard ducks with their baby ducklings, or to just decompress in nature, occasionally catching a glimpse of dragonflies in the stream. I was sitting on a bench, smiling like a fool, when an old man walking wearing a cap and walking his dog came up to me.

"Can I join you?" the man asked.

"Yes, please do," I said, sensing he wanted to talk to somebody.

We were exchanging the normal pleasantries, talking about the weather, when he turned to me. "Where are you from? Belgium?"

"No," I said, holding back my smile. This was the first time somebody hadn't asked if I was English. "I'm from the U.S. Los Angeles and Chicago."

His jaw dropped. "What are you doing here? In Cugnaux?"

"I'm married to a Frenchman," I said, patting the head of his dog.

"Aren't you bored? There is nothing to do here," he huffed. "Guess where I'm from?" he asked. "Can you tell me the name of the beautiful island off the coast of France?"

I took a wild guess. "*L'île de Porquerolles?*"

"Bah," he said. "I'm from Corsica. I still have a house there, just meters from the sea. I'm moving back there for good one day. The biggest mistake I ever made was marrying a Frenchwoman from Cugnaux. There's nothing to do here," he repeated. "It's flat and it's boring."

"I love it here. Really I do. In a few hours, we can drive to the Atlantic coast, or the vineyards, the Mediterranean Sea or the mountains. We can explore old castles and beautiful villages, visiting ruins…"

"I'm still moving back to Corsica." The old man shrugged. "Your French is very, very good, by the way."

"*Merci*," I said. "*Merci beaucoup.*"

At home, Jean-Luc was rummaging through the refrigerator. I sneaked up, hugging him from behind, my arms looped under his, my hands resting on his broad shoulders. "What are you looking for?" I asked.

He turned to face me, holding the eggplant we'd picked up at the market in the morning. "I wanted to make a *tian Provençal* to go with the barbecued lamb."

"Do you need my help?"

"You remember how to prepare it?"

"I remember everything," I said. "Now, let's get to it."

Jean-Luc pulled me in for a hard kiss. I withdrew from the embrace and raised my brows in surprise, pointing to the ceiling. "The kids are upstairs," I said, and he laughed his warm, teasing laugh.

I shot him a sideways glance and grabbed two cutting boards and two knives from the sink, laying them down next to the pile of gleaming vegetables in front of us. I picked up a *courgette*, thinking about zucchini with its French name. So much had changed in three years. I'd even started dreaming in French.

Wordlessly, side-by-side, we sliced up the tomatoes, red onions, eggplant, and zucchini, placing them in a ceramic baking dish in tight rows. The end result was a vibrant display of alternating colors of green, deep purple, and two shades of red. The kitchen smelled of summer, sweet and fresh. I handed Jean-Luc the *fleur de sel* and pepper while I crushed the garlic. A little olive oil and some *herbes de Provence,* and our glistening creation was ready for the oven.

"We work well together," I said.

"It's only a vegetable dish." Jean-Luc placed the *tian* in the oven, setting the timer for forty minutes. He popped his lips and shrugged his shoulders. "It's simple."

"It's more than simple." I grabbed a serving platter, placed the lamb leg on it, and seasoned the meat with *herbes de Provence* and a little olive oil on autopilot. "It's perfect."

Jean-Luc's eyes flashed with understanding. "Anything can be built when you have the right tools. And we've built more than a few hundred meals together; we've constructed a new life."

I eyed the bracelet on my wrist, the amethyst heart that had rested on my pulse ever since he'd given it to me on our second anniversary. Yes, here I was, living a new life in the here, in the now, right where I was supposed to be.

"*Je t'aime,*" I said.

"*Je t'aime, aussi, mon coeur,*" he said.

JEAN-LUC'S TRADITIONAL
TIAN PROVENÇAL

Prep time: 15 minutes

Cook time: 35 minutes

Serves: 4 to 6

Great for: side dish for pork, chicken, and lamb, or stand-alone vegetarian meal

Wine suggestion: Bandol Blanc or rosé

- 2 red onions, peeled and sliced
- 1 clove garlic, peeled, de-germed, and finely minced
- 2 zucchini, skin on, sliced
- 6 tomatoes, sliced
- 1 large eggplant, sliced
- 1 healthy pinch *herbes de Provence*
- 1 healthy pinch *fleur de sel* or other coarse salt, to taste
- Freshly ground black pepper, to taste

Preheat oven to 400°F. In a skillet over medium heat, add a dash of olive oil, along with the onion and garlic, cooking until translucent, about 5 minutes. Place the onions in the bottom of a 9 x 12 baking pan. Drizzle with olive oil. Place the vegetables, alternating tomato, eggplant, and zucchini, in the pan on top of the onions until the whole baking dish is filled. (The vegetables aren't layered, but stacked sideways like a spine.) Drizzle the vegetables with olive oil. Season with *herbes de Provence*, a bit of *fleur de sel*, and pepper, and bake for 35 minutes. Serve with rice or quinoa.

Kathy's Goat Cheese
and Balsamic Glaze *Tian Provençal*

Prep time: 15 minutes
Cook time: 35 minutes
Serves: 4 to 6
Great for: side dish, vegetarian meal, or for anyone who loves tomatoes and cheese
Wine suggestion: Sancerre Rosé

- 1 log goat cheese, sliced*
- ¾ cup balsamic vinegar

Preheat the oven to 400°F. Prepare Jean-Luc's *tian*, and after the vegetables have been placed in the dish, add in the cheese slices. Bake for 25 minutes.

10 minutes before serving, in a small pot, heat the vinegar over high heat for about 5 minutes, until it reduces to a syrup-like consistency. Carefully pour over the vegetables and bake for another 5 minutes.

* *Feta cheese is also delicious in this recipe.*

JEAN-LUC'S SIMPLE *POT-AU-FEU*

Prep time: 30 minutes

Cook time: 3 hours in a Dutch oven or 1½ hours in a pressure cooker

Serves: 6

Great for: winter family dinner

Wine suggestion: a hearty Bordeaux

- 1 tablespoon extra virgin olive oil
- 1 cup *lardons*
- 2 cloves garlic, peeled, de-germed, and finely minced
- 3 pounds lean stewing beef, brisket, or rump roast
- 2 marrow bones (optional)
- 2 cups beef stock
- 1½ teaspoons black peppercorns
- 3 cloves
- 1 bouquet garni (p. 132)
- 4 carrots, peeled and sliced in 2-inch rounds
- 3 to 4 leeks, sliced in 2-inch rounds
- 3 celery stalks, roughly chopped
- 2 onions, peeled and quartered
- ¼ cup flat parsley, finely chopped, plus extra for garnish
- ¼ cup tarragon, finely chopped, plus extra for garnish
- 6 medium red or gold potatoes, halved
- ½ cabbage head, quartered and heart removed (optional)
- 2 rutabagas, peeled and quartered
- ¼ cup chives, finely chopped, for garnish
- Whole grain or Dijon mustard, for serving
- Salt and freshly ground black pepper, to taste

Heat up a Dutch oven or a large pot with the oil. Cook the *lardons* with the garlic until brown, and remove with a slotted spoon, setting aside onto a paper towel. Season the beef with salt and pepper, and, in the same pot, sear the beef on all sides until brown. Add the garlic mixture back into the pot, and place the marrow bones (if using), beef stock, peppercorns, cloves, and bouquet garni in the pot, seasoning with salt and pepper.

Add in the carrots, leeks, celery, onion, parsley, and tarragon, and then add enough water to cover the meat and vegetables. Bring to a boil, then lower the heat to a simmer. Cover with a lid and cook for 2 hours. Add the potatoes, cabbage (if using), and rutabagas to the pot. Cover and simmer for 1 hour.

If using a pressure cooker, once the beef is prepared, add all the ingredients to the pot at once, cover, and cut the cooking time in half.

Remove the bouquet garni before serving, and season with salt and pepper. To serve, place the beef on a carving dish and cut into individually sized portions. Place the meat in bowls and cover with the broth and vegetables. Garnish with parsley, chives, and tarragon. Serve with a baguette and mustard on the side.

JEAN-LUC'S CHERRY CLAFOUTIS

Prep time: 15 minutes (plus 20 minutes of rest time)
Cook time: 30 to 35 minutes
Serves: 6 to 8
Great for: easy and delicious dessert
Wine suggestion: Rosé d'Anjou

- 1 pound fresh cherries*
- 1 cup all-purpose flour
- 1 teaspoon baking powder
- ¾ cup sugar
- 1 tablespoon vanilla extract
- 1 to 2 pinches ground cinnamon
- 2 pinches salt
- 4 eggs
- 1½ cups whole milk
- Confectioners' sugar, for garnish

Preheat the oven to 350°F. Grease a ceramic baking or pie dish. Place the cherries in the dish. In a large mixing bowl, combine the flour, baking powder, sugar, vanilla, cinnamon, and salt, then fold in the eggs. Add the milk, little by little, using a handheld blender or whisk, mixing the batter until smooth. Set aside for 20 minutes. Pour the batter over the cherries until covered. Bake for 30 to 35 minutes. Dust the clafoutis with confectioners' sugar. Serve warm or at room temperature with a dollop of whipped cream and vanilla ice cream.

> * *Jean-Luc, Isabelle, and most French insist that a clafoutis isn't a cla-foutis unless the pits are kept in the cherries supposedly giving the dish a nuttier flavor. If you decide to pit the cherries, a rebellious friend of mine, Jacqueline, suggests adding 2 tablespoons of almond liqueur and ¼ cup slivered almonds to the batter.*

JEAN-LUC'S STRAWBERRY SOUP

Prep time: 10 minutes

Cook time: 30 minutes (to chill in refrigerator)

Serves: 4

Great for: summer, when you're pressed to come up with a quick dessert

Wine suggestion: Banyuls

- 4 cups fresh strawberries, stems removed
- 1½ cups *crème fraîche* or sour cream
- 2 teaspoons vanilla extract
- ½ cup brown sugar
- Fresh basil leaves, for garnish

Place all the ingredients in a food processor or blender. Pulse, mixing until creamy. Chill in the refrigerator for at least half an hour. Serve in bowls, and garnish with fresh basil leaves.

A CRUMBLE FOR ALL

Prep time: 15 minutes

Cook time: 35 to 40 minutes

Serves: 6 to 8

Great for: anytime, depending on what fruits are in season

Wine suggestion: Gaillac or Muscat

- 1 cup all-purpose flour
- ¾ cup brown sugar
- 1 teaspoon salt
- 1 stick unsalted butter, sliced in chunks and softened
- 12 cups apples, peeled and cubed*
- 2 tablespoons lemon juice
- 1 teaspoon ground cinnamon, powdered ginger, or ground nutmeg
- 2 teaspoons vanilla extract
- 2 tablespoons rum (optional)

Preheat the oven to 400°F. To make the topping, sift the flour into a large mixing bowl, and add the brown sugar and salt. Mix the butter into the flour mixture with your hands until the mixture looks like breadcrumbs.

In a 9 x 12 ceramic or glass baking dish, place the fruit with the lemon and spice of your choice, adding in the vanilla and rum (if using). Toss until the fruit is well coated. Sprinkle the crumble mixture over the fruit. Bake for 30 to 35 minutes, or until the topping is firm. Serve with a dollop of whipped cream or vanilla ice cream.

* *Here are some of my favorite fruit combinations, depending on what is in season: apples and pears; apples, currants, blackberries, raspberries, rhubarb, and strawberries; or apples, peaches, kiwi, and apricots. Mix as many fruits as you like, remembering that apples (about 6 to 8 cups) give a nice texture to the dish.*

FRUSHI

Prep time: 20 minutes
Cook time: 30 minutes
Yield: 4 rolls
Great for: Stepmother's Day!
Wine suggestion: Haut Médoc or St. Emilion

FOR THE RICE:

- 2 cups sushi rice
- ½ cup rice wine vinegar
- ⅛ cup sugar
- ⅛ cup mirin

FOR THE FRUSHI ROLL:

- 1 pound duck breast
- Freshly ground black pepper
- 4 sheets nori
- 6 to 8 tablespoons cherry compote (p. 298)
- Pickled ginger
- Soy sauce

In a strainer, rinse the rice until the water runs clear. In a small saucepan, heat the vinegar, sugar, and mirin, whisking until the sugar dissolves. Cool to room temperature. Cook the rice with equal parts water to rice. Transfer the rice to large mixing bowl, and pour the vinegar mixture over rice, folding it in until evenly distributed. Cover the bowl with a warm, wet towel. Set aside.

On a cutting board, pepper the duck breast, then slice it

into ¼-inch strips. Cover a bamboo sushi mat with plastic film, wrapping it tightly. Cut a quarter of a nori sheet off with a pair of scissors. Take the larger portions of nori and lightly toast each sheet by waving it over a toaster or heating it in a pan. If the nori turns light green, it's been toasted too long. Set the sheets aside.

In the same pan, cook the strips of duck to your liking, leaving the fat on (for now). Once cooked, move the duck to a cutting board, and set aside. Place 1 nori sheet on the covered bamboo mat, rough side up, and cover with rice. Carefully flip the sheet over on the mat, placing the rice side down. Trim the fat off a few slices of duck, and place them on the edge of the nori closest to you. Place 1 or 2 tablespoons of cherry compote over the duck, then roll! To cut the Frushi, cover the roll in plastic wrap. The first cut should be in the center, moving outward, ending up with 6 pieces. Garnish each roll with a slice of pickled ginger and a cherry from the compote. Serve with soy sauce.

CHERRY COMPOTE

Prep time: 10 minutes
Cook time: 20 minutes
Makes 1 cup
Great for: Frushi!

- 2 cups stemmed and pitted cherries
- 2 oranges, juiced
- ½ lemon, juiced
- ⅛ cup brandy or Cognac
- ⅛ cup sugar

Place the cherries in a small pot over medium-high heat. Add the orange and lemon juice, the brandy or Cognac, and the sugar, stirring in evenly. Bring to a boil, then reduce heat. Remove the cherries with a slotted spoon, place in a bowl, and set aside. Continue to simmer the liquid for another 10 to 15 minutes. Pour the juice over cherries. Let sit to cool until ready to serve. Store in a mason jar in the refrigerator for up to 2 to 3 weeks.

EPILOGUE

EVERY TIME SOMEBODY LEARNS THAT I live in France, nine out of ten times they will say, "Oh my God! You are *so* lucky. I love Paris."

To which I reply, "I do feel lucky, but…I don't live in Paris."

"Where do you live?" they ask, confused. "Provence?"

"Well, by car, I'm seven hours south of Paris," I explain. "I live in a small town thirteen kilometers outside of Toulouse. Cugnaux. In southwestern France."

An eyebrow usually lifts. More questions, like "Do you love living in France?" ensue.

Today, my answer is a wholehearted yes. Yes, I do.

My perspective toward life, love, and family has changed. My dreams have changed. And change can be very, very good. In six years of marriage, Jean-Luc and I have had *maybe* five arguments—mostly due to the frustrations of home renovation projects. Perhaps it is the way in which we communicate. Perhaps it is the way of the bonobo chimps. Whatever the case, we work well together. We've had our ups and our downs. It's called life. Real life. In the end, our family is a true family, and the dynamic is strong. So we must learn to let our hearts soar with the dragonflies and hummingbirds and to focus on the tiny, beautiful things in life. Because when it comes to life and love, there is no such thing as perfect; we must find the beauty in every moment, diving right into every second with no fear or regrets, and go with the flow.

Je vois ma vie en rose.
Toujours, la famille! Et, encore, l'amour.

HOW TO HOST THE PERFECT BOOK CLUB

B ook clubs are a great way to find new reads, to get together with the gals (and/or guys), to have a lively debate over a bottle—or two—of wine, and, in our case here in the south of France, to *speak* (and read) our mother tongue on a regular basis. My book club has expanded to include twenty members from all corners of the globe, including two French gals, though most meetings cap off at about eight people. We may come from all walks of life, but we share one thing in common: a love for books.

Once a month, one of our members chooses a read, and the rendezvous takes place at her home. The amazing Kristin from South Dakota went above and beyond when Gillian Flynn's *Gone Girl* was the pick. She came up with snacks based on the plot of the book—"She's Nuts" (nuts), "Olive You, Olive You Not" (olives), and the "Sweetest Revenge" (a dessert). She even made tiny, handwritten signs for all of the treats. So, for *How to Make a French Family*, that's what I'm recommending for you to do! Get creative and have some fun! Host a French-themed discussion!

Here are some ideas to get you started:

> **Music:** Play "La Vie en Rose" by Edith Piaf and other well-known French classics.
>
> **Wine suggestions:** In the summer and spring, choose a nice crisp white or a rosé. In the fall

or winter, a hearty red. *Mais*, French, *bien sûr*. A
bubbly Badoit or Perrier with a wedge of lemon
or lime or a refreshing drink like iced tea are
great non-alcoholic drink options.

Snacks: Choose something from the recipes
included in this book. Tiny quiches are always
a hit. Check out page 125, "How to Host a
French Dinner Party," starting with the *apéro*,
for ideas. The only limit is your imagination. I
quiche you, or I quiche you not!

Also, every book club (well, mine does) needs discussion questions
to keep the conversation on track. Alas, the reading group discussion guide for *How to Make a French Family* can be found on the
following page.

Finally, I'm available for book club meetings via Skype should
your group want to ask me questions. Shoot me an email at
slverant@gmail.com to set up a date/time. Please be aware of the
time change since I live in France. If the timing is impossible, your
group can send me questions ahead of time, and I'll answer them in
a YouTube video or via email. *Voilà! Voilà!*

Happy reading, happy discussions, and *bisous* from a small town
outside of Toulouse.

READING GROUP GUIDE

1. Samantha faces more than a few obstacles when she "leaps" into her new life in southwestern France. Have you ever moved to a new place or lived in a foreign country? What kind of challenges did you face? How did you overcome them?

2. When Samantha is craving a taste of home, she makes a tuna noodle casserole (which doesn't go over well with the kids). If you were away from home, what food would you crave the most? How do you think you would react if you were faced with picky eaters like Samantha's stepchildren?

3. Food is a way of life in France, and Samantha prepares meals to communicate her love to her family and friends. How do you convey love to others? Do you cook?

4. Parenthood, as we know, isn't easy, and Samantha becomes an "instant stepmom" practically overnight. How did her relationship with Max and Elvire change over the course of the book?

5. Samantha overcomes quite a few fears in the book, including speaking out loud in another language, flambéing, skiing, and scuba diving. What fears have you overcome? What would you do if fear was not holding you back? How do you kick fear to the curb to accomplish what you want to do?

6. Samantha says "dreams change." Have you ever thought you wanted something only to find out your ideal situation has changed later in life? What was your childhood dream? What are your current dreams and desires?

7. Samantha made the mistake of not reaching out to others when she first landed in France and struggled to find a group of her own. What is the importance of finding a group of people to connect with—separate from your partner's? Have you ever encountered any difficulties when seeking out new friends? How do you overcome them?

8. Jean-Luc and Samantha travel all over the Pyrénées in southwestern France. What is on your travel bucket list? Where do you want to go? How will you make these plans happen?

9. Life is full of ups and downs, and Jean-Luc and Samantha deal with three consecutive miscarriages, a seedy renter, and the declining health of an aging parent in the time span of one year. Still, they maintain a somewhat positive attitude, even when difficult situations threaten to tear them apart. What do you do to shift your perspective when life hands you lemons? How do you remain communicative in your relationships, no matter how difficult the subject matter is to discuss?

10. Samantha makes it clear that she doesn't want to live a life filled with regret, and she takes many risks throughout the book. What risks are you happy that you took? What were the stakes, and what was the outcome? Would you take that risk again?

11. How do Samantha's perspectives toward love, life, and family change by the end of the book?

12. And, finally, what, in your opinion, are the ingredients for making a happy family?

ACKNOWLEDGMENTS

Here's to Team Seabiscuit!

I'd like to start by thanking Anna Michels, my fabulous editor. Thank you for believing me in the beginning and plucking my first book out of the slush pile. And, thank you for believing in this book too. I'd also like to thank the Sourcebooks team, especially Dominique Raccah, my publisher, copy editors extraordinaire Cassie Gutman and Elizabeth Bagby, and foreign rights maestro Sara Hartman-Seeskin. Thanks to my agent, Jennifer Barclay, for her unwavering support and sage advice. *Merci mille fois!*

I raise a glass of champagne to my parents, Anne and Tony Platt, and to my two best friends in the entire world, Tracey Biesterfeldt and my sister, Jessica. Cheers to family!

A special shout goes out to my beta readers, Susan Blumberg Kason and Pam Ferderbar. Thanks for cheering me on! I'd also like to thank my Paris Authors' Group, especially our token male, chef Didier Quémener (a.k.a. DQ Flambé), who gave us his recipe for *pâte brisée*. And I can't forget chef Mary O'Leary. This girl has never measured. Thank you for looking over my recipes! Yes, chef! A *merci* also goes out to Jacqueline White for her lovely additions to the clafoutis recipe. *Miam, miam!*

A huge and heartfelt thanks goes to the Toulouse *Les Chicks*—Monique Nayard, Oksana Ritchie, and Trupty Vora. I couldn't have survived France without your friendships. Love you gals!

Tons of love goes to Jean-Luc's family, his parents, Marcelle and André, his sisters Isabelle and Muriel, and to their spouses, Richard and Alain, and their children. To my adoptive French parents, Christian and Ghislaine, and to all of Jean-Luc's friends: Thank you for welcoming me into your family.

As for Jean-Luc, thank you for changing my dreams and filling my world with love. *Je t'aime.* This book is dedicated to Max and Elvire. Having both of you in my life makes me the happiest woman in the world (especially when you clean your rooms).

I've made so many new friends on this journey, *and* I can't put into words how much all of these new friendships mean to me. Really, it's impossible. Can a simple thank-you suffice?

So, thank you for joining me on this family adventure. Now put this book down and go appreciate the tiny, beautiful things in life. Dragonflies. Hummingbirds. Roses. After that, pop open a bottle of bubbly and celebrate your world. I'll join you for a virtual toast. *Merci mille fois!*

ABOUT THE AUTHOR

S AMANTHA VÉRANT IS A TRAVEL addict, a self-professed oenophile, and a determined, if occasionally unconventional, French chef. She lives in southwestern France, where she's able to explore all of her passions. In addition to this memoir, she's the author of *Seven Letters from Paris*, the story in which she recounts how she married a sexy French rocket scientist she'd met in 1989 but ignored for twenty years.

Photo © Susy Barrat

For photos and videos of the recipes presented in this book, visit the *les recettes* tab at www.samanthaverant.com.